£6

THE FRENCH RESISTANCE

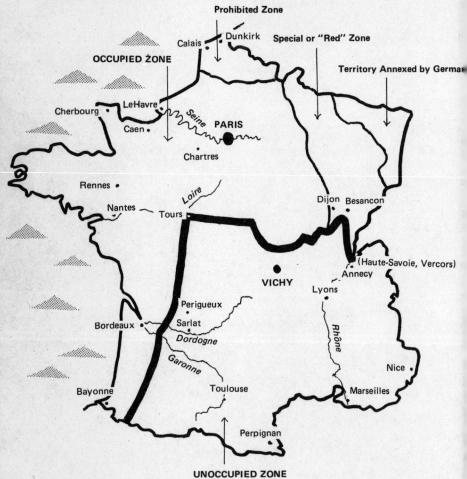

FRANCE, 1940.

Prohibited Zone

Special or "Red" Zone

Territory Annexed by German

OCCUPIED ZONE

Dunkirk

Calais

Cherbourg

LeHavre

Caen

Seine

PARIS

Chartres

Rennes

Nantes

Tours

Loire

Dijon Besancon

(Haute-Savoie, Vercors)

Annecy

VICHY

Lyons

Perigueux

Bordeaux

Sarlat

Dordogne

Rhône

Garonne

Nice

Bayonne

Toulouse

Marseilles

Perpignan

UNOCCUPIED ZONE

THE FRENCH RESISTANCE

1940 to 1944

by

FRIDA KNIGHT

1975
LAWRENCE AND WISHART
LONDON

SBN 85315 331 0 (hardback edition)
SBN 85315 335 3 (paperback edition)

Printed in Great Britain by
The Camelot Press Limited, Southampton

FOREWORD

This book is offered as a small tribute to comrades in the French Resistance. One cannot, of course, attempt to set down the complete history in twenty-odd chapters. My aim has been rather to recall how the Resistance was organised, how it was led, how it fought, how it won—and what happened after the victory. The facts are often glossed over or distorted—or, it may be, merely forgotten or unknown—in this country.

If I have in any way succeeded in presenting the salient features of that terrible and heroic episode, it is due largely to the help and encouragement of many friends to whom I am immensely grateful. Among them I must mention very specially those in the Dordogne and Lot valleys: Madame Jeanne Dayre and her family; Madame Emilienne Lagarde of Saint Julien de Lampon; M. Roussely and M. André Marty of Belvés; Madame Jean Lurçat of Saint Céré; M. Yves Péron, deputy of Perigueux; M. Castaigne of Limoges. In Paris I have had assistance and advice from M. Jean Cassou, M. André Tollet and M. Cukier of the Musée de la Résistance at Ivry, M. Francis Cohen, M. Dominique Bayle, and from the publishers, *Editions Sociales*, who kindly supplied a large number of books in their series on the Resistance.

In England I have received much kindness from scholars and historians, even those whose views may not always coincide with mine, and must particularly thank Professor M. R. D. Foot, Dr Henry Pelling, Professor Bryce Gallie, for giving me precious time to discuss thorny questions; Dr Tony Judt and Dr Don Symonds, Mrs Guy Chapman, Mrs Claudette Kennedy, Mrs Jean Pace and Dr Martin Bernal for providing valuable books and references; Professor and Mrs George Thomson for reading and criticising the typescript and my family for help and encouragement throughout.

My thanks are due to Dr Christopher Grieve (Hugh MacDiarmid) for sending me his poem from *Stony Limits*: to Professor Christopher Cornford for permission to quote unpublished translations by Frances Cornford of Aragon's verses, and to the British Museum MSS department for giving me access to these; to the University Library and the City Library of Cambridge; to the Librarian of the Institut français, London; and to the Council of Lucy Cavendish College, Cambridge, for facilities given me during the period of my research.

FRIDA KNIGHT

Cambridge, 1975

CONTENTS

1. 1934–1936 France against Fascism 9
2. 1936–1939 The Rise and Decline of the Popular Front 20
3. 1939, winter Phoney War 31
4. 1940, spring Invasion 41
5. 1940, summer Occupation 52
6. 1940, autumn Beginnings of Resistance 62
7. 1941 Zone Rouge 73
8. 1941–1942 Vichy 80
9. 1942 Free French in London 90
10. 1942, winter North African Problems 101
11. 1943 Fighting France 111
12. 1943 Mediterranean Liberation 123
13. 1943, winter *Nacht und Nebel* 130
14. Culture in the Resistance 140
15. 1943–1944 Maquis 150
16. 1944, June D-day and after 163
17. 1944, summer France aflame 175
18. 1944, July Paris Insurgent 184
19. 1944, August Paris Liberated 193
20. 1944–1945 Victory and its Sequel 204
21. Conclusion 216
   Abbreviations 221
   Calendar of Events 222
   Select Bibliography 236
   Index 239

Chapter 1
1934–1936
FRANCE AGAINST FASCISM

L'homme en cette époque agitée
　　Sombre océan
Doit faire comme Prométhée
　　Et comme Adam

. . . Il faut que le peuple s'arrache
　　Au dur decret
Et qu'enfin ce grand martyr sache
　　Le grand secret.
　　　　　　　　　　Victor Hugo, *Ibo*

Man in this troubled time,
　　Dark ocean,
Must act like Prometheus
　　And like Adam

. . . The People must tear free
　　From the harsh decree
and at long last the great martyr must learn
　　The great Secret.

The words "The French Resistance" inevitably call to my mind a faded but symbolic memory: the Champs Elysées one cold November day in 1940, and a multitude of young people, tense and quiet, many with tricolour badges on their jackets, heading in their hundreds up the avenue towards the tomb of the Unknown Soldier. How strangely alive it still is, this image of the first big Paris demonstration against the Nazis, which they said was communist inspired, and was so brutally put down! Since 1944 I have lived with that and other memories of those days—of the German occupation, of the "exodus", of the internment camps and the persecution of political prisoners, of the stirrings in the underground and the workers' secret organisation, the illegal trade unions, the strikes and sabotage—wondering when some English writer would record these things faithfully and in full.

The story of wartime France has, it's true, been presented to the British public from many angles, by politicians, historians, soldiers, journalists and former secret agents. But certain things have been misrepresented and much has been left unsaid; and in the absence of a better-qualified witness I feel a kind of obligation to try to fill some of the gaps.

What, in fact, was the Resistance? Was it, as some would have us think, first and foremost the legendary stand of General de Gaulle? Or the epic of S.O.E. (Secret Operations Executive)? Was victory in France due to Winston Churchill? Or to the U.S. Airforce? Or to the individual gallantry of the agents dropped by night, the heroism of those caught, the admirable achievements of individual groups? Of course it was won partly thanks to all of these, but far more to the defiance of millions of ordinary French people, some with weapons, most of them unarmed, who said NO to Nazi domination; and above all to the unity, discipline and devotion of the workers in town and countryside in their four-year struggle to defeat the Germans and eventually make a new and better France.

* * *

The story of those years has to be read as one episode of a world-wide battle against the scourge of our century—fascism. The complicated political situations and events of the Resistance can only be understood in the light of the attitudes—more or less pro- or anti-fascist—of the actors on the wide stage which was France in the nineteen-thirties and 'forties.

We ought to go back to 1871 for the historical beginnings of the chronicle, to the formation of France's Third Republic when the liberal bourgeoisie, after crushing the Commune, built up a system designed to prevent possible revolution and to keep the people in "their proper place".

There is no space here for such a study, important though it would be in explaining the events that led to World War II, the collapse of the Republic, surrender to Hitler and the Resistance of the 1940s; but it is indispensable to outline the situation in the preceding decade so as to see the relevance of the class divisions, economic upheavals, strikes and crises of those years to the political and military scene just before the German invasion.

For our purpose, then, the story starts in February 1934, at the height of the world economic crisis of that decade. Although the slump reached France later than the U.S.A. or Great Britain it hit that country as hard as any other.

In 1931 there had been 1,500,000 unemployed, while those in work suffered short-time, cuts in wages and widespread distress. Thousands of bankruptcies were recorded (13,764 in 1933, 15,052 in

1934); imports fell to a fraction of the 1929 level (textiles, for instance, from 1,679 million francs to 214 million in 1933); production was halved (silk, from 74 per cent of pre-war output to 35 per cent in 1933).

It was by fascism that Italy had for eleven years of economic crisis held down its working people and prevented revolution, and by fascism that the German capitalists hoped to solve their even deeper problems. From 1933 onwards, great industrialists and financiers supported Adolf Hitler and his storm troopers, the arms kings supplied weapons for the police state and embarked on a vast war programme in the name of German supremacy; the middle class were bamboozled by loud and lurid demagogy into acceptance of national-socialism; Jews and liberals were outlawed; communists were herded into concentration camps and the vast majority of the workers bludgeoned into silence.

This solution was thought rather too crude by the French extreme Right, but many of the wealthy conservatives infinitely preferred the thought of a police state to "popular power".

As the workers became more wretched, restive and militant, a number of fascist organisations emerged into prominence: the ex-Communist Jacques Doriot's *Parti Populaire Français* (P.P.F.), Colonel de la Rocque's royalist *Croix de Feu*, Charles Maurras' *Action Française*, Pierre Taittinger's *Jeunesse Patriote*. They were backed by right-wing politicians and financed by reactionary millionaires, some of them members of the Two Hundred Families, celebrated in France's economic history as owners of banks and industry. The "deux cents familles" were the *Conseil Général* of the Bank of France, its largest shareholders, and controllers of many key financial positions, of industrial groups including the *Comité des Forges*, of transport, commerce, the press, armaments.[1]

They would gladly have imposed a fascist regime to ensure their profits, had it been possible in the early 1930s, and would have had help from their opposite numbers abroad. But they were confronted with the united strength of the working class, the French Communist Party (P.C.F.), the *Confédération Générale du Travail* (C.G.T.) with its million-odd members, the Catholic unions (C.U.T.C.), the very vocal peasantry, imbued with strong Republican traditions. The conservatives of the French middle class, though all for law and order, and *contre le bolchevisme*, were on the whole highly patriotic and not inclined to fall for Hitler-type propaganda; the socialists— pacifist and anti-revolutionary—would still not accept anti-

republicanism at this time. None the less, the French fascist movement was growing, and it thrived on the crop of financial scandals of
the day which it was said were due to the rottenness of the democratic system. The most sensational was that centred round the forger
Stavisky, who at the beginning of 1934 was proved to have stolen
hundreds of millions of francs of private and public money with the
connivance of the Paris Préfet, Chiappe, and various politicians.
Stavisky committed suicide, in mysterious circumstances, and
Chiappe was sacked by Daladier. Popular feeling ran high and,
cashing in on this, the Government was blamed by the anti-democratic leaders, Doriot and Colonel de la Rocque, who called for
demonstrations against the Third Republic and its corrupt minions.

Their intention was to show the fascist flag, if not actually to take
power, by attacking the Chambre des Députés, symbol of decadent
democracy. In so doing they started a train of events which were to
have very long-term and violent effects on France.

*   *   *

On the bleak chilly night of Thursday, 6 February 1934, the
streets around the Parliament buildings were the scene of the most
serious riots witnessed in France for thirty years. In the dusk,
crowds of fascist supporters 40,000 strong gathered on the Place de
la Concorde and in the rue de Grenelle, shouting slogans, restlessly
stamping and swaying, and eventually surging forward spasmodically
towards the *maison sans fenêtres* to clash with the serried ranks of
police protecting the scared deputies within. To howls of "Down
with the Thieves!", "The Government must resign!", "Long live
Chiappe!", the rioters threw stones and railings torn from the *Place*,
set a bus on fire, and wounded over fifty of the 170 police guarding
the bridge across the Seine to the Chamber.

At 7 p.m. the *Action Française* formations crossed the river and
opened fire on the Parliament buildings from the front, while the
fascist Youth Groups and the Croix de Feu's followers made repeated attacks from the rear, repulsed after bitter clashes on both
sides by the Republican Guards.[2] The fighting went on till after
midnight, and only ended when the police dispersed the crowd by
firing, killing 16 and wounding 655. The fascist organisers had not
destroyed parliamentary government, but they had certainly made
their mark in blood, and badly scared the ministry.

Daladier, the Prime Minister, frightened out of his wits, resigned
next day, and President Jean Lebrun, yielding to the rioters' pressure,

called on the Radical Gaston Doumergue to form a government of the centre.

Sensing that the events of 6 February had been a win for the fascist leagues, the angry and indignant anti-fascist workers of Paris' Confédération Générale du Travail (Unitaire), the C.G.T.U. led by the Communist Benoit Frachon, called a general strike on the 12th, with a preliminary demonstration on the 9th. The latter was forbidden by the police, but none the less the workers turned out in force, Socialists and Léon Jouhaux's Confédération Générale du Travail (C.G.T.) members alongside Communists, for the first time together, all over Paris, in a highly significant display of unity. They were roughly put down by the police, who fired on them at the Gare de l'Est and in Place Voltaire, killing six people and wounding hundreds. It was said that out of 50,000 demonstrators 1,200 were arrested.

Nothing daunted, the two Trade Union Congresses, united and with the support of the Communist Party, continued to organise the strike of 12 February. This won an immediate and overwhelming response from the whole of France; 4,500,000 workers left the factories, over a million took part in demonstrations—150,000 in Paris alone and the whole working class won a feeling of confidence in its strength and power to resist the fascists, as well as a sense of the unity that could be achieved in action. Committees for united action sprang up all over France, pointing the way forward to the Popular Front that was eventually to come.

The events of February brought out clearly the alignment of forces in France: on the one hand, the lengths to which the fascists would go to attack Republican institutions (the *Chambre* being a symbol), the weak, even conniving, attitude of authority (the Préfet, Chiappe, was demoted, but the right-wing organisations continued with impunity); on the other hand, the February demonstrations showed the overwhelming power of the working classes when aroused, and this, while it terrified conservatives, inspired the Left to organise energetically for the further defence of the Republic and for civil and social rights. They had the sense of being backed by international solidarity—the Spanish workers called a general strike in .sympathy, and the British T.U.C. expressed support. Anti-fascism was a powerful cement, internationally—as a 30,000 strong Paris meeting for the liberation of the German anti-fascist, Ernst Thaelmann, showed—and nationally. While workers organised for their defence, leading intellectuals formed a Vigilance Committee, led by the distinguished physicist Professor Paul Langevin and Paul Rivet, director of the *Musée de l'Homme*, and supported by André Gide, André Malraux and many other eminent writers and academics. Those who held back from united action with the communists were, as often happened, members of the French Socialist Party. In 1926 and 1928, they had refused to join forces to fight Poincaré, in 1932 they had boycotted the World Committee against War and Fascism, in spite of appeals by Romain Rolland and Henri Barbusse, and in 1933 they firmly rejected the proposals for a united front. But the events of early 1934 created a new and urgent situation, and after much discussion between the socialists and the P.C.F. a "united front pact" was signed on 27 July 1934.

Throughout 1935, tension increased on the French political front. On 6 February the fascist Leagues (still at large) organised an anniversary commemoration service in Notre-Dame Cathedral, hoping to show that officially they had the Church behind them. On 10 February the Left countered with its own demonstration, of 100,000 people in the Place de la République, honouring their dead of 9 February 1934. It was a year of mammoth popular meetings: in March 200,000 turned out to a Commune memorial meeting at Père Lachaise cemetery; 500,000 to the first gathering called by the Front Populaire at the Mutualité, half a million to the 14 July demonstration at the Bastille—all tremendous occasions, gay and enthusiastic, and testifying to the hope and confidence in popular control to change and build a better France.[3]

Following Mussolini's attack on Ethiopia in October, popular fury was aroused by the Hoare-Laval agreement virtually whitewashing Italy. In view of the increasing arrogance of the fascist powers, the French Radical Party agreed to join the Socialist and Communist parties, taking the decision at its 1934 autumn congress and bringing 180,000 members' support to the People's Front. It was agreed to fight the next election on a common programme.

In view of the closing of the ranks on the Left, the French Parliament at last dissolved the fascist Leagues.

The news from abroad of Hitler's remilitarisation of the Rhineland, in March 1936, added fuel to the anti-fascist campaign. The Sarraut government (which had succeeded that of Daladier and Laval) was dissuaded by British pressure from doing anything effective in protest, and popular anger mounted rapidly at the fascists' impudence and the French authorities' inaction. The elections of April/May 1936 were fought largely on the question of the fascist threat, and they produced a sweeping victory for the Front Populaire parties: out of 618 seats, 378 went to the Front Populaire, the Socialists increased their representation from 101 to 146 deputies, the Communists from 10 to 72.[4]

A Popular Front government came into power on 4 June, headed by the Socialist Léon Blum, pledged to a programme of sweeping reforms, defence of civil liberties at home and of peace abroad. The Communist Party and the C.G.T. decided not to participate in the government, but said they would give it their support and co-operation.

On 10 May, Blum announced some of the measures proposed by his government which would be implemented "gradually". The industrial workers, enthusiastic for the reforms and impatient to see them put through not "gradually" but rapidly, showed their strength and support for the programme by their most effective form of demonstration—widespread and united strikes for the higher wages promised and so desperately needed.

A wave of sit-in strikes began on 26 May in Paris aircraft factories and surged across the country till over a million workers were striking or occupying their premises. Men and women slept on the shop floor, organised factory committees, kept everything clean, tidy and in order, sang, danced, and enjoyed their great sense of power. As an American writer observed, "even the leaders of the C.P. and C.G.T. were taken by surprise by that spontaneous wave of jubilation. . . . The workers were good-humoured, damaged nothing in the occupied factories and hadn't the remotest idea what to do next. But their demonstration of the fragility of owners' control threw owners into panic."[5]

Some employers adopted a prudent attitude, like Prince Jean de Caraman-Chimay, head of the Veuve Clicquot Champagne firm, who "had a suit tailored from blue workman's overall material and was driven to work in it wearing a red carnation" (*Observer*, 5 May 1974); but most capitalists stayed out of sight awaiting developments.

Before the full Popular Front programme could be made law, and to speed things up, an emergency meeting was held on 7 June at the Hotel Matignon in Paris, between the C.G.T. and the French Federation of Employers, under Blum's chairmanship. There the strikers' demands were put forward, and conceded by the unwilling bosses who had no other choice. Within a few hours of this "Matignon Agreement" legislation was passed in the Chamber of Deputies, establishing in principle the following measures: *(a)* the 40-hour week without loss of pay; *(b)* a fortnight's paid holiday yearly; *(c)* collective agreements in every workshop; *(d)* restoration of wage cuts inflicted by recent government decrees.

Wages as a result rose immediately, in normal cases from 10 to 15 per cent, but in sweated factories and workshops sometimes by up to 50 per cent.

In some areas the workers demanded still more, and in spite of the Agreement they continued to strike in an effort to ensure satisfaction of their demands—half a million miners in northern France, 100,000 textile workers, plus wage-earners in the dress-making and restaurant trades staying out through the summer months. In June, Maurice Thorez, leader of the P.C.F., called for an end to strikes and emphasised the importance of proletarian discipline—but many people held out till the end of September.

Right-wing politicians grumbled at the sight of "men and women workers going off on Saturday mornings on their tandems, wearing matching sweaters and calling this 'progress'," as Paul Reynaud put it,[6] complaining that owing to all this French armaments production was falling behind Germany's war effort. Robert Schuman (of post-war celebrity) moaned about "the disastrous impression on other countries produced by . . . our tolerating the four-months' occupation of our factories"; General Gamelin was shocked by the groups of workers he saw at the tram stops in the Paris suburbs, raising their hands in the clenched fist salute as he passed; a Belgian minister on a visit to Paris expressed horror at having to carry his cases down the hotel stairs himself because the porters were on strike, and asked Paul Reynaud, "Isn't it excusable to have anxieties about France?"[7]

The workers themselves had no such anxieties. They had won great victories by their actions, and trade union membership rose in three months from less than a million to $2\frac{1}{2}$ millions. Within a year the C.G.T. had five million members, enjoying holidays with pay, and the 40-hour week. These advances strengthened the whole Front Populaire. Under the watchful eye of the C.G.T. (now uniting the whole trade union movement) unwilling employers were forced to carry out the agreements. Other parts of the programme were quickly implemented; the *Office du Blé* (regulating the price of grain) was created, the fascist Leagues outlawed, arms firms nationalised, the hydra-headed Bank of France brought partly under government control, and the influence of the Two Hundred Families greatly curbed.

Anyone who was in France during the summer of 1936 must remember the heady atmosphere, the cheerful faces in the working class quarters, the optimism of left-wingers among the intellectuals, the enthusiasm of the political meetings. I vividly recall a packed demonstration at the "Vel d'Hiv" (the Vélodrome d'Hiver, a vast hall much used for Paris mass meetings) and a hilarious evening at the "Cabaret du Front Populaire" with its scarlet curtains and its ribald impersonations of right-wing leaders. Everybody joined vociferously in the chorus (to the tune of *La Carmagnole*) of the hit song which went: "M'sieur d'la Rocque avait promis/de chambarder la bourgeoisie;/Mais il a raté son coup, et ça y est, c'est à nous— Ah, ça ira, ça ira, ça ira . . .".

In contrast, the highbrows discussing "la Volonté du Mal" at the Abbaye de Pontigny, where eminent intellectuals of Right and Left met annually for philosophical and literary sessions (to which I went under my old father's scholarly wing), were cautiously optimistic. The enlightened liberals who dominated the scene (Professor Brunschvicg, and his wife, Undersecretary of Blum's Ministry of Health, Raymond Aron, and Jean Wahl) considered themselves firm supporters of the Popular Front against fascism; while the younger members of the party, typical of that generation, were not at all afraid of revolutionary prospects, and would stay up most of the night confidently discussing the bright future of a socialist France which would defeat the forces of evil.

But many of the French middle class were less happy. There was a deep seated fear of "bolchevisme" which led to confrontations in classrooms, cafés, offices, and in city streets. A great many professional people, white-collar workers, businessmen, conservatives and right-wing socialists alike, distrusted the Front Populaire, which was said to be communist-organised. The conservative press stirred up their fears with shrill anti-Government propaganda. Even the moderate *Temps* habitually called the Popular Front programme "revolutionary", as did the liberal historian Daniel Halévy. It was constantly suggested that Moscow was running France, and right-wingers and fearful liberals alike expected imminent revolution. The silent majority of those days was inclined to be anti-fascist, but on each side of the amorphous mass the lines were drawn in 1936 between the social classes of the French, clearly foreshadowing the 1940 position.

There were on the extreme Right those very highly placed persons whose interests lay in preserving capitalism at all costs, and who would welcome fascism—and even Hitler's National-Socialism—if it offered them protection from "popular power". On their flank were those small property-owners who feared bolshevism more than fascism and might be temporarily misled into subjection by the hope of saving their stake in the *status quo* or (as in the case of many sincere socialists and pacifists) of avoiding war. On the Left there were the communists, 5 million strong, determined to change the system but hoping for social revolution by democratic means; and with them the great majority of the working class and its allies, the people who would at whatever cost defend the freedom and independence of France against the fascist danger.

In face of the great popular advances of 1936, the preservation of the *status quo* and survival of their vast private possessions depended on how far the financiers and industrialists would be able to undermine the attempts to build a socialist economy, wreck democratic institutions and cause a national crisis leading possibly to war—always a convenient way out for capitalism *in extremis*. The international monopolists would of course be ready to step in when needed, and the press and media (owned mainly by the Trusts) could be used to sway public opinion. The police and armed forces were of course still reliable—but one never knew.

In the meanwhile, the Right decided to lie low. Though things were not going their way at home, the prospects abroad were favourable. In Germany and Italy, the spectre of revolution had been firmly laid, and Hitler and Mussolini could be expected to be satisfied in their territorial appetites without harm to French capitalist interests. It was hoped that Hitler might be tempted by the rich wheat lands and oil wells of the Soviet Union, and in any case the danger of an attack on the West was negligible while Germany had so many unfulfilled ambitions elsewhere.

So the reactionaries bided their time, keeping their cadres together, building up Franco-German friendship committees, trading with Japan, digging-in in colonial administration, and cursing the Front Populaire, which went confidently forward with its plans for a free, fraternal and egalitarian France.

NOTES

1. D. N. Pritt, *The Fall of the French Republic* (London 1941) p. 25
2. G. de Benouville, *Le Sacrifice du Matin* (Paris, 1947) p. 66

3. Pritt, op. cit. pp. 64–67
4. A. Werth, *The Destiny of France* (London, 1937) p. 274
5. R. Paxton, *Vichy France* (London, 1970) p. 247
6. R. Reynaud, *La France a sauvé l'Europe* (Paris, 1947) p. 388
7. ibid. pp. 393, 400

Chapter 2

1936–1939

THE RISE AND DECLINE OF
THE POPULAR FRONT

Come, let us put an end to one thing
Now that science gives us the power,
And make it impossible for any man
To exercise for another hour
An influence that depends
On economic pressure to gain its ends

Come, let us finish the whole damned farce
Of law and order on murder based,
On the power to coerce and starve and kill
With all its hypocrisy, cruelty and waste,
And safe from all human interference give
Every man at least ample means to live.

Hugh MacDiarmid (from *Stony Limits*)

On 14 July 1936 over a million people gathered in the Place de la Bastille in a great show of support for the new Popular Front Government. The vast crowd was at the same time expressing its solidarity with the recently formed Frente Popular in Spain where, as in France, a combination of liberals, socialists and communists had been voted into power. French anti-fascists were jubilant at the prospect of democratic change for their poor backward neighbour, and the massive meeting went off in an atmosphere of great good humour and optimism, unhindered by right-wing thugs or police interference.

Four days later came the news of a coup by the exiled Spanish general, Francisco Franco, against the Frente Popular. The government in Madrid was pushing ahead its programme of mild and long overdue social reform, but even this was too "revolutionary" for the reactionary Junta in Morocco. (The excuse given by the fascists to the outside world was that the anarchists had taken things into their hands and were about to launch a revolution.) Counting on Mussolini and Hitler's promised support, Franco had landed on 18 July in southern Spain and army officers were rallying to his Junta and taking over in the garrison towns, crushing the local people's attempted resistance.

The Madrid government appealed urgently to France to send arms and the supplies which they were entitled to and ready to pay for. While Italian warplanes flew over Spain, Mussolini's troops disembarked on the coast and German warships steamed towards it to land Nazi technicians on Franco's side; but Léon Blum, under pressure from the British Conservative government, decided on a cautious policy of non-intervention and forbade the dispatch of war material to Spain, announcing the ban on 8 August 1936.

There were massive and spontaneous pro-Spanish Republic demonstrations all over Paris; campaigns for "Arms for Spain", and relief committees mushroomed everywhere in France, and indeed in all non-fascist European countries, where decent people were deeply shocked by the reports of naked aggression and ruthless crushing of all opposition.

As news came of Franco's advance under the protection of the fascist powers, the French reacted with increasing vigour: money was collected for food and milk and medical aid (notes and coins were flung into Republican red-yellow-purple flags carried by sympathisers through the streets); appeals went out for clothing and comforts for the victims of Hitler's bombing raids; the International Brigade was formed and headquarters set up in Paris to recruit hundreds of young anti-fascists. There was a deep common longing to do something effective, even among drop-outs like Sartre's character "with an oddly ardent look" in *The Age of Reason*: "I wanted to get there but it couldn't be fixed."[1] A great many did get there and they stopped the fascists from taking Madrid in 1936 with the cry of "No pasaràn!" and "Madrid sará el tumbo del fascismo!"

Some of France's best intellectuals took the Republican side, proclaiming the threat to all freedom of thought should fascism prevail on the peninsula—for it would not stop at the Pyrenees. Writers and poets published impressive work in praise of the heroic Spaniards, journalists and film-makers produced documentaries (André Malraux's *Jours de Mépris* was a valuable contribution, and even more so were the planes that he smuggled into Spain), high-power left-wing delegations visited Madrid and returned to speak passionately to mammoth meetings, pleading for arms and supplies for the Republic. The French Right early on showed itself to be pro-Franco; as André Chamson wrote, "Our right-wing press has joined Italy's and Germany's, our nationalists have attuned their actions to those of Hitler and Mussolini. The working class fraternity has played its full part for the Spanish Republic, while liberal-democratic support has been sentimental and theoretic."[2]

Léon Blum and his colleagues' support could hardly be called even that, though at the time his government was at the peak of its success. A few Ministers of character saved their own personal honour by helping the Spanish people—Pierre Cot, the Aircraft Minister, for instance, arranged for some 300 planes to reach Spain via other countries, and in this he was assisted by Jean Moulin, later an outstanding leader in the French Resistance. With a few more of their courage in the government, the Spanish Republic might have been saved. Paul Baudouin says in his *Diaries* (p. 57) that Daladier and Gamelin were prepared to send French divisions to Catalonia but the right-wing militarists' views prevailed. Pétain told Baudouin, "If I had not been there Gamelin would have agreed to it. I that day prevented a catastrophe in which the Popular Front would have involved France."

On the wider international front, Blum talked to the U.S.S.R. leaders that summer about forming an alliance against fascism, but it came to nothing; in the meantime, Germany and Japan signed an anti-communist pact, and the latter prepared to invade China while the Western powers looked the other way.

For some months, the French capitalists were in retreat and made a number of concessions. They could not set up an effective opposition in Parliament, and it was even admitted in June by the representative of the *Comité des Forges* that they had no intention of playing the classic Parliamentary game because "the driving force for action quite clearly lies outside Parliament"—a reference to the fascist Leagues, to be resuscitated in due course under new names.

There was, however, one means of disrupting the Front Populaire which the Right could use immediately, with help from the City of London, if not from the British government itself—the weapon of financial pressure. This was effectively used on 25 September, to bring about the devaluation of the franc. In conjunction with the City of London the French bankers started a rapid export of capital, until by the autumn 40 milliards of francs had "taken flight". Blum surrendered to the pressure, agreed to devaluation, and thereafter had to make concession after fatal concession to the financial oligarchy. By calling in the right-wing Paul Baudouin (later Foreign Secretary in Vichy) to advise on financial matters, Blum installed the enemy within the camp.[3]

At Baudouin's instigation, a "pause" was announced in the Popular Front programme, and many economic and social measures were suspended at the employers' demand. In June 1937 60 milliard francs had taken flight, and the banks refused to grant credits. The Senate defeated Blum by 168 votes to 96 on 21 June, and Blum, instead of putting up a fight against this high-handed resistance to the majority will, resigned. He was succeeded by Camille Chautemps, prime minister in 1933–34, who acted as premier with the support of various Socialist colleagues.

In spite of right-wing pressure and unscrupulous campaigns against the Popular Front the latter won more votes in the autumn local elections than before. Its supporters were fiercely determined to preserve their gains and to defeat fascist plots against them. Thanks to their vigilance, a large-scale Cagoulard conspiracy to overthrow the government and launch civil war was exposed in time and collapsed on 15 November. It was revealed by Marx Dormoy, Socialist Minister of the Interior, that the Cagoulards under their leader Eugène Deloncle had detailed plans for taking over Paris; they had connections with influential members of the General Staff, possessed stocks of German and Italian weapons and had access to plenty more through their friends in the Army.[4]

The leaders were arrested, but later released and, thanks to their powerful connections, were never prosecuted. Some of them emerged into high posts in June 1940, as we shall later see.

But to return to September 1937. The atmosphere of Paris in that late summer heat was politically as well as physically sultry. I remember my strong impression at that time, on the way back from a month in the press office in Madrid, that the French people would not let Spain down; their belief in eventual victory, and anger at the betrayal by the "democracies" was manifest in slogans, on hoardings and in street demonstrations. Every day the Spanish Pavilion at the international exhibition at the Chaillot Palace was packed with pro-Republicans queuing up to look at the films and paintings of the war, coming away from Picasso's *Guernica* with fists clenched in anger at the shame of France's disloyalty. Nobody would accept the thought that the fascists might conceivably win.

André Chamson, just back from the Writers' Congress in Madrid, wrote of "the extraordinary, terrible human experience being lived through there, of misery and death, joy and hope, combined", and declared in a white heat of prophetic indignation: "What I saw there convinced me that, if the impossible happened—and it could only happen by the mad complicity of France and England—and Franco were victorious in this struggle, the certainty of European war would be established."[5]

Alas, the "mad complicity" prevailed. During the winter of 1937, more and more German and Italian material poured into Spain, which was avowedly being used by the Wehrmacht "as a laboratory to try out its new material, especially its Stuka bombers", as the German Commander Beck later told General Gamelin.[6] Meanwhile, the Spanish coast was blockaded by fascist ships to prevent Soviet arms reaching the "reds". The Teruel offensive in December won new positions for the Republicans, but these were lost in February 1938.

The battle of the Ebro raised the people's hopes, but all the courage of the legendary Fifth Brigade and the Internationals could not prevent the Franquists with their vastly superior armaments cutting through into Catalonia. The Spanish people had their backs to the wall, and their friends held their breath.

By the spring of 1938 Hitler was satisfied that "the democracies" would not intervene, and that Franco would win. He turned his attention to the next objective—the reunion of the German-speaking peoples of central Europe with "The Fatherland". Nazi troops entered Austria on 12 March and the consolidation of German overlordship there proceeded throughout the summer, while the Führer made threatening noises about the German minority—the Sudetendeutsch—in Czechoslovakia.

In the unsettled national and explosive international situation, the French government (still nominally Front Populaire) fell and changed rightwards several times—Blum succeeding Chautemps and being succeeded by Daladier in April 1938.

On 29 September, Neville Chamberlain flew to Munich with Daladier to meet Hitler, and signed away the independence of Czechoslovakia—handing over her proud people and her splendid army and fortifications in exchange for an empty hope of "peace in our time".

In France disillusion and disgust against the connivance in British appeasement were widespread. "Compared with this Munich butchery, the Hoare-Laval plan looks like a piece of delicate surgery", wrote a French journalist, André Simone.[7] And Konni Zilliacus, a British M.P., observed that, in return for unlimited servility, the French Right openly relied on the fascist regimes to bolster them up against their own people. "Anyone who wants France to stand by her treaty obligations or to help Spanish democracy or to oppose the fascist powers in any way is promptly called a warmonger. . . . The state of confusion and defeatism among the

French masses since the Czech betrayal is indescribable. . . ."[8] In Spain too the Munich agreement caused dismay to the internationally conscious Republicans who were deeply disillusioned by the "democracies'" behaviour, and by the League of Nations' order for withdrawal (on 21 September) of the foreign volunteers of the International Brigades while Italians and Germans remained in force to fight for Franco.

In the European parliaments there were still a very few anti-fascists who raised dissident voices, nearly all of them Communist. In the British House of Commons William Gallacher's was the only protest when Chamberlain made his announcement. And in the *Chambre des Députés* on 5 October, out of 693 members only 75 voted against the Munich pact. Seventy-three of these were Communists.

By then the Front Populaire was in its last stages. Its decline had begun in January 1938 with an attack on the franc. Chautemps, in office since June 1937 with Socialist support, tried to win the banks to his side by surrendering to right-wing demands. The Socialists refused to back him in his manœuvres and he resigned on 14 January 1938. Four days later he returned to office (nobody else being willing to take over) on a solely Radical ticket. He got a unanimous vote from the *Chambre* thanks to his fulsome promises to introduce Old Age Pensions and other reforms not yet achieved by the Popular Front. The Left backed Chautemps because they hoped thereby to help the ailing coalition, the reactionaries because they knew the hollowness of his declarations.

After a few weeks, under renewed pressure from Britain and the banks, Chautemps demanded "exceptional powers"; with these he set out to put the clock back: now, far from offering pensions he proposed to cut down social services, to tamper with the 40-hour week to the detriment of the workers, and to withdraw much else of the Front Populaire programme. This was too much for the deputies to swallow and on 13 March 1938 Chautemps gave way to Blum, who, while behaving very feebly in international affairs, at least did not carry out his predecessor's threats at home. He was again subjected to financial pressure and wrecking tactics by the right-wingers who wanted to split the Radicals from the Left bloc; foremost among the critics were Pierre Laval and Paul-Etienne Flandin, who hinted at the suppression of parliamentary government and dissolution of trades unions (measures introduced by them as Vichy ministers two years later). Blum was supplanted in April by Daladier and by mid-

1938 it was evident that democracy was being betrayed in its own house; the vacillating bourgeoisie and liberal centre had swung over to the reactionaries, while the Socialist leaders were acting as conscious or unconscious agents for French and British capitalist interests. This became clear when Daladier on 14 November issued a *décret-loi* abolishing many Front Populaire decrees and doing away with the 40-hour week, on the pretext of balancing the budget.

The C.G.T. called a 24-hour strike in protest on 30 November, and this was widely supported by the angry and resentful workers in spite of ruthless suppression of their demonstrations by the police. When the Chamber met again on 8 December 1938, Daladier was warned by the reactionaries, his only remaining supporters, that he must now take his orders from them.

*   *   *

For each concession to reaction at home there was one made on the international front. At the end of 1938, to match Daladier's pact with the French Right, his foreign minister Georges Bonnet signed a Franco-German pact, or "statement of entente" with von Ribbentrop, his opposite number in Germany, solemnly recognising "as permanent the frontier between their countries as it is presently drawn". Bonnet explained to his ambassadors in various European capitals that "the struggle against Bolshevism" was the basis of the Berlin–Rome Axis, which therefore made the Axis respectable; and as to Spain, "the action of Germany had from the beginning been inspired solely by the struggle against Bolshevism".[9]

Every concession to Hitler was of course made in the hope that the Nazis would attack the Soviet Union. From the beginning of 1939 on, it seemed that war was inevitable—Hitler had to break out somewhere. The right-wing governments put their efforts from now on into turning the coming war away from the West and towards the U.S.S.R. in the East.

*   *   *

In the spring of 1939 the Spanish Republic collapsed, from lack of arms, thanks to the collusion of the "democracies" with the fascist powers and in spite of all the popular movements in its support.

Hundreds of thousands of refugees poured over the Catalan border into France, regiments of *milicianos* along with the populations of whole villages, grandfathers, babies, young mothers, children, in mule-carts, pushing barrows or carrying on their backs the few poor odds and ends they had been able to save and bring with them in their headlong flight. The French government—again, one supposes, with the aim of pleasing international reaction, and Hitler—sent police and army men to receive them and to herd them into detention camps on a bare desolate stretch of coast between Sète and Banyuls. There, behind 9-foot-high wire fences, guarded by Moroccan soldiers, rifles at the ready, on a waste of grey sand swept by piercing east winds, the remnant of the Spanish people's army and their families were left to rot. Fending for themselves, the refugees put up little shacks of wood and corrugated iron and sheltered as best they could.

The French authorities provided a sort of bean soup and swede mush *(rutabaga)* to keep the refugees from starving, and rows of wooden barracks were gradually erected, giving the impression that the Spanish were expected to be there for a good while. Fortunately, the Aid Committees quickly moved in to Perpignan (the nearest town) and supplied extra food, clothing and blankets; French sympathisers organised homes and jobs for many refugees, and invitations from abroad poured into committee rooms, so that after a few weeks of hectic activity a considerable number were evacuated to Chile, San Domingo and Guatemala, as well as to England, Belgium and the U.S.S.R.

As a volunteer in the British relief office I saw the departure of S.S. *Sinaia* to Mexico, carrying 5,000 sponsored by our Committee, waved off by the Duchess of Atholl and various pro-Republican British M.P.s, to the strains of *God Save the King* and the *Himno de Riego*. The symbolic (if slightly incongruous) scene was to me the most heartening sight of that sad time.

But for many months the shame of the camps continued, the worst disgrace being the removal of Communists and International Brigaders to out-and-out concentration camps at Vernet-les-Bains (described by Arthur Koestler in *Scum of the Earth*) and to Gurs in the western Pyrenees, where they stayed virtually forgotten by the outside world for more than two years.

The French authorities who had to bear the brunt of the Spanish exodus were, of course, faced with an enormous problem and could not have been expected to offer luxury accommodation; but they did seem to go out of their way to make life difficult, if not unbearable, for the unfortunate refugees. M. Daladier had other things on his mind: the international horizon was dark with storm clouds. On 15

March 1939, Hitler had seized the whole of Czechoslovakia and, it was obvious, was looking for new territory to take by force of arms. Poland appeared to be marked as the next victim, and could only be saved by agreement with the Soviet Union. The British government began to negotiate with Moscow, but used delaying tactics, sending a minor Foreign Official—by land—without the authority to conclude a pact (which indeed the near-fascist Polish-government would not accept as it necessarily meant involving the Soviet Red Army in its defence).

Chamberlain and his friends in Britain still hoped against hope that Hitler would attack Russia. The French government acquiesced in giving the Nazis a free hand in the East, but they went through the motions of pretending they would resist, and M. Bonnet warned Abetz, the German Ambassador in Paris, that if war broke out the French nation would rally to the support of the government. "Elections would be suspended; public meetings stopped; attempts at foreign propaganda of whatever kind would be suppressed and the Communists brought to book *(mis à raison)*."[10] Daladier saw to it that when war was in fact declared these promises were carried out—this was action after his own heart.

All through 1939, while the Left struggled to keep some popular unity and to save the remnants of the Spanish republic, the French right-wing movements were on the offensive. Fascist and anti-semitic secret societies were formed, to further Franco-German friendship: the most reactionary leaders of the Croix de Feu and Action Française in conjunction with the France-Allemagne Association, all busied themselves in preparing a wooden horse by which the Nazis would be helped to take France over when the time came. A police dossier, dated between September 1938 and May 1939, reports the comings and goings between Paris and Berlin of such characters as Darquier de Pellepoix, Fernand de Brinon, Count Jaunez des Marrés (whose wife, Elisabeth Buettner was secretary to the infamous Nazi propagandist Julius Streicher), all of them in high society, with connections in the top ranks of Army and Air Force whom they were able to bribe and subvert by munificent German subsidies. Of Madame des Marrés, the police reported: "This woman, whether or not engaged in military espionage, works for the International Centre of German Propaganda, charged with providing financial resources for those in France occupied in anti-semitic and racist activity."[11] Later we read details of this activity—campaigns against "the Jewish peril", the organisation of propaganda, and of groups of provocateurs and terrorists: "all means, even the worst, were to be employed".[12]

It is unlikely that the net result of this repulsive effort won Hitler many disciples, though it may have lined the pockets of his supporters and enabled them to publish their news-sheets: Darquier's *La France Enchainée*, supported by Céline, Coston's *La Libre Parole* and Legrand's *Le Défi* (which he claimed had 9,000 subscribers, many of them Army and Airforce officers).[13] But it was a fact that such racist and pro-German propaganda was not discouraged, let alone banned, by the French government which frowned on left-wing activity and literature. This is not perhaps surprising when one learns that the Minister, Bonnet, and Laval had themselves created a substantial fund to support the campaign for "Franco-German Understanding", which was based on two groups, one led by Déat and Bergery, another around Laval and Adrien Marquet, Mayor of Bordeaux.[14]

Their path towards collaboration—the shape of things to come— was smoothed by the anti-communism of many educated French, and by the apathy of others. The working class was in retreat, the hopes of 1936 frustrated, its unity lost through the cowardice of its so-called leaders, who had surrendered to reaction.

The sudden bombshell of the news that the Soviet Union had signed a non-aggression pact with Germany, on 30 August 1939, threw the Left into further disarray, shocked the middle-of-the-roaders into anti-sovietism, and gave the Right an opportunity to take the offensive, posing as patriots, which of course delighted them.

The government allowed no explanation of the pact to leak through press or radio: nobody was permitted to point out the obvious truth, that the U.S.S.R. could not wait indefinitely for guarantees from Britain and France, that she had to take measures for her own protection. The Communist deputies' letter to the President, explaining this, was suppressed and its authors suspended. *L'Humanité* had already been banned for anti-Government head-lines some weeks earlier, and its 100,000 readership remained in darkness.

Suddenly almost the whole French middle class decided that the patriotic thing was to be anti-communist. It was an illuminating experience to be at a conference of intellectuals at Pontigny that week. There had been discussions on the problems of refugees, led by humanitarians and sociologists of repute, and I had gone there to represent the National Joint Committee for Spanish Relief. Thinking some of the younger participants at least were sincere anti-fascists, I expressed my belief that the Soviet Union had acted in self-defence. Alas, the Socialist "universitaires" and writers turned on me, and I realised that beneath all the liberal talk deep-rooted anti-communism prevailed.

It was with a heavy heart that I packed my bag on the morning that mobilisation was decreed in France—1 September. Hitler's troops had crossed the German–Polish border on a trumped up pretext of provocation[15] and were waging *blitzkrieg* against the Poles, while Russian troops were advancing into Bessarabia. Although there was little that her Western allies could do to help Poland in time to save her collapse, France and Britain on 3 September declared war on Germany.

War—without Czechoslovakia and without the Soviet Union— under Chamberlain and Daladier! How could it really be war against fascism? This was the question which hung over Europe that threatening autumn, and which got a very dusty answer.

NOTES

1. J. P. Sartre, *The Age of Reason* (Penguin Books, London, 1961) p. 6
2. A. Chamson, *Rien qu'un Témoignage* (Paris, 1937) p. 95
3. D. N. Pritt, *The Fall of the French Republic* (London, 1941) p. 96
4. ibid. pp. 100–101
5. Chamson, op. cit. p. 98
6. P. Reynaud, *La France a sauvé l'Europe*, I p. 442
7. A. Simone, *J'accuse* (Paris, 1942) p. 209
8. K. Zilliacus, *Why we are Losing the Peace* (London, 1939)
9. Pritt, op. cit. p. 115
10. *Livre Jaune*, 1939 p. 146
11. *Police Report*, 1938–39 p. 9
12. ibid. pp. 41–46
13. ibid.
14. Simone, op. cit. p. 233
15. See P. Reynaud, op. cit. p. 599. At the Nuremberg trials in 1946 one of Heydrich's lieutenants said that a dozen concentration camp prisoners had been put into Polish uniforms and, under Himmler's orders, forced to attack a German train on Reich territory. They were shot down, and Hitler proceeded to announce an "unprovoked aggression" and ordered the invasion of Poland by the Wehrmacht.

Chapter 3

PHONEY WAR

> Go to the war, workers, go to the war,
> Heed not the socialists but wallow in gore;
> Shoulder your rifle, workers, don't ask what it's for,
> Let your wife and children starve and go to the war.
>
> Clydeside Ballad 1915

In England people were taking the news more phlegmatically than the French, though the same sort of stunned confusedness competed with a show of organisational zeal. Nobody could quite believe that we were actually at war or visualise what Nazi *blitzkrieg* might mean. The deep shelters that had been demanded by the Left were non-existent, and we were assured by Chamberlain's government that Anderson Shelters and brown paper pasted over windows would preserve us. Barrage balloons like huge sausages hovered over London as a symbol of British readiness should the Luftwaffe appear; volunteers were called on to join Dad's Army, take on war work, man A.R.P. canteens; ration-books and gas-masks were issued (the latter soon relegated to the attic or glory-hole).

The Spanish Aid organisations and more recent Czech refugee committees met to discuss their future. It was decided that the National Joint Committee should be wound up and the Basque children sent "home", except for those who were orphans or had no known relatives in Spain.

In mid-December 1939 my turn came to go with a convoy of repatriates—a sad journey with a heart-breaking goodbye at the end as our little friends walked across the bridge over the Bidassoa river to Irun, to be received by Franco's Guardas Civiles in their tricorn hats and black cloaks, menacing symbols of the new fascist regime.

On the way back from Hendaye to Paris I got off the train at Pau to take some Christmas parcels to International Brigade prisoners in Gurs camp. On that bitterly cold and misty day the rows of barracks behind barbed wire fences looked very grim indeed. The French officers in charge were polite, but clearly had no sympathy for the "reds" in their care. There were some 20,000 detainees there, facing a bleak future. They were a small sample of the multitudes of left-wing prisoners in camps all over France, most of whom had been arrested in September and during the following months on charges of "treason"—i.e. for supporting (or not denouncing) the Soviet-German pact, which had been made the pretext for widespread suppression of the Left.

In the round-up of Communists and fellow-travelling trade unionists many mayors and town councillors had been imprisoned. Typical was the Mayor of Boucau (Pyrenées-Atlantiques), Jean Lanusse, whose story is worth quoting. He was taken from a sickbed to the police station where his son had been beaten up by the gendarmes for the crime of giving out anti-fascist leaflets. Lanusse found several Communist colleagues there under arrest, and was himself handcuffed and taken to Bayonne where he spent several weeks in prison without any charge being brought; released, but under surveillance for eight months, he was deported to North Africa in April 1940 till the end of the war. His friend, André Moine, a trade union leader, was at the same time given four months' solitary confinement in Pau prison after a meeting where he spoke in defence of the Soviet Union, then put in *résidence forcée* till he too was deported. Moine found the mental anxiety of his ordeal almost as bad as the physical sufferings: "The deep uncertainty and fear in our troubled minds were increased by chauvinist agitation"; but throughout every trial "most prisoners kept their belief and confidence in the victory of the working class".[1]

Hundreds of similar stories came to light later, but even at the time anyone with left-wing connections knew that terrible things were happening. In my own experience, friends disappeared without trace and it was impossible to write or get into touch without falling under suspicion. The witch-hunt and atmosphere of fear and uncertainty affected almost everyone; even Paris, city of light, was dark, anxious, xenophobic, as I discovered on returning to work there in January 1940 for a Spanish committee whose organisers had gone into hiding.

The rational voice of the press was stifled. On 26 August (well before war was declared) *l'Humanité* had been banned for its headline "Unity of the French Nation against the Nazi aggressor!" and since then had not appeared.

All socialist papers were heavily censored. The right-wing press was pessimistic and said little of interest; the only information available pointed to France's disarray and to the likelihood that despite the police-state situation Hitler would choose his moment to attack.

The French were told by Daladier's government to pin their faith
to the Maginot Line; Pétain and the General Staff proclaimed its
invulnerability and gave no hint of action in the field. As Winston
Churchill wrote, "The authority of the aged Marshal Pétain had
weighed heavily . . . in discouraging what had been quaintly called
offensive weapons." It was generally known that the Maginot Line
was too short to prevent invasion in the north and "it was extraordinary that it should not have been carried forward at least along
the River Meuse. . . . But Marshal Pétain had opposed this exten-
sion."[2]

"Maginot Line mentality" was prevalent among conservatives, but
intelligent people were beset by doubts, as is clearly reflected in
André Maurois' memoirs. Visiting the Belgian front as an observer
in late 1939 he reported, "The line was terrifyingly weak—there were
little concrete casemates supposed to be connected by an anti-tank
ditch, but these were few in number, and the ditch would only be
effective if it were commanded by anti-tank guns. Only there were no
guns. There were trenches of the 1914 type, but in the mud of
Flanders the parapets collapsed; and what use were these miserable
entrenchments against giant tanks or concentrated bombardment?
The censorship did not allow (journalists) to voice any criticism;
nevertheless the facts were indisputable and certainly known to the
enemy! On the frontier a thin line without density and lacking
indispensable weapons, behind this line, nothing—no reserves, no
mass of manœuvre. Such was the terrifying picture."[3]

And although Maurois saw on the Line itself "fine soldiers who
inspired confidence" and splendid armaments, he reflected that if the
Germans broke through elsewhere "all this force would become
useless and this magnificent army would be imprisoned".[4]

The politically conscious workers realised the fatal flaws in French
military thinking from the beginning, and as reports arrived of
bombings in Poland they remembered the air-raids in Spain, which
now more than ever appeared to have been used as a Nazi practice
ground. They knew that the army command was reactionary and
bureaucratic, and sensed that it was also out-of-date and inefficient.
The modern weapons that they should have been producing were
obviously not considered important: the personnel of the Renault
armaments factories was reduced that autumn from 30,000 to some
7,000—the workers having been mobilised in September and kicking
their heels in provincial barracks for months on end.[5]

It was clear too that the political direction of the "war effort" left a great deal to be desired. Big capitalists had been allowed to send their money "to safety" abroad, and 80 milliards of gold had been exported.[6] Renault went on making cars for tourism instead of tanks; major industries were not directed to produce war material;[7] profiteering and corruption were widespread—among other instances, the French steel magnate M. de Wendel was sending trainloads of iron ore to his cousin Herr von Wendel in Germany and receiving handsome emoluments for this service.[8] At the same time, the workers were suffering harsh privations. The social legislation of the Front Populaire had been scrapped, the working week extended to 72 hours, and unlimited overtime imposed without extra pay. Women filled the places of mobilised men at very low wages, and in some factories the men were sent back to work on soldiers' pay—$1\frac{1}{2}d.$ a day!

The cost of living index rose, according to the right-wing *Peuple* (25.1.1940) in five months by 25 to 30 points.

The wage-earners could do nothing about it as they had been deprived by the suppression of their organisations of their rights to protest or strike: 629 unions were dissolved by the government during the first months of the "war", and many of their secretaries and delegates arrested as Communists. The vacancies were no longer filled by election, and all appointments had to be vetted by the Ministry of Labour. All this almost unbelievable business was carried out with the assent of the French Socialists, whose predominant feelings appeared to be fear and hatred of the Communists.

All anti-fascist organisations were hard hit by the decrees and arrests of their active members. The Aid Spain Committee looking after Republican exiles in France had plenty of jobs for a friend with a British passport (thanks to which one was not likely to be whisked off to a French detention camp); and after a brief return visit to London to collect a few belongings I went to work in *drôle de guerre* (phoney war) Paris for as long as fate or Hitler would allow, signing on at the university for morning classes in French civilisation as a safeguard against unemployment.

It was not a cheerful scene. My friends there were suffering badly from the oppressive atmosphere, the censorship, and the disappearance of comrades and colleagues. There were tragi-comic touches—the liberal philosopher in his officer's *képi*, braid and badges, shivering in the outpost of Massy-Palaiseau; the Sorbonne lecturer extolling 1789 while looking nervously round for informers in his classroom; in contrast, my old landlady's discovery of a book by

Karl Marx in my room—she threw it into the Seine and gave me twenty-four hours' notice to quit!

*　　*　　*

The Soviet Union's short war with Finland (December 1939 to March 1940) over the bases in Karelia which the U.S.S.R. needed to ensure the safety of Leningrad, caused a new wave of governmental Russophobia in France and (slightly less) in Britain. There was talk in late 1939 of bombing the oil wells at Baku so as to maim the U.S.S.R., and at the Supreme War Council, Churchill (then First Lord of the Admiralty) tells us, the main subject of discussion on 5 February was Aid to Finland; plans were approved for the preparation of three or four divisions to be sent via Sweden. "As might be expected the Swedes did not agree to this, and the whole project fell to the ground", says Churchill. "Later M. Daladier without consulting the British Government agreed to send 60,000 volunteers and a hundred bombers to Finland. In view of the ceaseless intelligence reports of the steady massing of German troops on the Western front this went far beyond what prudence would allow. However, it was agreed to send fifty British bombers. But on 12 March, Russian armistice terms were accepted by the Finns—and all the plans were cancelled."[9]

The defeat of Finland was fatal to the Daladier government; and on 21 March a new cabinet was formed under Paul Reynaud, pledged to an increasingly vigorous conduct of the war.

The "drôle de guerre" proceeded according to Hitler's plans throughout the spring of 1940. The Germans, firmly entrenched in Poland after committing unspeakable atrocities against workers, Jews and the Gipsy minority, were building up for further invasions —of Denmark, Norway, Holland. They had laid mines along the British North Sea coast, and Churchill urged reprisals: but he could not get the French to adopt his plan of mining the Rhine by the R.A.F. in March 1940. The President of the Republic himself had intervened, forbidding any aggressive action which might draw reprisals on France. "This idea of not irritating the enemy did not commend itself to me", says Churchill. "Good decent civilised people, it appeared, must never themselves strike till after they have been struck dead. In those days, the fearful German volcano and all its subterranean fires drew near to their explosion-point. There were still months of pretended war. On the one side, endless discussions about trivial points, no decisions taken, or if taken, rescinded, and

the rule 'don't be unkind to the enemy, you will only make him
angry'. On the other, doom preparing—a vast machine grinding
forward ready to break upon us!"[10]

Thus threatened, the French government could devise no better
form of patriotic activity than persecution of the Left. Here, their
record was impressive. The mammoth mopping-up operation
against the French Communist Party (P.C.F.) was reported by M.
Sarraut to the Senate on 19 March: "300 Communist municipal
councils suspended; 2,778 elected councillors deprived of their seats;
443 public employees belonging to the P.C.F. dismissed along with
many others from their positions; the publications *L'Humanité*
(circulation 500,000) and *Ce Soir* (250,000) suppressed, along with
159 other Communist newspapers. 629 trade unions dissolved;
11,000 raids made on premises which might serve for Communist
meetings. 675 political groups disbanded." M. Sarraut also boasted
that by 7 March 3,400 militants had been arrested, and the hunt was
still on. Numerous foreign accomplices had been interned in
concentration camps or deported. In all, 8,000 individual sentences
had been passed on Communists.[11]

Lack of space precludes comment, but it may be pointed out that,
given the political situation in France, it was inevitable that the
ruling class should use the excuse of a war to suppress their formidable left-wing opponents. Reaction has always tried to maintain
its power by the most unscrupulous misrepresentations of the attitude of liberals, radicals, socialists or communists (according to
period). In France in 1940 the reactionaries sought to destroy every
progressive element by screaming "Communist", making the term
synonymous with "traitor" and meting out the appropriate treatment, regardless of truth or justice.

One of the most anti-democratic acts of the Daladier government
was the purge of Parliament, in which the seventy Communist
deputies were deprived of their seats, thus disenfranchising $1\frac{1}{2}$
million voters. The excuse was that the deputies had in October 1939
formed a "Workers' and Peasants' Group" and had written a letter
to M. Herriot, the President, giving their views on the Soviet-
German Pact and asking for a debate on it. Both these perfectly
legal actions were said to be "propagation of slogans of the Communist Third International", connection with which was now dubbed
a crime—just as Thiers, the butcher of the Paris Commune, dubbed
it a crime to affiliate to the First International. And just as the 1870
patriots (including Gustav Courbet and Blanqui) were tried and

punished for this crime, so were their descendants of 1940.

The indictment, conduct and circumstances of the Deputies' trial were so outrageous by any standards of justice that it was thought better to hold the proceedings in secret; but French law demands that all points of procedure be discussed in public, so there was a twelve-hour hearing in open court before the judge ruled that the trial should proceed in *huis clos* (in camera).

On that first day, 20 March, a friend took me along to the Palais de Justice where I managed to squeeze into the gallery among the relatives of the accused, anxiously waiting to see their dear ones who had been in custody for several weeks, and to hear them speak—for it was rightly assumed that the accused would not miss the chance of justifying themselves in public. In fact the court turned into a forum for the deputies, who made hard-hitting attacks on the prosecutors. They followed the example set by Maître Willard, their lawyer, who belaboured the authorities and declared that there was no precedent in French history for a political trial taking place behind closed doors. "The trials of Danton, Babeuf and Blanqui were all public. The judge may say 'we are at war', but during the last war there was no case of a trial being held in secret."[12]

The defence had called three Ministers as witnesses, but Herriot claimed immunity as President of the Chamber, and Daladier as a Minister, while Bonnet, subpoenaed, pleaded illness (in fact he was well enough to speak at the Radical Party Congress next day). It was obvious from the start that the accused were not to be allowed any concessions whatever; but they seized the opportunity to make long stirring speeches in protest against their treatment by the pro-fascist government and exposing the "fifth columnists". François Billoux indicted the whole internal and foreign policy of the ruling class, claiming that "we Communists were the first to warn of the danger of international fascism. . . . For years we urged the French government to save the peace and independence of the country by efforts to unite all men of goodwill throughout Europe." If they sabotaged such efforts they would bear the responsibility for the war which would then break out. Billoux insisted that "Neither the Communist deputies nor Communism is on trial here . . . the real culprit is the capitalist regime which, in Jaurés' words 'bears war within itself as the cloud bears the storm'."[13]

Despite all demands for a public hearing, from then on the trial was held in secret. On the last day, 3 April 1940, the Tribunal gave judgment. All thirty-two deputies were sentenced to five years' prison, 4,000 or 5,000 francs' fine and the loss of all civil and political rights. Nine tried in their absence (including Maurice Thorez, Gabriel Péri and Jacques Duclos) received the same penalties. Only the four war-wounded, one of them the totally blind Jean Duclos, got suspended sentences, as did three renegades—Parsal, Vazeille and Bèchard. For a whole year the deputies were sent from one French prison to another, suffering appalling indignities and worse conditions than common criminals; on 25 April 1941 they were transported to Algiers where they were imprisoned till 1943 in the notorious and horrible Maison-Carrée gaol.[14] In his book *Le Chemin de l'Honneur* (Paris, 1970), Florimond Bonte gives details of conditions there, including the fact that ninety prisoners died per month from sickness and malnutrition, out of a population of 1,200.

Little information on the trial was published, but through the two witnesses from England who attended it, the story of the Deputies' courageous stand and cruel punishment got out. Democrats outside France were shocked by the savage persecution and even more by the sequel of the trial. On 8 April decrees were promulgated in France imposing the death penalty on "every Frenchman who takes part willingly in an attempt to disaffect the Army or the Nation . . . with the aim of hampering national defence". This, it was explained, would strike both at "communist" and pro-Hitler propaganda! Thus any critic of the government or whosoever had unpopular opinions could be put to death for expressing his views.

Moreover, "preparing, stocking or supplying instruments of Communist propaganda" became a crime punishable by death. A leaflet would count as such an "instrument"; "stocking" i.e. possessing one, was a capital offence; "preparing" covered the mere collection of facts and figures about social conditions—also a capital offence.

A group of eminent British writers, among them G. B. Shaw, H. G. Wells and E. M. Forster, sent a letter to the English press protesting strongly against the new French decree "which makes the propagation of Communist and 'defeatist' opinions an offence punishable by death". "We are convinced that the world cannot be saved from Nazism and the barbarous repression which that term implies by imitating the standards and methods of that abhorrent regime."[15]

Inside France no voice was publicly raised; the Communists and their friends were muzzled, and the Socialists consented. Decent liberals were disturbed but pleaded lack of information. Nothing,

apart from the official decree, was published in comment or en-
lightenment; although there were enough people with contacts in
camps and prisons to know something of the truth, during the reign
of silent terror it was impossible to organise protest or broadcast the
facts.

All I, personally, knew was gleaned from colleagues in the refugee
office, and from university people in and around the Sorbonne where
I was still attending lectures. One friend, once secretary to Henri
Barbusse, a very courageous and lively woman, told me many
stories of police brutality and corruption, and of the bravery of the
persecuted anti-fascists. One Sunday afternoon we went to put
flowers on Barbusse's grave in Père Lachaise cemetery. When we got
to the spot we found the headstone overturned and badly damaged.
Annette did not burst into tears, that was not her line. She only shook
her head in fury and said with bitter certainty: "They think they can
destroy his ideas by breaking his tombstone—but how wrong they
are!

*   *   *

All attempts to stifle the Left could not hide the fact that things
were very rotten indeed in the state of France. People were not consoled by the German radio which blared out nightly Goebbels'
assurances that the Reich had no quarrel with France and that the
French had been dragged into war at the heels of the British.

The utter failure of Chamberlain and Daladier's "switch the war"
policy was demonstrated by Germany's invasion of Denmark and
attacks on Norway in April. Daladier had had to resign in March,
and it was generally hoped that Reynaud who succeeded him would
live up to his reputation as a "true Frenchman of the Centre". Unfortunately Reynaud had no following in the Chamber, and could
not survive as premier except with the support of the extreme Right.
This was willingly accorded, under condition that he became a
smoke screen for their plans. The general popular impression that
Reynaud would stand firm and defy the Nazis was indeed useful to
them. (In fact he was very directly under Nazi influence, as his
mistress, Madame Hélène de Portes, was one of the most important
agents employed by Abetz, the German ambassador. Her salon was
a rallying point of the Fifth Column, and a centre for the Comité
France-Allemagne.) Hitler's friends in France were not yet strong
enough to impose a compromise with Germany at the expense of the
country or of Britain, but they waited in the wings, while Reynaud
promised a more vigorous war effort.

One hopeful sign was a reshuffle of the war cabinet, dropping the pro-German Bonnet; another was the agreement with Britain that "if Holland were invaded by Germany the Allies would be free to enter Belgium to assist Holland"; equally welcome to all patriots was the solemn declaration by the British and French governments, on 28 March, that "during the present war they would neither negotiate nor conclude an armistice or treaty of peace except by mutual agreement".[16] Weighty words—unfortunately not to be matched by deeds.

NOTES

1. A. Moine, *Déportation et Résistance en Afrique du Nord* (Paris, 1972) pp. 18–20
2. W. Churchill, *The Second World War*, Vol. I (London, Reprint Society, 1950) p. 382
3. A. Maurois. *Call No Man Happy* (London, Reprint Society, 1944) p. 259
4. ibid. p. 60
5. Pritt, *The Fall of the French Republic* p. 130
6. *Rapport Serre*, IV p. 860
7. *Le Parti Communiste français dans la Résistance* (Paris, 1967) p. 29
8. Pritt, op. cit. p. 130
9. Churchill, op. cit. p. 459
10. ibid. p. 460
11. Pritt, op. cit. p. 132
12. ibid. p. 140
13. F. Bonte, *Le Chemin de l'Honneur* (Paris, 1970) pp. 163–165
14. ibid. p. 317
15. Pritt, op. cit. p. 144
16. Churchill, op. cit. pp. 462–3
17. ibid. p. 463

Chapter 4
1940, SPRING
INVASION

... C'est alors
Qu'élèvant tout à coup sa voix désespérée
La Déroute, géante à la face effarée
... Se lève grandissante au milieu des armées,
La Déroute apparut au soldat qui s'émeut
Et se tordant les bras cria: Sauve qui peut!

Victor Hugo, L'Expiation

Then, suddenly raising her despairing voice,
Defeat, ashen-faced giant,
Arose ever-growing in the midst of the armies—
Defeat appeared to the soldier who would fight no more
And with wild gestures cried, Fly who may!

At the beginning of May 1940, the Germans, now firmly in control of central Europe, from Warsaw to Vienna, and (in the face of bitter popular hostility) entrenched in Norway and Denmark, turned their attention to Western Europe. On 10 May, the same day that Neville Chamberlain resigned from office and Winston Churchill became British Prime Minister, they attacked Holland and Belgium with heavy bombing raids (reducing Rotterdam to smoking ruins) and with powerful thrusts by their mechanised army. They advanced rapidly towards France, preceded by hundreds of fleeing Belgians.

The British Northern Army "sprang to the rescue of Belgium", in Churchill's words, and "poured forward along the roads amid the cheers of the inhabitants", while the French 7th Army advanced so rapidly into Belgium that it outran its ammunition supplies. But all this was no impediment to the enemy, who drove forward in force to the south of the Allied armies and side-tracked them, reaching the Meuse on 13 May and next day breaking through at Sédan with a massive combination of tanks and dive-bombing. "At almost all points . . . the weight and fury of the German attack was overpowering." By 15 May ten Panzer divisions had swept through the gap in the Ardennes, by-passing the Maginot Line (now shown to have been quite uselessly manned for eight months by all those "fine soldiers") and taking Laon and St-Quentin, sixty miles inside France.

Reynaud telephoned London on 15 May lamenting, "We have been defeated—we have lost the battle!" Churchill refused to accept this pessimism, but in fact the British Expeditionary Force (B.E.F.) were ordered two days later to withdraw from their advanced but useless positions to the Scheldt—an ominous, however necessary, decision.

The British Premier flew to Paris on 16 May and met Reynaud, Gamelin and Daladier: "Utter dejection was written on every face."

When Churchill asked, "Where is the strategic reserve?" Gamelin with a shake of the head and a shrug, said "Aucune"—"None". Churchill was dumbfounded: "What were we to think of the great French army and its highest chiefs? It had never occurred to me that any commanders having to defend 500 miles of engaged front would have left themselves unprovided with a mass of manœuvre."[1]

The situation deteriorated rapidly as the German armoured vehicles continued to pour through the gap towards Amiens and Arras, turning westward north of the Somme and heading towards the sea. On 20 May they entered Abbeville, cutting the communications of the Northern Armies and meeting little or no resistance. Nazi tanks advanced forty miles a day, accompanied by crowds of French prisoners, passing through scores of towns without the least opposition. Five British brigades prepared to defend Arras but had to withdraw under an attack by 400 tanks commanded by Rommel.

Several German divisions bound north-west drove the B.E.F. and the French First Army back under intense pressure of armour and aeroplanes towards the Channel, while the German 6th Army pushed up on the East to effect the encirclement of the Allied forces. In a bridgehead on the coast organised by Lord Gort, the British fought "with extraordinary tenacity" according to Rundstedt's diary,[2] but it was also with the courage of despair as the German trap began to close and 160,000 Allied soldiers were faced with capture and death unless they could escape by sea.

Elsewhere the other fronts were collapsing—the French armies in retreat all along the line, the ports mercilessly bombed by the Luftwaffe, the roads blocked by transports and by terrified refugees.

The rest of France knew little about what was happening, but it was obvious in Paris from 20 May onwards that things were very serious indeed. A strict censorship was imposed. No intelligible news came from the front, nothing disturbing percolated through the black-out. Journalists were given such directives as "Rien sur le bombardement du Havre. Rien sur l'Espagne et l'Italie." "Nothing on the probable evacuation of the British colony of Paris."[3] This was meant to reduce public anxiety, but in fact it greatly increased it. Paris newspapers were reduced from four pages to two, and on some days even to a single page, and that not worth reading. We were completely in the dark, and I recall the feeling of utter helplessness in the absence of any information, guidance or leadership. What was the government doing? people asked. Certainly not rallying their spirits or support.

Those lucky enough to get hold of the illegal *Humanité* on 17 May could have read a demand for action against the enemy agents at large, and for the release of anti-fascists so as to rally the people in energetic resistance to the German invasion. But appeals from the Left were in vain.

As things got worse, Reynaud turned to the extreme Right for help. On 18 May, as the Germans reached Arras without slowing down, the Premier announced that he was calling on "new and fresh forces" to save France in her hour of trial. These forces turned out to be the 84-year-old Pétain, appointed Vice-premier, and septuagenarian General Weygand, replacing Gamelin as C. in C.

The journalist Alexander Werth noted in his diary for that day, "Gloom at the War Office", and described Weygand as "a dapper little man full of vitality. . . . Gosh, what a job he's undertaking! . . . Pétain looks rather more solemn. Poor old boy—fancy being dragged into all this at his age."[4]

Pétain's appointment was not reassuring for anyone who looked at his public record. Although his image was constantly projected as the "Victor of Verdun", the less gullible remembered that he had been a defeatist even in 1917 and that Clemenceau had once said he had had "to kick Pétain into victory up the backside!" Since 1939 he had been ambassador to Franco in Madrid; there, his colleagues reported that if "not completely senile" he was losing his memory, "would forget everything from one day to the next", and made the most appalling diplomatic blunders. However, his legend persisted and he was after all well fitted to represent clerico-fascist interests in the Cabinet.[5]

The government was now amply stocked with "ultras"; besides Pétain the Maurrassien, and Weygand, self-proclaimed anti-Communist, there was Baudouin, who had acted for the banking oligarchy in 1937 in forcing the "pause" in the Popular Front programme; the pro-Franco Ybarnégaray; Reibel, known for his Croix-de-Feu affiliations. These were not people to inspire confidence;

pro-fascists themselves, how could they possibly wage an anti-fascist war?

A rumour went around that Bonnet and Flandin had been sent to a concentration camp, which seemed too good to be true; and journalists said that certain political quarters were agitating in favour of Laval becoming Foreign Minister. Werth commented in his diary, "Surely Reynaud can't agree to that—though with Mme de Portes' very curious influence as strong as it is, almost anything is possible. . . ."[6]

In the military sphere it was obvious, too, that all was not as it should be: on 25 May, as the Wehrmacht swung round encircling the Allied divisions in the north, fifteen French generals were deprived of their command. The news of this change of horses in mid-stream, or of generals in mid-campaign, was not reassuring to the general public. More bad news trickled through the censorship on 28 May when the King of Belgium ordered his army to surrender to Hitler. Leopold was generally considered by observers "as a bad egg—pro-Nazi, pro-Degrelle, pro-Mussolini; he had paid a mystery visit to London just before the Hoare-Laval plan was hatched, and he was thought to have had a hand in it. He had a German mistress, and the Nazis were said to have rewarded his collaboration by giving him a chateau. . . ."[7]

In Paris, news of the Belgian surrender was received with disgust, and in "snob" shop windows Leopold's portrait was replaced by those of the British Royal family. Reynaud vigorously berated Leopold and declared, presumably at Weygand's behest, that a new line had been established to hold up the Germans indefinitely on the Somme. The Supreme Allied Council issued a communiqué to the effect that they were "implacably resolved to pursue the struggle in the closest possible concord until final victory". But these fine words did not prevent the Germans storming on, ignoring the Somme, and in their northward pincer movement taking Dieppe, Boulogne and Calais on the west, and Dixmude and Nieuport on the east, of Dunkirk.

The Allied northern armies which had got to the coast through a narrow corridor, threatened on each flank by heavy German pressure, were gathering in and around Dunkirk on 26 May, and by the beginning of June nearly 400,000 troops were bottled up on a stretch of sand 15 miles long by 5 miles deep. The story of their rescue by a vast improvised armada from England is too well known to be repeated here, but it is perhaps worth mentioning the numbers involved: 338,226 men evacuated from Dunkirk beaches and harbour (26,175 of them French) in a fleet of 861 vessels, including 39 destroyers, 77 trawlers, 40 ex-Dutch Schuits, 26 yachts, 22 tugs and 372 "other small craft".[8]

Several thousands of French were left behind, and great quantities of arms and equipment fell to the Nazis. The escape operation could hardly be called a victory but it was a triumph of improvisation; it saved the bulk of the B.E.F. and proved the worth of the R.A.F. which beat back the Luftwaffe and provided the ships with air cover. It also showed the occupied countries of Europe the mettle of the British. Churchill's words, broadcast on 4 June, inspired resistance wherever they were heard and later found an echo in the partisan movements everywhere: "We shall fight on the beaches, on the landing-grounds, in the fields and in the streets, we shall fight in the hills; we shall never surrender. . . ."[9]

The only similar language used in France was that of the underground Executive Committee of the Communist Party who on 6 June through Professor Georges Politzer conveyed an appeal to the government "to transform the character of the war into a fight for national freedom and independence . . . create popular enthusiasm, order a mass rising, arm the people and turn Paris into an invincible fortress". Needless to say these words went unheeded by Reynaud and Company.[10]

Equally disregarded was the offer on 25 May by the Soviet government to supply war planes to help France in her dire need. A French diplomat sent to negotiate this failed to arrive in Moscow till 22 June.[11]

In the meanwhile, France was rapidly succumbing. The Germans, after mopping up operations on the coast, resumed their southward drive, meeting little organised resistance; fortified by eight Panzer divisions, they reached the Marne, and in two great thrusts turned the French defeat into a rout. By June 16, one thrust had reached Orleans and the Loire, while the other had passed through Dijon and Besançon (where over 400,000 men were surrounded and captured) almost to the Swiss frontier.

The armies defending Paris were scattered. The capital was declared an open city, and on 14 June the Germans marched in.

*   *   *

Before looking at the catastrophe of the fall of Paris, there are some observations to be made about the débâcle in general. How had it been possible for the Germans to overrun most of France in less than a month, seizing all her north coastal and industrial cities, smashing up her army, and taking the capital like a ripe plum? All accounts testify to the hopeless mismanagement of the French High Command: as Professor Marc Bloch wrote, in a white heat of anger during the late summer, "It would have been hard to find a single officer . . . who had the slightest doubt that, whatever the deep-seated causes of the disaster may have been, the immediate occasion was the utter incompetence of the High Command. . . . Our leaders . . . were incapable of thinking in terms of a new war. We interpreted war in terms of assegai versus rifle made familiar to us by long years of colonial expansion."[12]

Paul Reynaud, who had always pressed for a modern French army, wrote later that, "in May 1940 the motorised German divisions went through Pétain's front like a circus rider going through a paper hoop. Pétain saw this war as a repetition of 1914".[13] And Weygand admitted on 25 May that "France had made the major mistake of entering this war without the necessary material and without that basis of military theory which alone could have led to success," and that he himself was as much to blame as anyone.[14]

The lack of material was of course crucial as was repeatedly observed. What has not been said so often is that this situation arose from political attitudes, from wilful neglect by top military advisers who never intended to go to war with Germany and who considered the army mainly as a weapon for use against discontented colonies or subversives at home. As Bidault said, "of all the armies, the French was the worst prepared for combat, both materially and morally", while "the most complacent and cocksure about its strength, something which posters proclaimed on every wall".[15]

One basic flaw was the lack of liaison between the Allied Commands. "Faced with disaster . . . the two General Staffs gave up almost entirely any further pretence of collaboration." The British blew up bridges to cover their retreat, and prematurely destroyed the whole telephone system in some cities, seriously hampering the French. "They did not burn the petrol dumps; contrary orders about sabotage were issued to French and British forces. All this made for a fatal breakdown of morale." Concord between the Allies neared breaking point at Dunkirk when British had priority in embarkation. "When the British were safely embarked the sailors looked after the French with equal kindliness; but the fact that they were left till last . . . made the French very bitter and was later used by the

Germans to kindle anti-British feeling in their own interests."[16]

Many eye-witness accounts of the French retreat before the German thrusts testify to the ordinary *poilu*'s will to fight in spite of the lack of it among his superiors: "The men were worried: 'We've been betrayed by the Fifth Column', they said. It would not have taken much to turn that crowd of anxious men into real fighting troops. All they needed was an ideal, a leader, and trained officers. Left in the dark, they stumbled and fell. . . ."[17]

Marc Bloch's men did what they could to stop the Germans: "We never abandoned any of our petrol depots in a fit state to operate. The whole line of our retreat from Mons to Lille was lit by more fires than can ever have been kindled by Attila . . . can after can went into the flames."[18]

Groups of soldiers defended villages from the approaching Wehrmacht by sniping from rooftops and church towers. The individual courage shown amid the general "pagaille" and confusion is described by Jean-Paul Sartre in *La Mort dans l'Ame*:[19] his Mathieu was one hero among thousands determined to fight to the end (although the libertarian Mathieu would have denied any heroism in his obsessive machine-gunning); the Communist Brunet, in the same book, rounded up with thousands of soldiers into a prison camp, reflects the bitterness of those who were not allowed to fight on.

Although Sartre shows little liking for Brunet, a doctrinaire hard-line C.P. member and one-time International Brigader, his portrait indicates the lines on which the Brunets were thinking—never for a moment abandoning their ideals, and continuing to recruit and to organise wherever they found themselves, whether in prison or later in the underground Resistance of Nazi-occupied France.

In contrast, cowardice was rife among the officers, according to the many accounts of headlong flight with the commander's car outstripping the rest, positions abandoned, "everyone for himself" orders given by those in charge. The defeatism shocked Marc Bloch, who was convinced that military resistance was possible: "Our younger last-ditchers were right. They dreamed of a modern type of warfare waged by guerrillas against tanks and motorised detachments. . . . The invaders might have been badly mauled by a few islands of resistance, well sited along the main roads, adequately camouflaged, sufficiently mobile, and armed with a few machine guns. . . . Once we had produced confusion in the enemy ranks we could melt into the 'wild' and repeat the performance farther on.

Three-quarters of the men would have jumped at the chance of playing a game like that. But alas, the regulations had never en-envisaged such a possibility."[20] Bloch's words have a prophetic ring—he himself joined the Resistance soon after, but was tragically killed before he saw his ideas put into practice in the Maquis.

Whether Bloch's explanation of the débâcle—disastrous military top brass and methods—or whether Werth's assessment of its cause—Axis-oriented political leadership—is nearer the mark, one thing is clear: the authorities, civil and military alike, were deeply reactionary and had no faith in the people who were at the base of the national effort—the workers in factories and fields, the soldiers at the front; and the people sensed it, and rightly mistrusted their "superiors".

So disaster fell on France. The working people, bamboozled and betrayed, bore the brunt of the punishment. Thousands of politically-conscious trades unionists, who could have explained or protested or acted in an organised way to prevent betrayal by their rulers, were in prison: $2\frac{1}{2}$ million were in German P.O.W. camps; hundreds of thousands more, deliberately disorganised by the dispersal of their groupings, by chaos in the army, by the fact of being refugees, were in no position to defend themselves or their families. The glorious sunshine of that early summer seemed to mock France's dark despair, as the refugees roamed the roads, and the convoys of P.O.W.s were herded eastwards and nobody dared look ahead.

Perhaps the worst element in the situation was the appalling un-certainty, during the last days of the fighting. Up to the last, even as the Germans were in sight of Paris, its inhabitants did not know whether it was declared an open city, or whether to expect air bombardment or street fighting in its defence. The government gave no sign of leadership, organisation or advice, no call for resistance nor for orderly evacuation. I remember the rumours which circu-lated, that the government was leaving, had left, was going to stay. Nobody knew anything, but almost everyone hoped that this signal of defeat would not be given. When I saw the *Journal Officiel* being packed up and sent off in sealed vans it was pretty clear that the decision to leave had been taken. Then notices appeared on the walls and in the Metro carriages, adjuring the population to keep calm and ordering civil servants to remain at their posts. One teacher com-plained bitterly to me, "The authorities have gone off and we're told to stay. Nothing's organised, and nobody knows to whom we are responsible." The trickle of people leaving Paris soon became a *sauve qui peut* as it was learned that factories were being dismantled and equipment sent south with their workers, while prisons were emptied, and their inmates dispatched in cattle trucks to unknown destinations.

In fact, the government ministers decamped on 10 June, though this was kept very dark; they made their way to Tours, while the High Command settled temporarily at Briary near Orleans, where Reynaud called Churchill urgently to a conference on the 11th.

The defeatism of France's leaders was all too evident, according to Churchill, who wrote later of how he had urged the French government to defend Paris, emphasising "the enormous absorbing power of the house-to-house defence of a great city upon an invading army".[21] He also told them that British heavy bombers were in southern France, ready to strike at Italy who had declared war on Germany's side on 10 June. The local authorities had, however, forbidden the bombers to take off, for fear of Italian reprisals. Churchill then made various proposals for the defence of Paris, asking if it were "not possible thus to prolong the resistance until the United States comes in?"

The French cabinet was sharply divided (or appeared to be); Reynaud backed by Mandel and Campinchi talked of fighting on; and General de Gaulle, who attended the conference and made a good impression on Churchill, was in favour of carrying on guerrilla warfare. Admiral Darlan too expressed support and "promised solemnly that he would never let Germany get the French fleet".

But Baudouin, then Reynaud's (and later Vichy) Foreign Minister, visiting Churchill at lunchtime on 13 June, "began at once in his soft silky manner about the hopelessness of any French resistance".[21] And General Weygand "saw no prospect of the French going on fighting and Maréchal Pétain had quite made up his mind that peace must be made". Churchill then and there told Reynaud that "Pétain is a dangerous man at this juncture; he was always a defeatist, even in the last war."[22]

In spite of his efforts, none of Churchill's suggestions were taken up, nor was his invitation on 16 June to the French government, now in Bordeaux, that France should join Britain in a Declaration of Union under a single war cabinet, to carry on hostilities "against the power of the enemy, no matter where the battle may be".[23] To this, with its stirring conclusion "And thus we shall conquer", answer came that "forces in favour of ascertaining terms of armistice had become too strong for Reynaud", and any proposal for jointly carrying on the war had been rejected. "Weygand had convinced

Pétain that England was lost", and according to the Marshal, union with Britain would be "fusion with a corpse".

Some of the arguments used by Reynaud's ministers make enlightening reading: Ybarnagaray exclaimed, "Better be a Nazi province. At least we know what that means." Senator Reibel declared that Churchill's scheme meant complete destruction for France.

Although Mandel and Campinchi strongly backed Reynaud's proposals for carrying on the war from North Africa, the Prime Minister, faced with majority opposition, admitted he was beaten and handed in his resignation. "The combination of Marshal Pétain and General Weygand . . . had proved too much for weak members of the government, on whom they worked by waving the spectre of revolution."[24] This revealing phrase speaks volumes, and sums up the attitude of those who were presently to sign a most ignoble peace with the Nazis, surrendering France to Hitler rather than risk a people's victory.

On 14 June headlines in the Madrid journal *Informaciones* proclaimed "We salute the fall of Paris as a mortal blow dealt to the democratic regime." And that same day Spanish troops occupied Tangier. The Swastika flew over Hendaye, occupied by German Panzer divisions, while Marshal Pétain, new head of the French government, through the intermediary of the Spanish Embassy, requested an armistice. Franco's General Vigon, received by the Führer at Acoz, discussed Morocco. His army put up posters saying "Algiers and Oran for Spain".[25] Mussolini sent 32 divisions into southern France. As Churchill said, "The rush for the spoils had begun".[26]

NOTES

1. W. Churchill, *The Second World War*, Vol. II p. 52
2. ibid. II p. 76
3. A. Werth, *The Last Days of Paris* p. 65
4. ibid. p. 61
5. J. R. Tournoux. *Pétain and de Gaulle* (trans./London, 1966) pp. 90–91
6. Werth, op. cit. p. 95
7. ibid. p. 97
8. Churchill, op. cit. pp. 97 and 108
9. ibid. p. 109
10. *Le P.C.F. dans la Resistance* p. 49
11. Pierre Cot, *Lettres françaises*, 15 and 21 December 1966

12. M. Bloch, *Strange Defeat*, Oxford, 1949 pp. 25–27
13. P. Reynaud, *La France a sauvé l'Europe* (Paris, 1947) p. 497
14. Weygand, *Secret Documents of the French General Staff* p. 140
15. G. Bidault, *Résistance* (trans. London, 1967) p. 9
16. Bloch, op. cit. pp. 74–77
17. Bidault, op. cit. p. 11
18. Bloch, op. cit. pp. 65–66
19. Sartre, *Iron in the Soul* (Penguin Books, London, 1963) pp. 239 et seq.
20. Bloch, op. cit. p. 51
21. Churchill, op. cit. p. 136
22. ibid. p. 157
23. ibid. p. 179
24. ibid. p. 183
25. M. Gallo, *Spain under Franco* (trans. London, 1973) pp. 94–95
26. Churchill, op. cit. p. 120

Chapter 5
OCCUPATION

O mois des floraisons mois des metamorphoses
Mai qui fut sans nuage et Juin poignardé

Aragon, *Le Crêve-cœur*

Months of metamorphoses months when all uncloses
May that passed unclouded and June stabbed dead.

Trans. Frances Cornford

While the French ministers shilly-shallied, France was collapsing and Nazi occupation was becoming an appalling reality. On 13 June as Churchill talked to Reynaud in Tours the German army rapidly advanced on Paris, driving before it hundreds of thousands of refugees, a vast mass of misery which snowballed into millions as the Parisians joined the exodus. My personal impressions—as, having failed to get a lift out of the city, I watched the tragic scene—tallied exactly with those of many writers, from Simone de Beauvoir to Nevil Shute, and best summed up by Louis Aragon in his poem:

Je n'oublierai jamais les lilas ni les roses
Ni ceux qui le printemps dans ses plis a gardés
Je n'oublierai jamais l'illusion tragique
Le cortège les cris la foule et le soleil[1]

Never shall I forget the lilac and the roses
Nor the fallen lapped in Spring, as we marched on ahead
Never shall I forget those tragic hours of blindness,
The crowd; the cries; the sun; the sound of tramping feet.

Out along the road towards Vincennes they went, not knowing whither, the cars of the better-off at a crawl, the mass of poor tired folk on foot, pushing bicycles and hand-carts piled with belongings; old and young alike looked stunned and weary, those who had been on the road for several days utterly exhausted. Six million civilian refugees, plus the remnants of the Army, reduced the roads to chaos. There was nowhere to rest, no food, drinking water, petrol, except at exorbitant prices. On top of all the unspeakable misery, the Nazi planes machine-gunned the long procession, sowing panic and death. On seeing the crowds and hearing the tragic stories later, one could only ask how such a disaster had been allowed to happen and curse the authorities who had failed to foresee, or if they had foreseen, to organise an orderly evacuation of the city.

It certainly seemed better at the time, as an individual, to have stayed in Paris and faced the music—which was in this case the blare of brass bands, the tramp of jackboots and the singing of martial songs that went on day and night for several weeks after the Germans' arrival.

The Wehrmacht entered Paris in the early hours of 14 June, after a day filled with the sinister approaching rumble of cannon, the sounds of explosions, the sights of desperate humanity on the move, the darkness of a midnight sky in the afternoon. Rain fell in a steady downpour of thick black drops caused by the firing of oil dumps north of the city—evidence of some sort of resistance perhaps, but horrid and sinister none the less.

When, after a sleepless short night I heard the first German motorcycles roar into Paris, tearing through the empty streets, it was almost a relief to know that the end had come. Although new and terrifying prospects opened, at least one knew just who the enemy was.

It was bleakly satisfying to think "We knew it all along", as the collaborators came out into the open. Though many of them had gone with the government, the hard-line fascists were soon in evidence. The director of *Le Matin* was reported as welcoming Nazi officers at his premises, and a day later his newspaper appeared, advocating immediate and total collaboration. Soon others followed: *L'Œuvre* (once Blum's sheet) appeared with blatantly pro-German headlines, under Marcel Déat's direction, while *Paris-Soir*'s new editor—a fifth-columnist liftman—insulted his readers' intelligence with fulsome Nazi propaganda.

The take-over in Paris was swift and relatively painless, in the absence of most of the population and lack of organised opposition. On the afternoon of 14 June the Reichswehr made its triumphal entry with tanks, armoured cars, horses and field-grey troops—in their millions as it seemed—which I watched, with a heart like lead, parading up the Champs-Elysées. The requisitioning of public buildings was immediately carried out, and the Swastika run up over the Chambre des Députés and the Eiffel Tower while goose-stepping guards were posted at the entrances of ministries, museums and national monuments.

Paris came out in a rash of posters designed to calm the agitated French: "Faites confiance au soldat allemand." "Trust the German soldier", they urged. The troops had orders to behave correctly, and apart from the occasional "Spazieren, Fraülein?" women were not annoyed or molested. For the first few days there were no untoward incidents.

On the kiosks strange new journals appeared alongside *l'Œuvre* and *Le Matin: Aujourdhui, La France au Travail, Dernières Nouvelles de Paris*, German-inspired and hardly trustworthy but better than nothing at all to the news-hungry people. It was announced on Sunday, 16 June, that the Reynaud government had capitulated, and a new Ministry had been formed with the purpose of seeking an immediate armistice from Germany. By the night of the 16th Pétain was proclaimed President, Chautemps Vice-president, Weygand Minister of National Defence (!), Baudouin Foreign Minister, and Darlan Minister of Marine. (Laval became Vice-premier on 23 June and took over Foreign Affairs four months later.) For those who did not fancy German domination it was *sauve qui peut*. Mandel, Daladier and Campinchi made their way to Africa, but were arrested and sent back to be imprisoned by Pétain as "traitors".

A few politicians managed to get on to ships bound for England, among them Charles de Gaulle (described by Werth as "the colonel who wrote that important book on the mechanised army . . . Daladier couldn't bear him");[2] but most stayed in Pétain's entourage, accepting defeat as inevitable. So—for the time being—ended Churchill's dream of a united Anglo-French continuation of the war and his hopes that Darlan would direct the fleet to a British port. It was all reported in the Germano-Parisian papers causing much satisfaction to the Occupants, and heart-break to the battered and bleeding French.

This was the moment when morale touched rock bottom. Besides the physical damage afflicting the country, and the deep humiliation suffered, people sensed that the very structure of Republican France had disintegrated, leaving them at the mercy of a mortal enemy, on the edge of an abyss. Where were the forces that could save them and rebuild France?

A teacher, who witnessed the débâcle and the disappearance of professional and trade union organisation, wrote that all reports from colleagues were of complete disarray. "When Pétain's bleating

voice begged for an armistice, it was *l'effondrement le plus total*
(total collapse)." But there was hope to be found even then: "There
still existed among the workers a real force, temporarily unorganised
but which was soon to show itself in spite of arrests and persecution.
And there were some—very rare at the time—who had heard the
voice of an army man, de Gaulle, calling on radio London for the
regrouping of soldiers and officers. . . ."[3] News of De Gaulle's *Appel*
and of the organisation of the Free French Forces in London was a
great and welcome surprise, and struck a spark of hope in the down-
cast listeners who heard it, and who quickly passed round word.
Georges Bidault, then a prisoner in Germany, happened to learn of
it by the grapevine: "The fact that de Gaulle was isolated in London
did not bother me. . . . One man was talking about victory. He was
saying that France was not enslaved, that it had a whole empire
which could help to win the war. That was enough for me; although I knew almost nothing about the man, I was on his side."[4]
This attitude was typical of patriotic middle-class and Catholic
Frenchmen.

However, de Gaulle's words were mainly addressed to the armed
forces who were invited to rally to him; his advice to his civilian
compatriots was to stay quiet and wait. This was cold comfort to
those who were longing silently for a call to some kind of action
inside France.

The speech had other shortcomings. Perhaps not wishing to
alienate former colleagues, the General said that "the German
tanks, aeroplanes and methods surprised our military commanders
and brought them to their present situation." He thus almost
absolved the High Command which was responsible for the defeat.
He did not dissociate himself from the leadership or point out their
appalling political mistakes, but merely declared to the world that
France was not finished. This was enough to encourage many who
were desperately seeking for hope and reassurance for the future. But
for those left to face the future within France the *Appel* lacked
something which de Gaulle himself lacked: any contact with the
immediate concerns of the masses of French people handed over,
bound and gagged, to the invader.

The working classes were not included in de Gaulle's plans. For
them a different leadership was needed, and this was provided mainly
by the Communist Party which had kept intact, underground,
throughout the crises of the past year. As Charles Tillon, chief of the
F.T.P. (the Franctireurs-Partisans) the Communist guerrilla move-

ment which was born in the months ahead, wrote, "It was as well that the P.C.F. did not become Gaullist, despite temptations to sail with the wind, but pursued its own policy, the only correct one for the workers." The Communists saw it as their task to "assess events in relation to the new conditions forced on the working people by the occupation; to unmask Pétain's demagogy; to show that resistance could not be achieved outside France, without the French people. The struggle against fascism had to go on, in the teeth of police repression, spies and informers, betrayal by those newly promoted. The militants who had so far escaped the witch hunt started searching for each other, in the human forest . . . a silent storm was brewing in the gloom of a sinister fog. . . ."[5]

Between 19 and 21 June there were still soldiers holding out in pockets of resistance around Saumur and near the Loire. But on the 21st the German armistice terms were delivered by General Keitel to the Pétain government in Bordeaux and meekly signed next evening, putting an end to all armed opposition to the Nazis by France's military machine. General Huntziger, the head of the French Armistice delegation, described the terms as harsh, but thought they "contained nothing which directly offended against honour".[6]

To the average French man and woman, however, the terms laid down looked dishonourable in the extreme: two thirds of France to be indefinitely occupied and under German control; the French to pay the maintenance costs of Hitler's troops; all French forces to be disarmed, except for some 100,000 necessary for maintaining order (the so-called Armée de l'Armistice); all weapons and equipment handed over to the Germans; France's battle fleet, one of the largest in the world, to be disarmed under German and Italian supervision except for a few vessels needed to defend colonial interests (so much for Darlan's "solemn promise" to Churchill); any Germans— mainly anti-Nazi refugees—living in France to be handed back to Germany on demand.[7]

Huntziger demurred over some of the articles but to no effect. The Armistice terms with Germany were signed at 7 p.m. on 22 June and with Italy two days later. On 25 June it was announced that both agreements had come into effect, as from the previous night, and Marsal Pétain broadcast his famous speech—"I have made France the gift of my person"—telling the country what it must expect from him, his government and the Germans from now on.

Although most people in the north of France, handed over lock, stock and barrel to Hitler, heard Pétain with a mixture of disgust and cynicism, a fair proportion of the French in the Southern zone greeted the announcement of the armistice with relief. At least they now knew the worst. The Catholic population and the conservative middle classes accepted their fate and genuinely put their trust in the old Marshal's promises. The more clear-sighted centre opinion considered it was the best bargain available under the circumstances; at any rate France was not to be completely run by Hitler, so it was thought. But most wondered doubtfully whether Pétain could possibly hold out against further German demands that might be made. The working people of Lyons, Marseilles, Toulouse, with their rights destroyed and their living standards at rock bottom, could see no advantage in being ruled by their class enemies rather than by a national enemy. The division of the country by a demarcation line presaged severe personal hardship, sharp economic problems if not disaster, and it also deliberately presented difficulties in any attempts to organise a common anti-German front.

On 2 July 1940 Pétain and his entourage set up house in Vichy, a sleepy little spa which had for them the advantages of being central and by its nature well-cushioned against industrial unrest. The members of the French National Assembly, except of course for the Communists and those who had escaped abroad, voted on 10 July for the new Constitution thought up by Laval and his friends, with Pétain in supreme command. The votes were 569 for, 80 against; those against included Blum and Daladier (who were imprisoned) and Reynaud and Herriot (sent to house arrest near Nancy).

The new government (an amalgam of extreme right-wing politicians, businessmen and bankers, ensconced in overcrowded hotels where bedrooms and even bathrooms served as ministerial offices) aimed at perpetuating the regime of privilege and personal power which had brought its members to the fore in the pre-war years. As policy they offered a "national revolution" and a purge of decadent liberalism through a programme entitled "Travail, Famille, Patrie" (Work, Family, Country). This, in effect, meant continued hardship for the poor and austerity for the middle classes, with total subservience to the Germans in accordance with Hitler's plan for France as outlined in *Mein Kampf*.

*   *   *

In the weeks following the Nazis' takeover people were mainly concerned with getting back to their homes, jobs (if any) and some sort of normal life. The refugees returning to Paris found a strange city filled with the tramp of German soldiers, the raucous sound of their songs or the roar of their motor-coaches taking members of the Wehrmacht round the sights; the highest concentration of Germans at any one time would be in the neighbourhood of the Sacré Cœur and its night clubs, or the Eiffel Tower up which they clanked fondly believing it to be the work of a German engineer.

The Occupants set out to win the good will of the Parisians. They did not behave unduly aggressively; they set up centres to supply soup to hungry children (though it was noticeable that no Jewish child was served); they were polite in the shops, where they bought and paid for large quantities of luxury goods, confectionery and clothes (long since lacking in the Reich).

For a month or so popular reaction was one of surprise and relief, but the illusion of things not being so bad faded as the Germans settled in permanently. When the shelves emptied, as though a plague of locusts had descended, it was realised that the Germans' paper money (printed specially for the occupation) was worthless. Food disappeared from the markets, and great vans could be seen in *les Halles* loading up with vegetables and meat and heading off to the Reich. Petrol vanished, and Parisians, grumbling, took to bicycles unless they could afford the exorbitant prices of petrol on the Black Market. Unoccupied apartments were commandeered, prices soared, and unemployment increased alarmingly.

Discontent was very soon apparent, though manifested in a veiled manner. I heard a woman remark in the post-office, ostentatiously surrendering her place in the queue to an impatient German officer: "Laissez donc passer le monsieur—il est bien pressé d'aller en Angleterre!" (Let the gentleman pass—he's in a hurry to get to England.) People boasted of misdirecting "les doryphores" (Colorado beetles) by sending them off in the wrong direction or to nonexistent addresses. When the notice "Jewish-owned" appeared in cafés (in an attempt to protect the master race from contamination) the tables of the non-Aryan concerns were crowded, while people avoided those patronised by *les Boches*.

Still more significant was the defacing of German posters, and the chalked slogans which appeared on walls: "Vive l'Angleterre", "A bas les Nazis" and "VV Thorez". The gruesome pictures of Churchill's face in the middle of a huge octopus strangling France in its tentacles, which I saw one day plastered on the pillars of the Rue de Rivoli, were by the next morning torn or destroyed in spite of the announcement of severe penalties for "mutilation".

There were often scrawls of "vendu" (sold out) on advertisements of *l'Œuvre* and *Le Matin*. When I asked for a newspaper to wrap my cod in, the fishmonger said he never used one: "C'est pas assez resistant!" (It isn't resistant enough). These small signs of revolt, however unimportant, reflected a growing mood of opposition.

There were other, more open and telling expressions of the public mood, such as the boycotting of German-controlled cinemas. When the Nazi newsreels were shown the spectators walked out in a body, so the Germans had the doors closed to keep them in. There was a fine rumpus; in the darkness, the Parisians gave full vent to their feelings. Whistles, catcalls, "mort aux Boches!" greeted the Nazi chiefs' appearance on the screen. Closing the cinemas for a week was tried, and when re-opened the lights were kept on during the newsreels; the Parisians' response to this was to take a book or magazine to the cinema and read throughout the *actualités*—a form of protest to which the Germans could find no retort.

In the *Théâtre Français* when a break in the performance was announced, because of an air-raid by the R.A.F., "there was," said one spectator, "a storm of applause such as had not been heard in the old theatre for years, much to the astonishment of those Germans present."

Individuals often gave revealing glimpses of the prevailing mood. One such was the old *Croix de Feu* veteran whose son was in a P.O.W. camp in Germany and might have been released through a Franco-German alliance: "I love my boy and want him back," said the old man, "but I'd rather he stayed three years there than that he should come back at that price to live here in shame!"[8] Another interesting remark came from a White Russian, who, after visiting Rennes, complained, "It's appalling! They're all Gaullists there. They steal the German officers' weapons in the restaurants and cafés. The poor things—now they can't even take off their belts at mealtimes. . . ."[9]

These and innumerable other stories reflected the feelings of the French, which were deeply and unmistakably anti-Nazi. From these feelings it was a short step to organisation and action, as French patriots soon found.

Madame Germaine Tillion, a scientist working at the Musée de l'Homme, where in the early autumn the first non-political activist group was formed, wrote later: "We were only a handful in 1940, but were we not already representative of a large section of French opinion? For my part, I believed this from the first day, and none of my comrades ever caused me to doubt it. . . ." This group began, Mme Tillion says, in a meeting of "a few old friends who decided to see each other regularly from then on 'pour faire quelque chose' (to do something)". Sometimes people who hardly knew each other would realise that they were reacting to events in the same way, while others would drop former friends whose attitude did not match their own. "The armistice produced an instantaneous cleavage throughout France, but the majority in every section of society were against the Occupation."

Later, Mme Tillion's group was followed by many more, which became networks, or *réseaux*, doing underground work for the Resistance. The recruits to the Musée de l'Homme group were mainly Mme Tillion's trusted personal friends and *their* friends. The main tasks in those early days were to help escaping prisoners, getting them false papers and clothing, to enable British subjects to cross to the Southern zone, to hide Jews on the run, and of course to recruit others. Members of the group were mainly middle class. Mme Tillion writes that, "All parties were represented among us, from left-wing socialists to monarchists—with the exception of the Communist Party. Why this exception? Because our recruiting was carried out before June 1941, at a time when the P.C.F. was in an extremely false position *vis-à-vis* the Resistance."[10]

With all respect and admiration due to the Musée de l'Homme group, whose bravery and patriotism were beyond praise, one may wonder how they could so signally have failed to understand the Communist position, or why they considered it "false". To anyone who has followed the course of events, it seems strange, indeed, that so many writers, often themselves in the Resistance, should malign the Communists with talk of "collaboration up to 1941", "honeymoon period", "pro-Hitler position", in disregard of known facts. Mme Tillion understood one thing, however—that divisions might well arise in a group containing non-political intellectuals and monarchists and ardently revolutionary workers. She writes, a little acridly, that "I suppose the P.C.F., having its own organisations, saw to it that its men did not stray into formations which were not under its control".

Brave and patriotic as Mme Tillion is, she ignores the facts when she names her network, "the first Resistance in the Occupied Zone"; for it is quite clear—as I hope the next chapter will show—that many weeks before it was formed the Communists were already actively resisting in their own way.

NOTES

1. Aragon, *Le Crêve-cœur* (ed. *La France Libre*, London, 1944) p. 56
2. A. Werth, *The Last Days of Paris* p. 87
3. P. Delanque, *Les Enseignants* (Paris, 1973) p. 84
4. G. Bidault, *Resistance* p. 79
5. C. Tillon, *Les F.T.P.* (Paris, 1962) p. 37
6. Gen. Weygand, *Memoirs*, III pp. 249–257
7. G. Warner, *Laval* (London, 1968) p. 184
8. A. Weil-Curiel, *Eclipse de la France* (Paris, 1947) pp. 142–143
9. ibid. p. 169
10. Mme G. Tillion, *Première Resistance*, Bulletin du Musée de l'Homme May 1958, pp. 6–7

Chapter 6

THE BEGINNINGS OF RESISTANCE

... Quand nous étions des étrangers en France
Des mendiants sur nos propres chemins
Quand nous tendions aux spectres d'espérance
La nudité honteuse de nos mains

Alors alors ceux-là qui se levèrent
Fut-ce un instant fut-ce aussitôt frappés
En plein hiver furent nos primevères
Et leur regard eut l'éclair d'une epée ...

Aragon, *La Diane française*

When we were foreigners in France, a host
Of beggars on the roads of our own land;
When each held out to hope's unhappy ghost
The naked shame of a beseeching hand;

Ah then those men who rose, and rose to fight
Even for an instant, felled as they would rise
They were our primroses in Winter's night
The lightning of a sword was in their eyes ...

Trans. Frances Cornford

About a month after de Gaulle's broadcast, a trade unionist friend told me that Thorez and Jacques Duclos were still in France and organising underground activity. They had on 10 July made a statement which had been printed as a leaflet and was circulating widely among workers. While not specifically mentioning the Germans, this was clearly a call for national unity against both the foreign invaders and their puppets. "The great hopes of national liberation lie in the people alone," it proclaimed. "It is only around the working class, with its confidence and courage, that a front can be built, for freedom, independence and national renaissance."[1]

This *Appel* was the first public sign of the continuing existence and struggle of the Communist Party. And it had an immediate effect on the morale of militant workers, especially those who were back on the shop floor in the big engineering factories now turned over to production for Germany. It was like a shot in the arm for them to learn that in spite of persecution, dispersal and terror the structure and leadership of the Party still survived. Members were proud to think that theirs was the only political body which had not dis-integrated during the events of the last year.

Isolated members were contacted by the central committee, and received directives to form *réseaux* or networks consisting of groups of three persons, linked through a single responsible person with other groups of three. Trade unions, too, met secretly to re-form their organisations and plan activity against the Nazis. Support could best be won by rallying the working people in defence of their rights and of their living standards. The soil was ready: misery and unrest were widespread. There were in July 1940 600,000 unemployed registered in the Paris region alone. The dole was a pittance—6 francs a person, 12 francs per family—and quite inadequate for the needs of a household where children had to be fed, clothed, shod. Rations were almost below subsistence level: 350 grams of bread a day, 350 grams of meat and 40 grams of cheese weekly per family, while milk, eggs and fish were virtually unobtainable except on the black market. German promises that the people would not suffer, and the Marshal's pleas that France should accept her fate, were shown to be hollow cynicism, and workers were urged to depend on their own efforts to win their rights, in leaflets which began to be duplicated and circulated even before the end of June 1940. Police records stated that during July nine underground organisations for printing and distributing "tracts" had been destroyed—but did not give the number of those which remained intact and multiplied. Ninety militants were reported arrested in the Paris region during the same period—but again, nobody said how many were still carrying on the good work.

On 10 July the Vichy government announced agreements with the Germans on the internment of dissidents, and other repressive measures. They were answered with a campaign, led by the trade union illegal news sheet *Vie Ouvrière*, for setting up *comités populaires* in Paris factories, aiming to unite workers both in resisting the Occupation and in promoting their own interests. The question of improving wages and shortening the working day was a vital one, and so was the matter of providing for the half-million unemployed. The workers were to be shown that the enemy was still the same as before: their employers (Renault, Wendel, Schneider) might be French, but they were hand in glove with the occupants, producing almost exclusively for the Nazi war machine.

Throughout the summer Thorez's *Appel* circulated, along with other illegal leaflets; the Communist Youth movement brought out its own paper, *L'Avant-Garde*; the illegal *Humanité* appeared ten times a month, in 140,000 copies. The accusation made against the Communist Party that it approached the German authorities in an endeavour to get permission for *Huma* to appear legally[2] is misleading and has been strenuously denied by the P.C.F. This was certainly never the policy of the Party which officially disassociated itself with any such moves—and which regarded as unthinkable the suggestion that the Communists should co-operate with the Germans in any way whatsoever.

Illegal and dispersed as they were, the Communists, for several months to come, put up the only organised and active political resistance in Occupied France. In late summer, party leaflets announced that *Brigades de Jeunesse* (Youth Brigades) were being formed, but as early as July young Communists had been re-grouping, holding meetings in the Bois de Vincennes under the guise of picnics and ball games, and even managing to collect two to three hundred youngsters for a meeting in the suburb of Garches. But as the French police, disorganised during June and July in the general chaos, became more efficient, acting under Nazi orders, the youth, like their elders, had to be warier, meet for their picnics in smaller numbers, and act in groups of two or three.

The youth were responsible for much of the leafletting and chalking of Paris and reports tell of many daring exploits: Jacques Grinbaum, aged twenty, of the 18th arrondissement, got himself a roneo and began to duplicate leaflets ". . . One night in July 1940 Jacques went out to chalk slogans on the walls of the fountains around the Sacré Cœur, including the words 'A bas l'Occupant' 'Vive l'URSS', and 'Vive la France'. Young people of the 11th district were the first to distribute Thorez's *Appel*, in July, in the Market of Alligre." Documents and witnesses speak of similar activity by young people in all parts of Paris: "In Saint-Denis young Communists were arrested for distributing anti-Nazi tracts in July"; nevertheless, "In August, anti-German leaflets went up during the night all over the town, including the police station, the H.Q. of the Légion d'Honneur, and the Town Hall."[3]

During August *L'Œuvre* carried threatening articles about the distribution of "Communist tracts", and reported 871 arrests and the seizure of thirty-five illegal printing presses (or roneos) since July. Many of those caught were young people, later to be executed as hostages.

The beginnings of the resistance movement can be traced in the controlled newspapers, not only in Paris but all over the occupied zone, reporting sentences of a week to six months' prison for all "manifestations hostiles aux Allemands". Even such minor offences as calling the Germans "sales boches", or spitting at officers, resulted in a year's imprisonment.[4]

In August and September more important misdeeds began seriously to worry the authorities. Sabotage, on telecommunications and railways, featured largely in official announcements. The Préfecture of the Eure Department proclaimed in early September an investigation into sabotage: 10,000 francs were offered for information. "All damage to telecommunications is forbidden under pain of death" came the grim German warning in the *Nord*, on 10 September. Even before this, the nineteen-year-old Pierre Roch had been arrested—by French police—for the crime of cutting military cables, and summarily executed.

The Nazi Military Commissioner for Northern France announced on 6 September that he "was obliged to intern the male population of mobilisable age in places where damage had been done by the inhabitants to military installations. . . ." He explained that, "in communes where security and order are threatened, the population of an age to carry weapons cannot be left at liberty". (One might well ask, who, if not the Herr Kommandant, had "threatened security and order"?) In Evreux, after someone had cut the Wehrmacht's cables, all men between the ages of eighteen and twenty-five were shut up in barracks from 6.30 p.m. till next day.

In spite of threats and drastic penalties the sabotage went on. Cables were cut all over the north of France, and on 17 September the Germans carried out the death sentence on Marcel Drossier, mechanic, of Rennes.[5] The warning went unheeded.

Besides cutting cables, many German vehicles were burned; Reichswehr soldiers were fired at; on 14 August a German post in the Bois de Boulogne was attacked, and the wood was closed to Parisians. In Royan, a German sailor was killed by an unnamed Frenchman. Reprisals came thick and fast, in the shape of arrests and of heavy fines on the local people: 3 million francs imposed on Royan, 7 million on Nantes, for two acts of sabotage (7 August and 6 September). Rennes had to pay a million francs and the village of Lumbres 100,000 for similar offences.

Such brief extracts from official reports give little idea of the political views of those involved; they were usually called "Communist", and whether or not this applied, the label made the accused more liable to severe punishment. It is clear, however, that resistance from July 1940 on was already a fact. Little by little the actions of individuals gave way to group activity; repressive measures increased as the organisation of armed struggle became effective and drew in the lone rebels whose brave protests were often futile because purely individual. The Communist Party took the lead in forming groups to carry out wide-scale sabotage, and this highly dangerous work was undertaken by reliable militants. The Secretary of the West Paris Federation, for instance, was sent to the Aube and other departments to organise *réseaux*. These set about helping prisoners to escape from P.O.W. or internment camps, distributing leaflets, recruiting support; but the most immediate task, now that it was recognised that armed struggle was on the agenda (in spite of Pétain's protests and de Gaulle's pleas for patience) was the collection of arms for the people's underground army one day to come into being.

People were already hiding weapons, as news items often revealed: *L'Œuvre* of 26 September cites a case, and between 26 August and the end of November, *Ouest-Eclair* reported thirteen sentences, amounting to sixteen years of prison for "detention of arms". One of the accused was a priest, one a student, the rest workers.[6]

But the main source of supply was the arsenal of weapons discarded by the French soldiers in retreat during May and June: guns, rifles and unused ammunition could be found in woods, gravel pits and ravines where they had been thrown.

The Préfet of the Aube Department noted in a private report in November that "the Communist Party has organised the collection of arms abandoned by the French army over all the territory. The formation of shock troop brigades of six to eight men is envisaged . . .";[7] a Communist report mentions that a lot of arms were found in the forest of Darnetz in Corrèze, which became a secret centre for the earliest organised armed resistance. By the end of 1940 twenty groups of three were active in the forest; but already wherever there were weapons, groups had sprung into being, ready to use them as soon as the opportunity came. As the activity of such groups increased the P.C.F. formed them into an "Organisation spéciale de combat" (O.S.) which, from its inception in early autumn 1940, became eventually the Franc-Tireurs Partisans (F.T.P.), leading element in the Resistance Army.

How, in view of these facts, can historians state that there were "no resisters of the first hour"? The reputedly well-informed Dr

Robert Paxton writes that "their number was minuscule and it was to grow even smaller during the first year" (June 1940 to May 1941). The early resistance groups, he writes, "posed no real problem for the regime. . . . The Germans carried out no 'grand operations of repression' in the first months, except against Communists, whose honeymoon period in occupied Paris ended with mass arrests on the night of 4–5 October 1940."[8] Apart from the distortion implied by the word "honeymoon", to say there was no repression except against Communists is like saying that the widespread sabotage and propaganda was of no importance because it was organised by one political party.

"Except against Communists"! when hundreds of militants were heavily penalised all over France, beaten up, tortured, shot. The writer might just as well have said, nobody suffered except the workers—but it happens that the workers are a fairly important section of the population. Two right-wing newspapers put the matter better. The London *Daily Telegraph* of 20 December 1940 reported that the only existing political party was the C.P., and more than a thousand of its members were arrested in November for distributing anti-German leaflets appealing to the patriotism of the French people. The *Journal d'Amiens* expressed anxiety about the strength of the Communist Party organisation, in March 1941: "There is a greater danger than is believed in high places. Of course, while the German army is on our soil, order will be vigorously maintained, but what about afterwards?"[9]

Although the Communists formed the only organised resistance at this stage, it would be quite wrong to suggest that there was little individual or passive opposition. Eighty deputies voted against Pétain on 10 July; Socialist mayors and Liberal generals showed their opinions, notably in Chartres and Lille; de Gaulle's stand was soon widely known and acclaimed, and the London radio listened to by millions. The importance of this passive resistance was that those who believed in France's survival during those dark days created the climate which made active resistance possible. It incidentally made life bearable for the few thousand foreigners trapped in Paris against their will, of whom I happened to be one.

For an Englishwoman, living in Paris through that summer was like a long wait for the sword of Damocles to drop. We were not persecuted, though we had to sign on every week at the local *poste de police*. We were fortunate in being provided by the American Chargé d'Affaires, who still had a Paris office, with subsistence, which in my case was eked out by giving unofficial lessons—a surprising number of people wanted to learn English, in spite of the Nazis' attempts to make German the first foreign language. There was never any ill feeling shown towards us by the French, notwithstanding German propaganda about "la menace britannique" to France's overseas territories, and the attacks led by Free French ships under British protection on the naval bases of Dakar and Oran in July, and again at Dakar in September when Vichyite commanders refused to let their vessels join the Allies.[9]

The anti-British posters everywhere—the one with Churchill's grinning face, the one "Remember Mers-el-Kebir" (the Oran base) and another, of a British officer amid starving French children captioned "C'est l'Anglais qui vous a fait cela!" (The English did this to you!)—had no noticeable effect. Churchill tells the story of peasant families near Toulon burying two of their sons, both killed by British fire at Oran: the parents "requested that the Union Jack should lie upon the coffins side by side with the Tricolour and their wishes were respectfully observed".[10] People understood why these things had happened, were glad that the British and de Gaulle were fighting back, and saw those actions, however much they hurt, as signs of hope.

Although British I had no difficulty in enrolling again for lectures at the Sorbonne when it re-opened in July 1940. This was much earlier than usual because of the threat of the Germans' requisitioning the buildings if not in use. Although many of the former staff had been dismissed for being left-wing or Jewish, the *recteur*, Roussy, still held his post and did what he could to keep up standards. He certainly had problems, what with Nazi-imposed changes of staff and curriculum, a scattered student population, and extra lectures, classes and exams to make up for those abandoned in June.

The university was a breeding-ground for resistance, and the students were soon bringing out their newspaper, *La Relève*. Both the Left and "non-political" youth co-operated in anti-Nazi activity, combining legal meetings and demonstrations with underground organisation. Led mainly by Communist students, study-groups were set up within the university framework, aiming at the defence of French culture in opposition to Vichyite and German plans for rooting out republican and radical ideas. Heckling and planned interventions disrupted anti-semitic lectures, and one New Order professor and his blackboard were pelted with eggs by the students (whose only regret was that eggs were expensive and rare in those days). In the libraries, boys and girls scattered leaflets among the books, on tables and staircases, and at night they slipped their propaganda under doors, and pasted notices on walls all over the Quartier Latin. *Recteur* Roussy was a good Frenchman and turned a blind eye to this activity. He could do little about German demands for changes, but his distaste for these was shown wherever possible. I remember one unpopular Pétainist lecturing in a very small room and lamenting that he had wanted to use the Great Hall but that a high university authority had not allowed it. This brought a storm of applause and cries of *Vive le Recteur!*, much to the professor's discomfiture; and his lecture thereafter was so noisily interrupted that he soon gave up and walked out.

I vividly remember, too, a more important demonstration, organised at the beginning of November in support of the great physicist Paul Langevin, who was arrested in his laboratory by the Nazis on 30 October.

Although Langevin was not a Communist (he joined the Party later, and was on the secret Paris Liberation Committee) he was very close to the Communist intellectuals Politzer, Solomon and Joliot-Curie. These Sorbonne professors had produced a pamphlet, immediately a best-seller in the university, showing Vichy's role in "raising ignorance into a State Institution and obscurantism into a national Credo"; and they were busy, in late October, producing the first number of a resistance journal *Université libre*, with Langevin's support—which no doubt accounted for his arrest at that moment.

There was a spontaneous reaction in the Sorbonne. The scientists immediately protested vigorously, led by Joliot-Curie who declared his laboratory closed till Langevin was freed. Communist students immediately got out a leaflet which began: "Students! . . . Professor Langevin's arrest is the public signal for battle by the obscurantists against culture and freedom of thought! Vichy's educational measures, the closing of the *Ecoles Normales*, the plans to close the university to French women, all point to a return to the lowest level of mediaeval civilisation. . . ." It ended with a call to young intellectuals to "Alert your comrades and your teachers! Demand Langevin's immediate release!"[11]

There was no problem about distributing the leaflet—nearly every student soon had a copy, and word went round like wildfire that there was to be a "manifestation" on Friday, 8 November. An enormous crowd assembled outside the Sorbonne shouting "Libérez Langevin". I felt a bit nervous as police and German soldiers swarmed around the edges of the crowd, but no shots were fired nor arrests made. The authorities were disturbed, however, and their newspaper *La France au Travail* complained that "just when Marshal Pétain is clearly explaining the policy of Franco-German collaboration, rumours and cunning underhand agitation are current in the Latin Quarter where judeo-masonic influences have been at work for some time. . . ." The paper warned against "the expression of patriotic feelings which would play into the hands of Jewish provocateurs".

Far from this deterring the students, who thought it very funny to be accused of being under judeo-masonic influence, they worked still harder for the success of their next demonstration. The order of the day, "All to the Étoile" was passed round and blackboards all over the Sorbonne carried the chalked message, "11 November 1940, 17 hrs. Champs-Elysées".[12]

An official communiqué that "no public demonstration will be tolerated" on Armistice Day did not prevent a mighty turn out, nor hundreds of wreaths on Clemenceau's monument (the biggest, of blue, white and scarlet flowers, bearing the words "La France Libre", had been deposited under cover of darkness by an envoy of de Gaulle).[13] Scores of groups of students, schoolchildren, teachers, from all over Paris and the suburbs assembled in the Avenue, carrying tricolour badges and flags, and red, white and blue bouquets, which the florists had—astonishingly—put on sale that day. Estimates of the crowd varied, from 3,000 to 10,000.

The Germans were ready within call, and the pro-Nazi French youth organisations had come along and were waiting to provoke the students and to point out their leaders to the French police. As soon as the march towards the Étoile started, cat-calls, abuse and scuffles occurred and arrests were made. As it continued, with the young people dodging the police, the orderly ranks were broken. Then, suddenly, German army cars appeared from nowhere, tearing up the Champs Elysées, scattering the procession, troops firing to right and left and throwing hand-grenades among the crowd. Over 140 arrests were made before the street was cleared, many people were wounded and, according to the very lowest estimate, five students killed.

Paris was staggered and outraged. This would have been a perfectly peaceful and legal assembly but for the provocation of the fascists; the effect of the encounter was to inspire greater hatred than hitherto and a far stronger will to resist, among all sorts and conditions of Parisians. The students, particularly, while suffering from the penalties imposed on them, were all the prouder for having asserted their faith in France in that massive, enthusiastic demonstration.

Reprisals were taken on several of the Lycées represented on the occasion, and the Sorbonne was closed for over a month. *Recteur* Roussy was sacked by Vichy, and students had to register weekly at the police stations; those who lived outside Paris had to leave the city and give up their university career.

Whether or not the November protests and demonstrations arose from a traditional patriotism rather than from a revolutionary base (as Dr Paxton suggests),[14] the authorities treated the whole thing as a Communist plot, and went on to arrest a large number of left-wing students whose names were found on one of the arrested demonstrators (so that from then on pseudonyms were used in the student "underground"). The arrests had the effect of actually increasing the membership of the student Communist organisation, and bringing a lot more young people to work alongside the militants.

As their secretary, Francis Cohen, wrote, "before then the only active political organisation was the Communists', but the events of that day brought a great many democratic and patriotic individuals into the movement; and this meeting of different tendencies was to be the essence of the French Resistance, and is what gave its historical significance to the 11th of November 1940".[15]

The Germans showed their true colours that day. They had been "korrekt" as long as it suited them, but for several weeks that autumn very harsh measures had been in operation. In October there had been a wave of brutal repression which swept many hundreds of Communist militants and trade unionists, along with the deputies Fernand Grenier and Henri Michels and dozens of city councillors, into the gaols of Fresnes, La Santé, and Mont Valérien.

The answer to the terror came from the *Organisations Spéciales* of the Communist Party, in a series of sabotages in factories—where (as at Ivry) sand and emery were often poured into machinery, and large tanks of oil set alight—and on the railways, where waggons loaded with food and other supplies for Germany were derailed or burned out.

The punishment for such misdeeds was death. Usually the saboteurs worked by night and were able to avoid capture; it was much more dangerous to operate in broad daylight, though often inevitable —one risked being taken as a hostage, like Bonsergent the young engineer, who paid with his life for one of his friends, guilty of having offended a German officer in the street. Paris was shocked by the news of this cold-blooded murder. Simone de Beauvoir wrote: "On 28 December as I went down the Boulevard Saint-Michel I saw a crowd in front of a hoarding with a big red poster:

AVIS

Jacques Bonsergent of Paris has been condemned to death by the German military tribunal for violence against a member of the German army. He was shot this morning.

Who was he? What had he done? I didn't know. But for the first time the 'correct' Occupants had officially announced that they had executed a Frenchman guilty of not having bowed the knee."[16]

I did not myself see the notice, as on 5 December, early in the morning, I had been picked up by the French police, and with some five hundred old men, women and children put on the train for the internment camp for "British nationals" in Caserne Vauban, Besançon.

NOTES

1. Tillon, *Les F.T.P.* p. 40
2. P. Novick, *The Resistance versus Vichy* (London, 1968) p. 47
3. A. Ouzoulias, *Les Bataillons de la Jeunesse* (Paris, 1969) p. 52
4. Tillon, op. cit. p. 43
5. ibid. pp. 54–55
6. ibid. pp. 61–62
7. Paxton, *Vichy France*, pp. 226–7
8. Paxton, op. cit. p. 38
9. Ouzoulias, op. cit. p. 36
10. Churchill, *The Second World War*, Vol. II pp. 390–392
11. Delanque, op. cit. pp. 108–110
12. Ouzoulias, op. cit. pp. 60–66
13. Weil-Curiel, *Eclipse en France* pp. 233–235
14. Paxton, op. cit.
15. Ouzoulias, op. cit. p. 71
16. S. de Beauvoir, *La Force de l'Age* (Paris, 1960) pp. 486–487

Chapter 7

ZONE ROUGE

Au nom des hommes en prison
Au nom des femmes deportées
Au nom de tous nos camarades
Martyrisés et massacrés
Pour n'avoir pas accepté l'ombre
Il nous faut drainer la colère
Et faire se lever le fer
Pour preserver l'image haute
Des innocents partout traqués
Et qui partout vont triompher
　　　　　Paul Eluard, *Les Sept Poèmes d'Amour en Guerre*

In the name of the men in prison
In the name of the women exiled,
In the name of all our comrades
Martyred and massacred
For not accepting darkness
We must drain our anger
And make the iron rise up
To preserve the high image
Of the innocent everywhere hunted
And who will triumph everywhere

To have the "enemy women" under its eye, the German Command had decided to collect them all in the "Zone Rouge", a tightly guarded area between the Franco-Swiss and Franco-German frontiers and a line stretching from the Ardennes south to Poligny in the Jura. The Demarcation Line dividing Occupied and Unoccupied France (Z.N.O.) lay some 10 miles to the south. Our camp was in the early-nineteenth-century barracks at Besançon, which had from June 1940 till the eve of our arrival been occupied by 20,000 prisoners of war captured among 500,000 others in the summer fighting. Their bequest of muck, filth and vermin made it more than unsuitable for the mainly elderly and very young who inherited the quarters; and a minor form of resistance consisted of demonstrations and protests led by our camp committee, which brought good results. The Germans, under our pressure, thoroughly disinfected the dormitories and provided clean bedding, and after two weeks the place was more or less habitable. The food, almost inedible at first, gradually improved and the epidemics of dysentery subsided as Red Cross parcels arrived to supplement the "rutabaga" mush and the *ersatz* coffee and *kunst marmelade*. The worst complaint was our lack of activity and freedom and of news from outside. Surrounded by the high walls of the barracks, guarded by tight-lipped German sentinels, our company of 5,000 "Britishers" (mainly non-English-speaking Maltese, Mauritians, Jews from Palestine, Gibraltese, Africans and White Russians) were effectively cut off from the rest of the world. There was little chance of knowing what was happening even in the locality, let alone on the international scene.

However the French P.O.W.s, and the Spanish refugees who worked under the Germans in the camp, passed on rumours gleaned from London and Swiss radio, and we learned of R.A.F. raids, fighting in North Africa, the invasion of Greece and the Balkans first by the Italians then the Nazis. The internees who had the luck to be taken into the town for dental treatment told us that the dentist as he filled their teeth had murmured congratulations on the reported R.A.F. raids on Germany. He also said that if anybody ever wanted help they could count on him; and the townspeople had seemed friendly, waved and said "Bonne chance!" to them as they were escorted between German soldiers through the streets. (Women dreaming of escape registered these facts with special interest.)

When the camp population was moved to Vittel, 30 miles north of Nancy and within 10 miles of the German border, we felt still more cut off, but even so there were certain events which could not be kept dark: for instance the mass arrests of foreign Jews in Paris in May 1941—tragic news for the non-Aryans in our midst, whose parents were Parisians but considered foreigners. (French Jews were not deported till later, though most lost their jobs or made their way to the Zone Non-Occupée—Z.N.O.—early on.)

What excitement, though, when we heard that Hitler had attacked the Soviet Union! We did not know just what this would mean, except probably even harsher persecution of French Communists; but we sensed, even behind the barbed wire, that this attack would be a turning point in the war. I could not believe, in spite of defeatist arguments, that the U.S.S.R. would be overrun. Hitler's defeat was, we sensed, as certain as Napoleon's had been in 1812.

In the camp we celebrated Russia's entry into the war at the same time as the *Fête Nationale*, on 14 July, with a demonstration in the hotel grounds, in which the French workmen and P.O.W.s joined with enthusiasm. The German sentries stood around grinning; *they* were under the impression that Hitler's eastern expedition would be a walk-over. They were panting to be off to the Russian front: "Lieber dort als hier", said one, "It will be a picnic!" When we asked why he thought so his solemn answer was "The Führer wills it; the Führer is always right". However, news trickled through the censorship that the Russians were resisting fiercely. The German soldiers began to feel less keen to leave the dull but peaceful camp, and the French were frankly jubilant. Wehrmacht officers came back from the front and made no secret of its being hell let loose there; it was rather ironic that we had first-hand news of their losses from the Germans themselves.

Letters from Paris during 1941 were, of course, strictly censored, although the significance of such sentences as "We spend a lot of time, not always profitably, in the market", and "We don't go to the theatre much, although the Schiller Theatre of Berlin has been here, and Serge Lifar is still dancing and Sacha Guitry acting . . ." was not lost on us. We had little idea of what was going on there, apart from the Jewish arrests. It was only later that I heard of how the Resistance movement was developing, in the factories, in the colleges, on the railways and—a new development—in small groups listening to Radio London, duplicating leaflets and generally spreading illegal anti-fascist propaganda. Our morale in captivity would have been immensely strengthened had we known of the growing opposition to the common enemy.

The Paris Préfecture announced on 5 April that 6,400 fines had been inflicted on concierges, shopkeepers, and houseowners who "ignored the Wehrmacht's orders and have allowed slogans or posters to be left on their walls".[1] To say, like Georges Bidault, that "Paris in 1941 was paralysed" was to underestimate the extent of the activity of those who affixed slogans, and the passive resistance of those whose walls flaunted them. Bidault thought "it would take a very long time to find men able or willing to risk their lives for the sake of a vague and remote victory", but as a returned prisoner, belonging to a disintegrated political party, he would hardly have found it easy to make contacts in the underground. Like many, he was pinning his faith to de Gaulle, yet had the impression that "the London group was very insulated and exclusive" because he received no reply to his many messages.[2]

To dwell for a moment on the Gaullist set-up, it should be said that in 1941 the organisation of networks was in its early stages, and the

General had not yet the facilities which he later insisted on getting from the British to build an effective movement. Up to mid-1941 he had not even a clear conception of what internal resistance might mean. "While consolidating our overseas base", he writes in his *Memoirs*, "it was of Metropolitan France that we were chiefly thinking. What to do there? How? With what? . . . Clandestine action was a field entirely new to us. No preparations had ever been made in France with a view to the situation into which the country had been hurled. . . . There was nothing to which our action could attach itself." The British, he said, simply wanted spies sent, to collect information. "But we meant to do better . . . to set up networks."[3]

De Gaulle's *réseaux* were a new element in the underground struggle. Gaullism became a focal point for groups of different political complexions attempting to win the allegiance of the French people away from the progressive Left and for a reformist policy in the future. Gaullism was basically conservative but was seen as opposition to Nazi imperialism, and therein lay its appeal to the bourgeosie. De Gaulle had in fact not offered the working class anything at all; his speeches were as anti-Communist as anti-German, and his British protectors were the Tory leaders. Many Frenchmen in exile refused to join him in the early days, and he on his side refused to associate with the Left: "M. Pierre Cot asked me to use him," he says, "but he was too notorious for this to be desirable." Catholic and Conservative, with his army upbringing, it was natural that de Gaulle should surround himself with like-minded colleagues, and distrust well-known Radicals let alone "Reds".

The General's Intelligence agents of the B.C.R.A. (Bureau de Renseignements et d'Action) were also naturally in contact with men whose views coincided with his, "some even with the *Cagoule* (the extreme right-wing society of Cagoulards, 'the hooded men') which, on its side, had not put all its eggs in one basket" as a left-wing writer observed.

In 1941, though, all this was not apparent to the average French patriot listening eagerly to radio London as a change from the Nazi-controlled news service. By the end of the year, too, the S.O.E., ordered by Churchill to "set Europe ablaze", was dropping British Intelligence Service (I.S.) agents into both zones of France, and the B.C.R.A. was soon to follow suit. These brave men and women did extremely dangerous work, mainly with individual groups, and many lost their lives or were tortured and deported. They worked for

Britain or for Gaullism at this stage, mainly without the co-operation of the workers and peasants who had their own forms of struggle, evolved in the earliest days of defeat, and were motivated by political ideals.

By the end of 1941 the Free French in London had won massive support among the middle classes, many thousands of whose patriots were undertaking any tasks within their power: sheltering prisoners, hiding agents, taking in mail, passing detainees into safety, at the risk of their own freedom or even their lives. This I can vouch for from my own experience, and when people say (as they often do today) that the average French citizen was not interested in the Resistance, I would refer them to the inhabitants of Nancy, or Besançon, Arbois, Lyons, Marseilles, who enabled me and my companion, when we escaped from the camp, to stay in those towns and to cross a great area of France under the noses of the Nazis and of the Vichy police. The families who took us in and hid us were very solid citizens; the cycle shop manager, the dentist (of Besançon) who got us our false papers, the Mayor who arranged for us to have ration cards, the veterans with whom we drank to victory on 11 November in a public café, the police officers who drove us to the demarcation line in an official car—they had nothing to gain, no special reason to be pro-British, their attitude was purely French and patriotic. They wanted France to be free and independent and they resented German occupation. Many had still-vivid memories of 1914–18, and some perhaps had the blood of the 1870 and even of 1789 republicans in their veins. They were not by any means all activists, but they all felt the need to say No; and this was the first step towards unity—which might have turned to true popular co-operation in anti-fascist struggle had not the representatives of the French ruling class in London decided that would be too dangerous.

Passing through the "forbidden zone" that chilly November, however, we witnessed a general agreement in all circles to do down "les boches". Those who enabled us to escape varied enormously—from the electrician who helped us out through the barbed wire, to the hotelier who overlooked our highly suspicious identity cards, from the Spanish refugee workers who gave up their rations to feed us, to the peasant family who hid us in a cupboard all night (in one vain attempt to cross into Switzerland), and from the photographer who took pictures for our false identity cards to the respected lawyer who put us up in Arbois.

It was a young worker from a local factory who guided us over

7 kilometres of wasteland to safety across the demarcation line—
every night this lad took the risk of being gunned down by German
guards as he conveyed escaping prisoners into the Unoccupied
Zone. Once in Vichy France, a farmer's wife fed us and a publican's
daughter gave us a bed.

Two well-dressed commercial travellers drove us to Lyons and put
us in touch with the U.S. consulate which provided laissez-passers.
To complete the variety of the social cross-section to whom we were
indebted, there was our hostess in Marseilles; she was, we were led
to believe, a flourishing 1941 *Boule de Suif* (her name was Madame
Morbelli, and she lived in the rue Sainte Victoire, which we thought
the best of omens) and she introduced us openly as "les dames de
Londres" to her many friends and clients.

If these worthy people—of no special political convictions—were
so courageous and dedicated as to risk their skins in helping us and
thus supporting the resistance how much more then is it certain that
the industrial workers (whom we did not happen to meet), anti-
fascist by social reasons from the start, were in their vast majority
"resistant"?

In conversations with our hosts and rescuers we learned a lot which
confirmed this impression. Everyone knew about the strikes and
sabotage going on in the factories and on the railways. People
talked about the miners' strike in the North, in May, and one
"fellow-traveller" in Marseilles even gave me details: 100,000 had
struck from 26 May to 9 June; "nearly 500,000 working days lost"
my informant exulted: "And imagine, they say the Germans lost
half a million tons of coal—as every lump of our coal goes to them or
their industry in France."

We heard other stories through friends who had recently made
their way south from Paris, Jewish socialists who had lost their
academic posts but managed to keep in touch. There had been mass
arrests of workers in July (seventy-two in the Aube department,
twenty-seven at Beauvais), and terrible reprisals after a German
officer had been shot by Colonel Fabien, a resistance leader, in
August: 400 to 500 Communists were to be shot for every German
killed, Keitel had announced. The execution of hostages brought a
wave of protest, and sabotage in factories producing arms for the
Russian front. Twenty-seven Communist hostages were shot at
Chateaubriant prison, twenty-one at Nantes, fifty at Bordeaux
after more German officers were killed, and a lightning strike had
taken place all over France in honour of the martyrs. Even in an Ivry

factory guarded by Germans, the workers had downed tools.

When we asked how our friend knew all this, we were told it was reported in the underground press, which now boasted many newspapers of a dozen different tendencies; besides the T.U. *Vie Ouvrière* and *Humanité*, there were the illegal Paris newspapers, *Resistance, Valmy, Défence de la France*, which somehow managed to cross the demarcation line, and in the Z.N.O., *Libérateur* and *Combat* (of Lyons), *Franctireur, Progrès* and *La Marseillaise*. Most people got hold of an underground leaflet or paper at some time, and passed it on, so that the circulation was considerable; and everyone "of course" listened regularly to "la Bé Bé Cé" (B.B.C.).

It was through Radio London that people in Vichy France learned that de Gaulle's Committee, *La France Libre*, formed in September, had been recognised by Britain (and hence by the other Allied governments in London) as the *de jure* government of France—news which gave us some small cheer at a time when it was badly needed. The official recognition that France was undefeated was immensely important to morale; for me perhaps even more so in Z.N.O. (Pétain's territory) than in the Zone Rouge, where one was face to face with the national enemy rather than up against the sham patriotism of Vichy, with which I was soon to become familiar.

NOTES

1. Tillon, *Les F.T.P.* p. 85
2. Bidault, *Resistance* p. 75
3. De Gaulle, *The Call to Honour* (trans. Collins, London, 1955) pp. 154–156

Chapter 8
1941–1942
VICHY

Fantômes fantômes fantômes
Général sans armée Amiral sans bateaux
Payés bon prix se levant tard se couchant tôt
Fantômes fantômes fantômes
Faussaires fossoyeurs nervis et négriers
Porte-plume buvant à tous les encriers
Fantômes fantômes fantômes
C'est Vichy-Grande-Grille On vent à la criée
Le chair de la Patrie au choix crue ou grillée

Aragon, *Le Musee Grévin*

Ghosts, ghosts, ghosts
General without armies, Admirals without a fleet
Well paid to rise late, sleep early
Forgers, gravediggers, crooks, slave-traders
Pens that drink at every inkwell
The Vichy steak-house, auctioning off
France's flesh, roasted or raw . . .

The two months that I spent in Vichy France during the winter of 1941–42 convinced me that the man in the street there was by no means as pro-Pétainist and anti-British as was often supposed in the North.

Naturally, feelings in Z.N.O. were not so violently Germanophobe, as the jackboots were not visible, and Pétain's velvet glove had up to then hidden the mailed fist which later hit out at the growing opposition. *Bienpensant* businessmen and devout Catholics had accepted the regime thankfully in 1940 and some still expressed the belief that "le père Pétain" had saved a third of France in the nick of time from both the Nazis and a Communist revolution. Many middle-class politically neutral men and women took the situation for granted and tried to live as normal a life as possible.

This was not easy, at least in the towns where consumer goods were scarce and food was short and nasty, even in restaurants. Most meals in December 1941 were based on carrots. I recall a typical menu: *Potage Paysanne* (carrots and water); *Filet de Bœuf garni* (carrots plus a small scrap of meat); *Macédoine de légumes* (mainly carrots), or simply *Carottes Vichy*. There was no oil for cooking, no wine, no meat, no coffee, very little fish (owing to the scarcity of petrol for the fishing boats). As to other necessaries of life, soap was ersatz—all the stocks of the famous *Savon de Marseille* having been requisitioned for Germany like so much else—grapes, fertilisers, leather (shoes were soled with wood). Coal was down to 35 per cent of pre-war supply, petrol to a tenth of the 1939 level. There was a black market for what little existed in good quality foods and cosmetics, and that, of course, increased the scarcity and pushed up prices for the average citizen, who unless he had relatives in the countryside (and even then) found it very difficult indeed to feed and keep his family.

I feared that the British blockade would make us unpopular; but on the contrary, in shops and offices we were told "C'est naturel!" and "If food comes into the port it's sent straight on to Germany"; and people said they preferred to tighten their belts to feeding the Boches. In spite of French colonial losses due to British action, the average person wished us well.

I met one Marseillais who had a son "overseas", and whose broad wink indicated that the latter had joined the Free French forces; and several casual acquaintances told me they would willingly go to England and help carry on the war—"how could it be arranged?"

Others longing to get out of Vichy France were the expatriate Poles and Austrians who sat around in cafés, patiently waiting for their papers to be "regularised" and for visas for New York or Latin America to be issued to them. They lived in a constant state of tension, knowing the fate that had overtaken too many of their compatriots sent to death camps in Nazi-occupied central Europe.

The Vieux Port quarter of Marseilles was a favourite haunt of the dispossessed and those on the run, and not long after our stay in the city it was drastically "cleaned up"—pending its total demolition by the Germans, who blew it up in their 1943 purge of the homes and haunts of "undesirable elements". These unfortunate foreigners were no threat to Pétain, but their presence was a constant reproach, and in the uncertain climate of opinion could not be tolerated.

There was no denying the fact, however, that the Vichy government was for the moment firmly entrenched (under the protection, of course, of invisible German bayonets). It seemed to me at the time a ministry of sinister but faceless men. Pétain had gathered around him, under the nomenclature *Etat français*—the Republic being dead and buried—an unsavoury collection of fascists and fifth-columnists, Maurrassiens and followers of Colonel de la Rocque, not one of whom could claim distinction of any kind. As Dr Paxton says, it was "a whole 1930s underworld of anti-semitic, anti-parliamentary agitators". The most extreme of them found jobs in the departments of propaganda and of law-and-order: Darnand the policeman, Paul Marion, Franco's friend Ybarnégaray, Henriot, Darquier de Pellepoix. In the more respectable administrative posts were a few of the Third Republic's elite who had voted for Pétain in July 1940; while most of the eighty who had not thus voted were in limbo, and Blum, Daladier, Reynaud and Mandel (later murdered by Darnand's *milice*) in prison, Pierre Pucheu, of the Comité des Forges, Flandin, the neo-monarchist Raphael Alibert, and Georges Bonnet were given high positions. Laval in the early days had the important post of Deputy Prime Minister; quarrelling with other ministers, he was dropped in December 1940 but returned to Vichy in April 1942 as Foreign Minister as well as Home Secretary.

Pétain's position as head of government was secure, and all decrees were signed by him personally, as sole arbiter of France's destiny. But the government was absurdly unstable: "Ministries came and went at speeds even more dizzying than at the worst moments of the Third Republic."[1] Between June 1940 and 1941 there were four ministers of Foreign Affairs, five of the Interior, five of Education, six of Industrial Production. In the propaganda department, there were eight ministers for Information and fifteen for Radio between 1940 and 1944! This of course made for extraordinary inefficiency. Vichy's policy, internal and external, vacillated continuously. The two firm elements throughout were Pétain himself and the authority of a powerful police, which inhibited public expression with its threat of punishment by special courts and its unremitting witch-hunt of "subversives".[2]

Most of Pétain's promises failed to materialise; the golden prospects that collaboration would result in the release of the P.O.W.s, in reduction of Occupation costs, in an easing of the demarcation line (so that divided families could be reunited), all these faded as time went by, as did hopes of a less rigid administration.[3] Living standards steadily deteriorated, and when complaints were voiced they were answered with the counsels of despair: "La France a été vaincue", and she must bear the consequences.

Vichy's programme, such as it was, consisted of a hotch-potch of clerico-fascist measures under the slogan "Travail, Famille, Patrie" which captioned the hundreds of huge posters bearing the Marshal's placid, lugubrious face. (De Gaulle's comment on Pétain's slogan was "Work? He lost the habit long ago. Family? He's an old libertine. Country? The Saviour of Verdun turned traitor." In France a popular distortion was "Travail forcé, 200 Familles, Patrie trahie"; another was "Trahison, Famine, Prisons".) Religion was given high priority. Pétain returned to the Roman Catholic Church the property confiscated in 1905 and reintroduced its power into French education, declaring an end of the "Godless school". A great effort was made to indoctrinate the young with Pétainist ideas, and youth organisations were set up which provided camps and clubs and uniforms for children, who paraded all over the Z.N.O. singing "Maréchal, nous voilà!" Jean Guéhenno noted in his diary that the Vichy Zone "is a strange land where everyone from children of six upwards, regimented into groups from 'youths' to Veterans, wearing Francisques (an axe crossed with a Marshal's baton), and symbols of the Legion, seemed to be in uniform". But support for these organisations was never great, and it dwindled as time went on—from 25,000 nominally in 1940 to 8,000 in 1944.

In the field of industry and labour, Vichy proved dismally incompetent. Production was at a very low level throughout its administration, partly owing to the material difficulties of the situation, partly to the conflict between businessmen and bureaucrats, each of whom wanted control. A certain degree of monopolisation was carried out, to rationalise industry, but Vichy was always hamstrung by the requisitioning of materials and skilled labour, and the closing down of plants by the Germans. Unemployment was rife, and Pétain's only solution in 1940 was to dissuade women from working and to intern all foreigners of eighteen to forty-five years old. The latter measure killed two birds with one stone—it *(a)* reduced the "excess of labour in the economy", and *(b)* got rid of "undesirable" and possibly subversive aliens (Spaniards and anti-Nazi Germans, Austrians and Czechs) while pleasing Franco and Hitler in the process. At the same time, 15,154 out of 500,000 Frenchmen naturalised since 1927 had their citizenship revoked. 6,307 of these were Jewish, many of them exiles from Hitler Germany.[4]

So began the "purification" of the French nation. It escalated rapidly in the following years, with anti-semitic measures such as the exclusion of most French Jews from the services and from many professions. Only 2 per cent were allowed to practise medicine, law and architecture, 3 per cent permitted to study in universities. Jews were banned completely from the Department of Allier where Vichy is situated.

The Pétainist handling of industrial affairs was equally obscurantist. The restrictions of workers' long-standing rights were spelled out in the government's *Charte de Travail*, which was published on 4 October 1941: No right to strike, no political functions, no worker-participation whatever in industry. The "illegal" C.G.T. made its feelings clear in widespread leaflets and underground newspapers; but in 1941 and 1942 there was so much unemployment that it was not easy to ask workers to risk getting the sack or to face arrest by breaking the new fascist labour laws.

At the same time as it antagonised the industrial workers, Vichy made advances to the peasants. The Marshal's ideology was expressed in a speech of 12 October 1940 which was an attempt to launch "family agriculture", as "the principal economic and social base of France", on a wide scale. Pierre Caziot, a backwoodsman of the Third Republic, was in charge of promoting the "return to the soil" by granting subsidies to families who would restore abandoned farms, and by organising the *Chantiers de la Jeunesse* which put all French youths of twenty-one years old in rural work-camps for eight months at a time.

These measures again fulfilled a double purpose—supplying man-power in the absence of thousands of peasants still in German camps, and placating Hitler by accepting the rural role designated for France in *Mein Kampf*.

It struck many young Frenchmen (perhaps all who were not sold on the Marshal's and Barré's ideas of utopian rural society) that all this was retrograde, that Pétain was putting back the clock. However praiseworthy the ideals of hard work and the simple life, surely, they thought, in the modern world France needed more than a peasant economy based on family groupings. Caziot's legislation did, in the end, take into account some of the objections. He made it easier to regroup scattered parcels of land into unified farms, and provided some agricultural training for prospective farmers, with other concessions for those who needed further persuasion to return to the soil. But for one reason or another the propaganda failed to induce Frenchmen to go back into agriculture or to keep them there; only just over 1,000 families settled under Caziot's scheme. A *Charte Paysanne*, or Landworkers' Charter, drawn up on 2 December 1940 to improve marketing methods, did not attract any more support, and Caziot's plans gave way to those of more modern thinking. He retired in 1942, and his successor Jacques Le Roy Ladurie introduced direct state control into agriculture, but to little effect: Vichy's problems were insoluble.

Fertilisers, machines and workers were lacking, and though farmers had enough for themselves they could not feed the whole Zone. The black market became the answer for the rich, while the poor went very hungry indeed. As Roger Martin du Gard wrote to André Gide, "There are whole families who have nothing but their daily bread ration each day: *C'est fou ce que les gens peuvent avoir faim* (It's crazy how hungry people are)."[5]

The sickly concern expressed in Pétain's propaganda did not blind people to the hard facts of life. Promotion of the Christian virtues of resignation and the founding of loyalist youth clubs did not endear Vichy to the man in the street, nor did the drive to increase the population by extolling the "Family", abolishing divorce, urging procreation and exhorting mothers to stay at home. The German ideal of *Küche, Kirche, Kinder* (Kitchen, Church, Children) did not appeal to the women, particularly when extra income was badly needed to make both ends meet.

In mid-1941 even the Marshal himself commented on the growing discontent and admitted that a "malaise is gripping the French people—the authority of my government is contested, its orders poorly executed". Nominally Vichy still exercised authority over the whole of France in matters of law and order, and it is not surprising that Pétain was worried by the increasing protests, widespread circulation of illegal newspapers, ever more open defiance.

General Speidel, Nazi overseer in Paris, reported 54 acts of sabotage in July, 73 in August, 134 in September, and 162 in October 1941. Assassinations of Germans were becoming frequent, and culminated that year in the shooting of the Feldkommandant of Nantes.

The ferocity of the Nazi reprisals (1,615 arrests in Paris and a million francs' fine) and the taking of hundreds of hostages, horrified the country; North and South alike were appalled by the brutality of the German authorities, and even if everyone did not approve of individual attacks on enemy soldiers, it was only collaborators like M. Jacques Nordal who saw them as the result of directives from Moscow. Nordal later wrote about "the sinister period of summer and autumn 1941 when the voices of de Gaulle and Pétain were united in reproving the senseless gestures which were paid for by France alone".[6] Perhaps neither realised that the "senseless gestures" were the acts of men who considered themselves still at war—legitimate armed attacks on a ruthless enemy.

De Gaulle's attitude to the partisan attacks was indeed one of disapproval; his decree of 23 October was that the Occupants were not to be killed, "for the one reason that it is at present too easy for the enemy to reply by massacring our temporarily disarmed fighters. When we are ready to pass to the attack, orders will be given." We will later look more closely at the General's position *vis-à-vis* the partisans; for the present it is Vichy that concerns us.

Pétain's public reaction to the executions was one of grief and shock; he was also much concerned as to the effect that the partisans activity would have on the Nazi authorities, and foresaw a hardening towards all Frenchmen, even his own supporters. He broadcast an appeal to everybody to keep the peace: "We have laid down our arms. We have no right to take them up again to stab the Germans in the back!" But privately Vichy ministers saw some advantage for themselves in the elimination of Communist and "terrorist" activists, and instead of asking for clemency from the Germans they tried to get the role of public executioner into their own hands. The Minister of the Interior, Pucheu, saw a chance of gaining more authority for the French police in the North, and he insisted that the French instead of the Germans should carry out the punishments, as a gesture of collaboration and of semi-independence. Pucheu also promised Abetz that instead of random hostages only Communists would be executed. Special legislation was rushed through by Darlan, Premier at the time, setting up special sections for courts martial, empowering the government to act exceptionally toughly with Communists and anarchists. (As any opposition to the regime was identified with Communism, the net was clearly spread wide.)

The Ministers had an additional reason for uneasiness and wanting revenge: several of their own colleagues had been attacked during the summer—Laval and Marcel Déat injured by a would-be assassin on 29 August, and Marcel Gitton shot on 5 September. So the Paris "Special Section" went to work and sentenced a number of Communists to death for infraction of the 1939 decree dissolving the Party. But the Germans were not satisfied with the comparatively paltry numbers produced by Vichy's courts, and in the end the Nazi Command went on choosing its hostages itself.[7]

Throughout his first year in power Pétain had managed to keep up the appearance of saving part of France from total occupation, and, while "collaborating", of defending the interests of the nation. He had respectable links with the outside world—an American and a Soviet Ambassador (till June 1941) in Vichy, and French diplomats in most of the neutral countries, in Washington, D.C., in Canada and

in the Vatican, where Pétain was smiled upon.[8] Vichy also boasted
that the Empire was intact and loyal to the Marshal—if only the
"traitor de Gaulle" and the British would stop making trouble. This
window-dressing did not disguise the lack of economic achievement,
the failure to get German concessions, the fratricidal repression; and
many of Pétain's admirers began to lose faith in him. When he gave
his blessing on 7 July 1941 to the *Légion de Volontaires contre le
Bolchevisme* and sent them off wearing German uniforms to fight on
the Russian front, there were sharp reactions among even the
moderate. Some prominent Catholic leaders disapproved of his
anti-semitic policies; Cardinal Saliège, for instance, openly protested when Pétain condoned the sending of Jewish transports to
Nazi death camps in December 1941, and later, when deportations
became part of official Vichy policy.

A great many intellectuals, even conservatives, became restive
under the obscurantist policies introduced into schools and universities, which were regarded by Pétain as "foyers empoisonnés"
largely responsible for France's defeat, possibly the principal agents
thereof. Vichy condemned French education *en bloc*: Away with
it! Down with Descartes and the spirit of criticism! Up with
Pétain's "moral schooling"! Special lectures and meetings were
organised to promote this, and a crop of books came out laying
down the precepts of the new education. To quote a couple of
extracts: "It is tragic that (the teachers of) this generation, corrupted
by political madness, should corrupt succeeding generations. . . ."[10]
"The immense majority of teachers can be won for the National
Revolution . . . they will turn to the Marshal who has said that New
France needs servants inspired by a New Ideal."[11] "In restoring our
vanquished country, we have to renounce intellectualism, the spirit
of scientific research, and to develop a *general education*."[12]

Although most teachers somehow got round the new rules, and
many failed to display the Marshal's portrait or else stuck it up in
a cupboard, it was impossible to avoid the all-pervasive propaganda
put out by Vichy, the posters, films and publications spreading
Pétain's philosophy. Nothing opposed to it was permitted, and the
vigilantes-type *Légion de Combattants* virtually took over "culture"
in the Z.N.O., choosing and censoring books and films and forbidding public functions that displeased them, such as the lectures of
André Gide, cancelled at Nice in May 1941.

In late 1941 and the beginning of 1942 it was clear to any observer
in Vichy France that support for Pétain rested only on the most

reactionary elements, and on the police and its paid agents in the Milice. There were enough of these, ruthless and unscrupulous, to enforce temporary silence on the majority of the population, who had as yet little in the way of organisation or leadership. The underground movement in Z.N.O. was dispersed and ineffective; but it seemed to me, travelling through Pétain country, talking to friends and even to strangers, that when the spirit of non-acceptance was canalised and organised it would become a formidable movement. Wherever we went we were asked, "A quand le deuxième Front?" and told "Ne vous en faites pas, we are ready for the British and de Gaulle". People carried crossed fishing-rods *(deux gaules)*, so we heard, and I personally saw "V" chalked on walls, and picked up one of the coins which was circulating with a tiny *de G* stamped under the words *Etat français*—small but meaningful indications of opinion.

In Marseilles, people offered us hospitality without thought of possible danger to themselves; one family, Catholic and comfortably off, were Pétainist ("the Marshal's playing a double game") but pro-British, and brought out their last reserves of olives and old wine to toast *la victoire*. In another home we found we were two in a series of escapees being given lavish hospitality: our hostess, Madame Fiocca (later renowned as Nancy Wake, S.O.E. heroine), had helped many an English officer to get out of France and was in touch with embryo networks reaching from Nice to Toulouse. She took us to several Marseilles bars where she was extremely popular, not least because of her outspoken anti-German attitude. When thoroughly cheerful after an evening out, Nancy would march home down the Canebière, arm-in-arm with us, singing "Rule Britannia" at the top of her voice—and the local gendarmerie, in spite of my apprehension, conveniently turned a deaf ear. Later, when the Germans occupied the Southern Zone, Nancy had to get out of Marseilles and escape across the Pyrenees to England, leaving her brave husband to a terrible fate at the hands of the Nazis. But in January 1941 they felt no fear of denunciation, surrounded as they were by good friends who shared their loyalties and complete confidence in Germany's and Vichy's defeat.

The last French family we talked to, in Toulouse on our journey towards London (via Spain, Portugal and Ireland), were relatives of Jean Cassou, the writer, then incarcerated for anti-Pétainist propaganda in the local gaol. They were deeply depressed by their situation as Jews, but sustained by the kindness of colleagues in Toulouse university, who had in protest against Vichy's anti-semitism got our friend, an ex-Sorbonne professor, a post in their campus. At his parents' temporary home we met Professor Friedmann, also exiled from Paris, who was active in the recently-formed local resistance group. As far as I could gather, its action was limited as yet to listening-in to Radio London and illegally circulating mimeographed information sheets. Friedmann asked me to convey "something very important" to the *Porte-parole de la France Libre* (de Gaulle's radio spokesman) in London, and handed over a packet of Gaulloises cigarettes, one of which contained a secret message rolled up inside. I was adjured to deliver this as soon as possible, and not on any account to smoke any of the cigarettes on the journey home.

The last words spoken to me in Vichy France were by this friend on Toulouse railway station as our train steamed out: "Tell them in London to open the Second Front soon—we are ready and waiting for them!"

NOTES

1. R. Paxton, *Vichy France* p. 199
2. ibid. p. 200
3. ibid. p. 222
4. ibid. p. 171
5. Gide, *Correspondence,* II, (Paris, 1968) p. 272
6. Tillon, *Les F.T.P.* p. 122
7. Paxton, op. cit. pp. 38–41
8. Weil-Curiel, *Eclipse de la France* p. 57
9. Tournoux, *Pétain and de Gaulle* (trans. London, 1966) p. 133
10. Delanque, *Les Enseignants* p. 121
11. S. Jeanneret, *La Verité sur les institueurs*
12. P. Crouzet, *La vraie Révolution nationale dans l'Instruction publique,* quoted Delanque op. cit. pp. 120–122

Chapter 9

FREE FRENCH IN LONDON

Puisque le juste est dans l'abime
Puisque'on donne le sceptre au crime
Puisque tous les droits sont trahis
Puisque'on affiche au coin des bornes
Le déshonneur de mon pays . . .
. . . Je t'aime, exil! douleur, je t'aime!

Victor Hugo, *Puisque le juste* . . .

Because justice is in the pit,
Because crime holds the sceptre,
Because all rights are betrayed,
Because at every street corner
My country's shame is advertised . . .
Exile, I love you, I love you, sorrow!

After so long in German-dominated France it was certainly a welcome change to be among the French in Britain where one could (I assumed) speak freely about Vichy's misdeeds and openly discuss the role and prospects of the resistance movement. The message from the Toulouse "underground" gave me immediate access to people at the centre of the Forces Françaises Libres (F.F.L.) in London. De Gaulle had his headquarters in Carlton Gardens, and various offices in the West End. Soldiers and sailors who had rallied to the F.F.L. were billeted in the suburbs, but they had a social centre of their own in London, while members of the administration could relax in a comfortable club in St James's Square.

The staff of France Libre were a disparate collection of individuals of various political colours, from the right-wing Palewski, the General's close adviser, and Colonel Wavrin (alias Passy), organiser of the B.C.R.A. (Bureau Central de Renseignement et d'Action, the secret service department), to the Socialists Georges Boris and André Philip. In the passages I glimpsed René Pleven, a conservative financial expert, the radical Mendés-France (in officer's uniform), Viénot, the diplomat, Crémieux, educationist brother of the writer Benjamin—all of very different opinions but temporarily united under the label *gaulliste*.

The first person I was introduced to was Maurice Schumann, tall, stooping, large-boned, a Jesuit I was told, enthusiastic organiser of the Gaullist radio service, and famous inside France as "la Porte Parole de la France Libre". Night after night he could be heard intoning "Le 250me—or 350me as it might be—jour de la lutte du peuple français pour sa libération!", after which came the words of encouragement, the latest news and the code messages. (My Gaulloise cigarette message had been decoded, they assured me, and the right answer broadcast on this programme to the Toulouse underground.) New arrivals from France were often asked to speak from Bush House on this wavelength; it was a nerve-racking test of one's accent, but I could only hope that my thanks to the friends in France for their help and sacrifice somehow got through to them.

The people in de Gaulle's entourage were, or said they were, interested in my recent experiences and impressions, and there was also a wide demand for first-hand news from occupied France among the British public. I spent a month that spring of 1942 writing articles, broadcasting and lecturing all over the place—Wales, Manchester, Scotland, Oxford—talking to big audiences ranging from factory workers to academics, and to army units in camps (even, once, to R.A.F. Command at Stanmore), always trying to convince anyone who would listen that what was needed was "The Second Front now". The words "Tell them to come—we're ready!" constantly rang in my ears.

I had the impression that the soldiers and airmen in the audience were surprised to learn that the French were not taking defeat lying down, and that they themselves would be glad to go into action in France; life in the English countryside was not their idea of waging war, and "the sooner we can have a bash at Hitler the better". As for nearly a thousand workers on the night shift at Ferranti's Moston factory (deeply involved in weapon production), they responded heart-warmingly to the stories of industrial sabotage and resistance to the Germans by their opposite numbers in France.

That summer the F.F.L. gave me a humble but satisfying job in the Information Department, reading and collating the French press, both legal and "clandestine", and the *Journal de Genève*, a useful Swiss source; from these we issued a weekly bulletin of the most important news items. I worked with Madame Soustelle, wife of the Head of the Department; she was a person of great charm and energy and we got on well (on the basis of mutual anti-Americanism; she had lived in Mexico and her favourite expression was "Abajo los Gringos!", Down with the Yanks.) We never discussed politics, apart from the day-to-day events, because we sensed our basic differences; but she was enthusiastic about the Red Army and its achievements, and assured me that her husband and de Gaulle were too: "Mon général thinks the British don't appreciate what the Russians are doing," she said. On the occasion of a victory celebration (of Stalingrad) in the Albert Hall, de Gaulle had looked disdainfully round the phlegmatic audience and said "*We* would do better than that!"—"He and my husband are in complete agreement", she added.

Jacques Soustelle was square, swarthy and vigorous. Everyone told me how brilliant he was as an anthropologist and politician. His drive and ambition had got him a long way; now only in his thirtieth year, he was de Gaulle's chief confidant, ran the information services and was also responsible for security. This (though I knew few details) was a difficult and arduous job, as plots and conspiracies played a large part in F.F.L. life, as in that of any group of exiles. De Gaulle's "police" were often accused of being over-conscientious, and strange stories circulated of second-degree methods being used in the basement of Duke Street, and arm-twisting in Carlton Gardens. My own experience was restricted to an unpleasant interview during which I was asked by two smooth plain-clothes policemen to give details of all my contacts in France; failing this I should lose my job in the Gaullist establishment, they said. I fobbed them off with a few invented names, and went straight back to report to Soustelle, who was furious. "I won't have these Gestapo methods used on my personnel", he declared, and promised me my inquisitor would be duly told off. Had I not known the Chief personally I would have been helpless. Soustelle was a good boss, and later I was very sorry to know that his success led him into such unworthy postures; it seemed a pity he had not gone back to anthropology where he might have done much good work instead of using his talents to promote French imperialism at its most "ultra" in Algeria. But that is another story.

Apart from our friendly little office, the atmosphere in Carlton Gardens was not altogether congenial. The life that most of the staff were leading contrasted too painfully with the grim existence in occupied France. Although many of them really suffered emotionally from the knowledge of what was happening inside their country, quite a few, it seemed to me, were not too concerned, particularly about the fate of the Communists who were rotting in the jails and camps. There were too many right-wing conservatives in de Gaulle's

entourage, wealthy ex-diplomats, well-connected people who did not
not know or very much care about the lamentable conditions of their
working-class compatriots. Naturally, professional men who had
been able to make their way to England, or who had British contacts,
were neither poor nor Left wing. There were few working-class folk
among the Free French, except for the soldiers who did chores in
the office buildings and whom it was a pleasure to talk to as a change
from the conversation of the élite.

It also struck me (rightly or wrongly) that really undesirable elements had too easy access to the offices and that some of the heavily
made-up young women who were given jobs by their uniformed boy
friends might be highly suspicious characters. It would be all too easy
for a female agent to make her way in, get access to confidential
files and do a lot of harm. Perhaps this was being over-suspicious;
but two years in occupied France made one suspect anybody not
outstandingly sincere or proven as a patriot. I think there were many
French in London who felt the same way, and mistrusted de Gaulle's
set-up. He was certainly not universally loved among the exiles:
Some were merely suspicious; others would not go near Carlton
Gardens; others, again, moved around in cliques, and published
journals to prove how authoritarian the General was; the left-wing
Socialist Louis Levy and the Gombault brothers, brilliant journalists,
who ran the newspaper *France*, bitterly resented the Gaullist
"monopoly" of patriotism. Then there was André Labarthe, waging
a non-stop smear campaign against the General; and Admiral
Muselier, who quarrelled violently with him over the Free French
Navy's action in Saint-Paul and Miquelon, which the Admiral had
advised against;[1] and a lot of other disgruntled members of the
armed forces who refused to take the oath of loyalty which de Gaulle
demanded. A whole group preferred to join the British Army to
bowing to the high-handed General; and there were even Frenchmen
who worked with the British Intelligence Service instead of the
B.C.R.A., which caused not a little bad feeling.

The I.S. department for Secret Operations in Europe (S.O.E.)
formed with Churchill's blessing to drop agents and organise pro-
Ally groups inside France, had better facilities and priority over the
Gaullists; and although eventually the two organisations had to co-
operate, no love was lost between them in the early days of 1941–42.
I was told by someone at the receiving end that de Gaulle's telephone
conversations with British security tended to finish with an abusive
"You peeg Eenglish!", and he certainly did not mince his words

when demanding his (or France's) rights from Winston Churchill himself.(I should mention, from personal experience, that he was impeccably courteous to his junior staff and never failed to salute the most minor employee on the doorstep of his office.)

In spite of all the dissidence, the General was undoubtedly the figurehead and inspiration of his movement, and had he not been so "difficult" and authoritarian he might not have succeeded in projecting his image, and keeping the limited power he attained. Given his background and upbringing, his attitude was to be expected; in fact, what was surprising was his realism *vis-à-vis* political opposites, his readiness to co-operate even with Communists from whom he so fundamentally differed. The Soviet Union's stand must have shaken some of his anti-communist prejudices, and the leading role of the P.C.F. in resistance opened his eyes to their bravery and resolution. Being intelligent, he understood that he could not afford to antagonise the working people, and so was prepared to go along with them so far, and for the time being.

De Gaulle always resented being dependent on the British, not only in the field of secret operations. Unfortunately for him, for many months during the war Britain was not specially interested in France. In December 1941 hostilities had become world-wide, with the Japanese attack on Pearl Harbour and the entry of the U.S.A. into the war. Battles were raging in the Pacific and in the Far East. In February and March 1942 Singapore and Java fell to the Japanese, who also threatened Australia from New Guinea. In North Africa Rommel was advancing in Tripoli and Egypt was at risk. The Red Army had to retreat before a violent German offensive in southern Russia.

The main British and American preoccupation was to save as much as possible of Western imperialist territory; and Russian requests for a second front, and the worsening plight of the occupied countries, were set aside as irrelevant in the global picture which demanded a military presence in Asia, Africa, the southern Mediterranean. Churchill did, however, admit that "large forces were occupying fronts where nothing was happening", and cynical left-wingers suggested that U.S. and British leaders had not abandoned their delaying tactics. Even Harriman had said the U.S. military leaders were consistently averse to any offensive action. "The chiefs of staff would have us wait till the last button has been sewn on the last gaiter before we launch an attack."[2]

The Second Front so urgently demanded by the U.S.S.R. and

longed for by the oppressed countries was not on the British agenda
for the time being. The massive bombings by the R.A.F. were advanced by Churchill on 10 May 1942 as equally effective. In June an
Anglo-Soviet-American communiqué mentioned the possible crea-
tion of a second front in 1942, but nothing materialised. Operation
Sledgehammer, which was promised to the Russians as a relief
operation, was supposed to land several divisions on the French
channel coast in 1943; but this was not done, even though by then
Hitler's crack troops had left for Russia, and fresh U.S. and British
divisions were already formed and ready.

The landings at Saint Nazaire in March 1942, and at Dieppe in
August, were welcomed by the local Resistance groups but were
disappointingly ineffective, resulting in heavy losses of Canadian
lives with little or no gain to France or the Allies.

No wonder the French population spoke of le Deuxième Front
with either exaggerated hope or with bitterness. When the London
Gaullists repeated, week in week out, optimistic words about
"débarquement imminent", many thought of it, not unreasonably,
as bluff. My impression was, however, that de Gaulle and his
supporters would certainly have joined willingly in any action which
brought relief to their hard pressed compatriots, in 1942 or 1943.

But it was not to be. The General had no means of carrying out
effective action, except in isolated parts of the French Empire.
Between 1940 and 1943 he visited West and Northern Africa,
Syria, Lebanon, etc. He did what he could to keep up morale and to
prod the British. He also took pains to show goodwill and give
token help to the U.S.S.R., publicly praised the Red Army, and sent
a squadron of Free French planes and pilots to Russia.

The Soviet Union returned the gesture by recognising Free France
and de Gaulle's authority, on 28 September 1942. This was welcome
news to the mainland French who heard it on the radio, and who
were watching the struggle on the Eastern front with tense interest.
France was being bled of her manpower as Hitler demanded workers
to replace Germans conscripted to fight on the Russian front. On 21
March, Sauckel, the Nazi labour chief, had demanded 350,000
workers, and the Vichy government had launched a "relief operation", "La Relève", for which they promised that for every three
workers sent to Germany one French P.O.W. would be released.
This was greeted with some scepticism, and the operation did not
produce the results hoped for by Vichy.

Following Hitler's attack on Stalingrad on 20 July, France was again told to tighten her belt. Laval, who in April had made the notorious statement, "Je souhaite la victoire de l'Allemagne" (I wish for Germany's victory), promised 350,000 more men to Sauckel, and on 4 September new labour laws were passed, compelling Frenchmen to go to German factories or face prison and even death.

For those of us working in the information offices, the reports of this emasculation of France made painful reading. My weekly bulletin of "documents" was filled with accounts of executions and "purges" and *rafles* all over France. It was the working people, particularly from "militant" districts, who suffered most. After the shooting by the Nazis on 7 March of Pierre Semard, foundation member of the P.C.F. and general secretary of the railwaymen's union, the popular demonstrations which broke out led to twenty hostages being executed. News of the first big-scale deportation of Jews on 27 February brought massive protests and in April a wave of reprisals—thirty-five patriots executed in the Pas-de-Calais, and thirty at Rouen. Following an attack on the notorious anti-semite Doriot at Rennes, on 10 April, fifteen hostages were shot in Paris and a curfew imposed. On 6 May, forty patriots were executed in Rouen, and on the 12th, twenty more, followed by large-scale arrests of partisans in Paris.

All through the summer of 1942 the terror went on: 22,000 Jews were arrested (by French policemen, to their shame) and taken to the Vélodrome d'Hiver prior to deportation and almost certain death in Auschwitz; it was bitter to think how this great hall had been the traditional meeting place for left-wing demonstrations in the 1930s. Protesters at Nancy were seized and fifteen sentenced to execution. In the Gare d'Orléans on 30 July a demonstration against the departure of a large convoy of deportees brought instant retaliation—200 patriots shot in France, and over 100 sent to an unknown destination in Germany. On 11 August, ninety-three inhabitants of the commune of Ivry were executed—imagine: as if in London the equivalent of nearly a hundred workers of Stepney or Bermondsey were taken up in a swoop and shot out of hand.

September was a black month too. On the 4th Laval's new Labour Law came into operation all over France, and on the 19th 116 executions were carried out, many for infringing the new law. Curfew was imposed in Paris from 3 p.m. on 20 September until next day, following attacks by partisans on German soldiers in the Marbeuf Metro, and at the Rex Cinema. In revenge, on 30 September, twenty-one F.T.P. members were sentenced to death.

These were only some of the major reprisals carried out on "Communists", known and suspected, which were reported in the press. French provincial newspapers which reached us via Switzerland carried brief paragraphs almost every day telling of the punishment of small groups or individuals, deaths and deportations by the dozen. All this, of course, besides the frequent arrests of members of resistance networks which we learned of only later, unconnected with Communist or trade unionist groups. There were by late 1942 a great number of these *réseaux* which had sprung up almost spontaneously since 1940 to carry on the struggle according to their means and ideas, and which by the end of the year were linked with the Free French or British I.S. In the north, many of the early groups had been quickly decimated, through inefficiency, indiscretion or treachery; new ones had arisen from their ashes, learning something, it was hoped, from the tragedy of their predecessors, but it was a costly lesson—the *Musée de l'Homme réseau* lost twenty-one members during 1941 and 1942, *Ceux de la Résistance* was wiped out except for one leader who thereafter was known as *Celui de la Résistance*.

Most of the groups began among friends; as the historian Henri Michel remarks: "Those who wanted action joined whatever movement was known to them. . . . Up to 1942, belonging to the Resistance meant making contacts, meeting others to keep up one's courage, laying foundations . . . passing on the word. Movements were quickly born and quickly disappeared. There were rapprochements unthinkable before the war—between Catholics and Communists, freethinkers and believers. . . ."[3]

The former political parties took many months to re-organise. Apart from the Communists, who had never stopped fighting, the groupings of the Third Republic had more or less collapsed. But there were individual Socialists and Radicals who took the lead in linking up with London, like Jean Moulin, Préfet of Chartres, or in organising their own districts like the Mayor of Roubaix who founded the underground newspaper *Voix du Nord* (produced in 5,000 copies weekly by late 1942, using paper, roneo, cars and petrol provided by the Town Hall). We received many illegal news-sheets in our bureau—*Liberté, Valmy, Socialisme et Liberté, Pantagruel, Résistance* and others—striking both by their political variety and their basic unanimity. We also had evidence that the students of the Zone Occupée were very busy. From the Sorbonne we received a newspaper *Défence de la France*, financed, we learned, by a friendly industrialist, and with a circulation of 100,000 copies. Students matched theory with practice too, in staging frequent demonstrations, leafletting their quarter, producing false papers and helping escapers to pass the demarcation line.

We got newspapers from the Z.N.O., too, of course; there was *Combat*, the organ of the Lyons group led by Georges Bidault, Claude Bourdet and others, and largely financed by London; in 1942 this appeared in 6,000 copies every ten days. There was *Libération*, of Clermont-Ferrand, with its strong trade union backing, led by Forgues and Lacoste of the C.G.T. and Viénot and Poimbœuf of the C.F.T.C.: Yvon Morandat, a young and dynamic Socialist, was their liaison with London. When he came to our office in 1942 we learned a lot about the movement in Lyons and central France. He thought "Combat", the biggest Gaullist group, was not sufficiently popular in character, too much organised from above, and his "Liberation" aimed at wider circles. Morandat hoped for more co-operation with other groups, such as "France Liberté" (a university based organisation much given to student demonstrations), "Franc-tireur" (Gaullist), "Le Coq enchaîné" (Freemasons and Radicals), "France d'Abord (intellectuals and military), "Témoin chrétien", and the short-lived "Père Duchesne".

Morandat, with his curly hair and cheery youthful face, was a hero I am proud to have met, and whose survival from the dangers of his work was one of the great reliefs of the war's ending. Another heroic character was Pierre Brossolette, a well-known Socialist journalist, who came on a mission from northern France to Carlton Gardens in early 1942. He was involved in setting up the Organisation Civile et Militaire (O.C.M.), an important *résau* in contact with Gaullist H.Q. and the B.C.R.A. through Rémy, a top agent, of the Centre Notre Dame, already doomed to disaster through Nazi infiltration.[4] I interviewed Brossolette for an English newspaper, and was deeply impressed by his intrepid personality and his obvious and passionate dedication. It was difficult to believe the news of a few weeks later that he had been caught by the Nazis and, rather than face torture and possibly give information, had thrown himself from the fifth floor of Gestapo headquarters to his death. But it was true—he was another of the many thousands to die for a belief, as we were constantly reminded by the messages that reached London.

1942 was the worst year for Nazi killings and atrocities. It was the year of *Nacht und Nebel*—"Night and Fog"—the title given by the authorities to their repressive operations—when darkness covered the face of France, and patriots struggling against it were swept off by the thousand into the even blacker night of Hitler's Reich.

The Germans were extremely nervous, constantly aware of the setbacks to their armies in Russia and of the increasing hostility of the people in the occupied territories. At the same time they were still strong enough to carry out full-scale repression, with their forces in France, as (there being no sign of a Second Front) a good part of the Wehrmacht could still be spared from Russia. As yet, the collaborationist police were on their side, waiting to see which way to jump—and though some French gendarmes resented and obstructed the enemy authorities, the majority in 1942 were carrying out the Germans' behests.

But already news of resistance in other countries—Holland, Yugoslavia, Norway, Greece—seeped through to the French patriots, encouraging and stimulating them. The shooting of the hated S.S. chief Heydrich (till quite recently in Paris), which happened in Prague on 27 May, brought silent satisfaction to every good Frenchman who learnt the news, even though it was followed on 10 June by that of the Lidice massacre in reprisal, which aroused deep sympathy and anger among the French.

Reports of the battle of Stalingrad, and General Von Paulus's setbacks that autumn, could not be stifled. Though the German authorities named it a criminal offence to listen in to Radio London, which made the most of the Russian successes, millions listened and began to believe that Hitler's defeat was actually in sight. Parisians, we learned, gleefully tormented the Germans, innocently asking soldiers when they were leaving for Stalingrad "to stop the Russians". Some wag of a cleaner, it was said, placed a large bone on a Nazi official's desk with a label saying "Stalingrad—il est dur à digérer!" (Stalingrad—hard to stomach). More importantly, on 20 September the anniversary of Valmy, as London Radio announced, "Aujourd'hui 822me jour de la lutte du peuple français pour sa libération", crowds gathered outside the municipal offices of towns all over France in massive demonstrations.

Hopes of a Second Front rose once more. They were not completely vain. Only, instead of landing on the French channel coast, at the beginning of November 1942, the Allies, American and British, disembarked in North Africa, on the outskirts of Vichy-controlled French Algiers.

NOTES

1. Churchill, *The Second World War*, III p. 521
2. R. Sherwood, *White House Papers*, Vol. I p. 395
3. H. Michel, *Histoire de la Résistance* (Paris, Livre de Poche) p. 33
4. Rémy, *Memoirs d'un Agent secret*, Paris, 1947

Chapter 10

NORTH AFRICAN PROBLEMS

Quarante mille en marche vers le bagne
L'étrange chaine et l'étrange convoi
D'Afrique vient qui tourne et l'accompagne
Un vent d'espoir dont blémit la campagne
Et la chiourme écoute cette voix

Un air ancien dont les Tyrans s'émurent
Sifle ce soir au simoun d'Algérie
Quarante mille en marche et qui murmurent
Cet air issu Marseille de tes murs
Quarante mille enfants de la patrie

Aragon, *La Diane française*

Forty thousand on the march to slavery
Strange file, strange convoy—
From Africa comes, turning and moving with it,
A wind of hope, blanching the scene
And the chain-gang hears the voice.

An old tune which the Tyrants feared
Is blowing tonight in the wind of Algeria,
Forty thousand on the march, humming
This air, born, Marseilles, in your streets,
Forty thousand sons of their country

The news of the Allied landings in North Africa on 8 November 1942 was hailed with joy by the majority of people inside France and their friends outside. Even if this was not the longed for advent of liberation on their coast it was a break in the stalemate, action instead of stagnation, a sign that the Americans had at last abandoned Vichy. Everyone waited impatiently for the news that de Gaulle had reached Algiers and was rallying the resistance forces there for an attack on occupied France. But it was not so simple. De Gaulle was not in the picture in those early days, and it was to be some time before the U.S. High Command even considered him as having any part in their plans—mainly because the Free French forces were numerically unimportant compared with the Vichyite army on the spot whom it was hoped to use against the Germans. The Americans looked on the operation as purely military; they failed to take into account the complex political and social situation of French North Africa, which

101

did not allow for quite such a simple takeover from Vichy and was to lead the Allies temporarily into something of a quagmire.

Since 1940 Algeria, Tunis and Morocco had been administered by staunch French imperialists tinged with racialism, whose policy did not noticeably differ in any way from Vichy's. The administrators saw their job as the protection of France's possessions, business and trade interests, while seeing that the "natives" kept quiet and produced wealth for the "mother country" in the form of crops, citrus fruit and olives from the fields, hides and meat from the animals, zinc, and iron ore from the mines. The mentality of the *Algérie française* bureaucracy, police and civil servants was, if not fascist, certainly not anti-fascist. Some 600,000 French colonialists lived comfortably in modern towns, the 7 million Algerian natives in urban or rural slums. The latter were miserably poor, those in the city factories scarcely better off. Education and health services hardly existed, except for Europeans. Politically speaking, there was conservatism at one end of the scale, a left-wing independence movement at the other, and mass apathy in the centre. A recent study sums up the attitudes that the Allies were to find on landing in North Africa: "Among the European populations, a very active and arrogant pro-fascist minority, especially around Oran, where the big land-owners were openly fascist. The working people followed the same tendencies as in France. . . : Resistance developed at different levels and in different forms according to the origins of the social strata."[1]

There were certainly numerous anti-fascists who could have been called on, had the Americans been interested, and who had already formed *réseaux*. From 1941 on, there was an Algerian underground press and organisation, mainly under Communist direction, which came out into the open on the night of the Allied landing (7–8 November) and was promptly suppressed by General Nogués, the Governor-general. However, soldiers in Algiers and Tunis spontaneously armed themselves with rifles and machine-guns and turned on the Germans and Italians in control. General Weygand estimated that 60,000 men offered their assistance to the Allies, in some cases with the support of their officers; but on the whole the higher ranks took their cue from their Pétainist superiors, and, after a costly show of defence of their positions against the Americans, came to an agreement with the invaders by which the Algerian military would take control and any popular movement would be suppressed.

The resistance groups were called on merely to help the military operations with information, weapons and small armed actions. "The Americans had no confidence in the resistance forces and did not supply the arms promised to the leader Jose Aboulker." There was a political motive in this, according to Moine: "It is clear that they aimed at setting aside the Free French, putting down the North African democratic forces and imposing a reactionary policy of the sort envisaged for France and Italy." In fact Aboulker's group carried out an extremely effective action on the night of the landing: "Between 1 and 1.50 a.m.", we learn, "400 armed civilians arrested Darlan, Juin (C. in C. North Africa), Mendigal (Chief of the Airforce) and several other generals and high Vichy officials. We took over H.Q., the Post Office, the Telecommunications Centre, Radio Algiers and the Governor's palace. At 2 a.m. Algiers was in our hands."[2] This prevented any effective opposition to the landings, which would otherwise have been attended by even more fighting and bloodshed.

However, co-operation from the Left did not suit the Americans' pre-conceived plans. Although Washington had suggested that some appeal to the popular African leaders be made, Robert Murphy, the U.S. envoy to Algiers, did not trouble; as he saw it—naturally enough, considering the circles he moved in—"the country is absolutely nazified, thanks to the collaboration . . . of the inhabitants, businessmen, functionaries, military. . . . No open opposition anyway; it was a big mistake to think we were going to be greeted as liberators."[3] Murphy's solution was to win over the collaborationist "élites", from Germanophile Pétainists to pro-Ally Pétainists, and Eisenhower backed him to the hilt. Alain de Sérigny, director of the *Echo d'Alger* (one of the "ultras" of 1960), wrote at the time that "a minority of the population is rejoicing (over the landing); the masses are passive; the army has accepted the landing, which it had been hoping for . . .".[4] But the pro-Ally resistants were not encouraged, and members were in fact arrested and gaoled if they ventured anti-fascist sentiments, for fear of offending the Vichyite authorities who had at all costs to be won over.

The question, once the landing was accomplished, was: Whom to deal with? It leaked out that Murphy and General Mark Clark were talking to Darlan, the only senior Vichy minister on the scene (who, so he said, had come to visit a sick son and was in Algiers quite by chance); captured by the Resistance, he had been speedily released by the Americans. This amazingly tactless move was explained by

Eisenhower to Washington on 14 November: "North African sentiments are not at all what we imagined. . . . Here the name of Marshal
Pétain represents something supernatural. . . . The military and
naval chiefs, and the civil governors alike, declare that only one man
has the right to represent Pétain, and that is Darlan. . . . If we
repudiate Darlan, the French will oppose us passively and sometimes
actively; the hope of co-operation in this region will be lost by us with
great expense of troops, etc."[5]

The Allies made a double miscalculation; on the one hand ignoring the democratic spirit of the people, and on the other hoping that
the Vichyites would co-operate; they reckoned without the traditional loyalty of officers to their General, and were surprised that the
reactions of the Pétainist administration (many of them military
men) were at first bitterly hostile. Resistance to the U.S. forces
between 8 and 11 November resulted in 6,000 killed or wounded,
many ships sunk or damaged beyond repair; 135 French planes
destroyed, 70 Allied planes shot down (see de Gaulle, *Memoirs*,
Unity, pp. 49–50).

The reactions in Vichy itself were of course still more violent; it
seems that here too Roosevelt had miscalculated when he hoped that
Pétain would accept his arguments for the Allied action. The
President sent a personal message to the Marshal which arrived at
4 a.m. on Sunday, 8 November, to the effect that the landings were
aimed at supporting the French authorities in North Africa, at
repelling possible German-Italian invasion of the Empire, and at
liberating France and her foreign territories from the Axis yoke.
Laval, then Prime Minister, arriving in Vichy at 4.15 a.m. (and
leaving Pétain to sleep on) drafted a bitterly indignant letter back to
Roosevelt accusing the U.S. of aggression. "France and her honour
are at stake," Laval wrote. "We shall defend ourselves. This is the
order I am giving."[6]

The Marshal was woken at 7 a.m., given the news of the landings
and told Laval's reply to Roosevelt, of which he approved. Then
began the tug-of-war across the Mediterranean. Pétain issued an
order to his North African followers to resist the Anglo-Americans;
from General Giraud (who had been convoyed, after escaping from
Germany, to Algiers and was with the U.S. Army in the sidelines)
came a broadcast calling to French forces to join the Allies. Darlan—
not yet engaged in talks with Clark—cabled Vichy asking for an
attack on Allied shipping. Laval sent off an appeal to Hitler for a
guarantee of France's territorial integrity. The Führer's answer was

a command (delivered by Abetz) to the Vichy government to declare war on Britain and the U.S.A. Laval, having failed to get the guarantee he wanted, hedged, and the Cabinet decided not to declare war, but to allow German flights over Africa while putting off granting the Axis any bases there.

On 9 November Laval travelled to Munich to meet Hitler and Ciano, the Italian Foreign Minister, leaving instructions in Vichy that "no negotiations must take place before his return". During his absence, confusion reigned. Requests for directives and orders flew between the perplexed colonial militarists in Algiers and Vichy. What if Germany should decide to invade? General Juin appealed for resistance to the Axis, but his subordinates refused to co-operate except under orders from General Noguès, their superior officer in France. From Bizerta, Admiral Derrien telegraphed requesting guidance, and was recommended to "adopt a passive attitude". Darlan, after much prevarication, at first called for air attacks on Allied ships, then decided to hobnob with General Clark and at long last appealed to the French Fleet to sail from Toulon and join the Allies.[7]

The Vichy government seemed to be faced with a three-horned dilemma—whether to call off resistance, to make a deal with the Allies, or to permit the Germans to land in Tunisia. In the end, Hitler, not trusting the French as comrades-in-arms, issued another ultimatum, this time that they should declare war on the U.S. unilaterally. This did not amount to much, as there was nothing that Vichy could do in the existing situation but wait and see. What they saw was General Noguès handing over his powers to Darlan on 13 November and the latter proclaiming that he had "assumed responsibility on behalf of the government and with the assent of the American authorities with whom I have agreed to defend North Africa".[8] This was followed by the surrender of Algiers to the Allies by General Juin, the defection of General Barre in Tunisia on 19 November, and the rallying of French West Africa to Darlan on the 23rd.

In the meantime the situation inside France changed swiftly and dramatically. On 11 November the German army units crossed the *ligne de démarcation* and occupied the whole of southern France except for Savoie and Corsica, which the Italians were ordered to take over. Mussolini's troops also occupied Nice, Cannes and Chambéry. There were now Germans everywhere, the heaviest concentrations being on the Mediterranean coast.

All this of course aroused the deepest resentment, and stimulated the spirit of resistance of those French who had not yet seen the Nazis at close quarters. Even Vichyist army officers put up a fight against the dissolution of their units demanded by the German authorities and carried out (with Pétain's express agreement) on 28 November. But at Toulon, despite a telegram from Darlan to Admiral Laborde, the latter did nothing about sending the fleet across to Algiers until much too late. On 27 November German soldiers surrounded the port, following Hitler's order: "Occupy Toulon, prevent the ships from leaving port, or destroy them." At long last—at 5.30 a.m. on the 28th—rather than let the fleet fall into enemy hands, Admiral Laborde gave the order to scuttle the ships, and within a few hours, after some deafening explosions, 250,000 tons of shipping were destroyed, including three battleships, seven cruisers and an aircraft carrier. An eye-witness wrote: "Dawn broke on a scene of indescribable desolation; every one of the magnificent vessels of the French Navy was lying on its side belching out thick black smoke."[9] Four submarines alone escaped and made their way to Algeria. The surviving naval officers and sailors were assembled by the furious Germans in the Place de la Liberté at Toulon and taken off to concentration camps, singing the *Marseillaise* and the *Internationale*.[10]

The scuttling made a tremendous impression inside France. A great many people saw it as a sign of Gaullism in action and waited impatiently for news that the General had arrived in Algiers and was rallying his forces for an attack on the mainland. But de Gaulle had not moved from London. Instead there was the disturbing announcement that—of all people—Darlan had been put in by the Americans to represent France: Darlan, who had been Pétain's prime minister for months, a collaborator and reactionary to the core. There could hardly have been a choice more unpopular among French working people than this traitor who had carried out Nazi orders from the start. The outcry from Frenchmen inside the mainland or in exile may not have surprised the Allies but its vehemence embarrassed them. They were however spared the need to solve their problem themselves, as on Christmas Eve 1942 Darlan was assassinated by a young Frenchman in Algiers, to the private relief of some, and public satisfaction of many more.

As his successor the Americans chose not de Gaulle but General Giraud, who had the distinction of having twice escaped from a German fortress but was otherwise politically and personally somewhat colourless. At the New Year he was installed as provisional Governor of Algiers. De Gaulle suggested an early meeting with him, but was turned down. The wrath of the London Free French naturally knew no bounds. At Carlton Gardens the whole Allied landing operation was seen as a plot to undermine de Gaulle and to forestall him in reaching France. How dared the Anglo-Americans assume the right to take control of French territory, putting in their puppet Giraud to carry out their wishes? The General's memoirs reflect his anger: "As for myself, submerged in seas of anger and disappointment, I was reduced to watching what had been one of France's major hopes sink out of sight"; but "among many such upsets I attempted to remain steadfast and unwavering".[11]

Churchill, who had been very uneasy about Darlan and had little faith in Giraud ("His power to command French allegiance was already exposed as a myth", he wrote), did his best, as he put it, "to unite the French resistance". He told Roosevelt on 27 December, "We ought to try above anything to bring them all together and have some French nucleus, solid and united, to work with." Roosevelt had written earlier, "I have hitherto enjoyed a quiet satisfaction in leaving (de Gaulle) in your hands. Apparently I have now acquired a similar problem in brother Giraud." It should, he said, be driven home to "these prima donnas" that "the situation is today solely in the military field" and approval of all decisions lies with General Eisenhower."[12] There is no indication that the President attached the slightest importance to the reactions of the people of France or of North Africa.

Winston Churchill was much more realistic about the importance of the resistance movement and the dangers of damaging it by excluding de Gaulle. He asked the President to invite the General to a conference in Casablanca in January ("the General was very haughty and refused several times") and himself brought pressure on de Gaulle to attend the conference through Anthony Eden; he wrote to the Foreign Secretary, "Here I have been all these days fighting de Gaulle's battle and making every arrangement for a good reconciliation between Frenchmen. If he rejects the chance now offered I shall feel that his removal from the headship of the Free French movement is essential to the further support of the Movement by H.M.G." This threat, which Churchill drove home to de Gaulle in the words, "If with your eyes open you reject this unique opportunity we shall endeavour to get on as well as we can without you . . .",[13] was probably realised by both men to be bluff—Churchill was well aware of de Gaulle's great importance in the eyes of French resistants and thus for the Allied effort. But de Gaulle deemed it wiser to comply, and on 22 January 1943 arrived in Casablanca where he met and talked to President Roosevelt and to Giraud. But no arrangement was made for giving him any authority yet in North Africa.

Nevertheless the obvious truth was at last recognised by the Americans: if the French nation were not to be bitterly disillusioned, it was imperative that some democratic French government, cleared of any ties with Vichy and Nazism, should be established under a well-respected leadership to sweep away existing abuses and to be seen as anti-fascist. A step in the right direction was taken when, on 5 February (none too soon) the French Communist deputies in the Maison Carrée prison were set free after nearly two years' suffering at the hands of their fascist gaolers. When released, several deputies published accounts of their inhuman treatment, how they had slept nine in a bare vermin-infested cell, cut off from the outside world, liable to recurrent attacks of typhus and dysentery. They were threatened with execution by a Légionnaire gaoler at the time of the Allied landings and, in spite of periodical promises of release, were only granted their freedom after an interview with Giraud on 27 January (held in a bedroom wrecked by a bombing raid the previous night).[14]

On their release the deputies immediately drafted and sent Giraud a list of proposed measures which should be applied without delay: the freeing of all anti-fascist detainees (10,000 in Algeria, 50,000 foreigners in Morocco, to name only part of the total); the abolition of all fascist laws; energetic measures against the fifth column; support for the Resistance inside France; a fair share in government programmes for workers and their organisations; satisfaction of the Moslems' lawful demands. The deputies pressed General Catroux, sent by de Gaulle from London, for assurances that North Africa would serve as a base for a national French army, thus increasing France's role in the war.[15] The last demand naturally met with a ready response from the London Free French who were looking forward to setting up their headquarters in North Africa before long. In the meantime (and indeed for the war's duration) the F.F.L. offices were needed in England to keep up the flow of information to and from France and co-operate with the Resistance—these services had to continue for geographical reasons, whether de Gaulle was in London or not.

Because he needed as much international support as possible to counterbalance American hostility, perhaps because he was now really concerned about unity in France, the General had at last agreed to co-operate with the French Communist Party. The Red Army's victories in the winter of 1942–43 must have seemed a good reason for showing friendliness towards the Russians' chief supporters inside France; another reason was, no doubt, the reputation that the Communists had earned for being the most deeply involved and hardest hit of all parties in the Resistance. It had to be recognised that in every repressive operation they suffered most. The most recent example was the Nazi evacuation and destruction of the Old Port of Marseilles, on 24 January 1943, when 40,000 people were turned out of their homes and herded into a camp at Fréjus. Two thousand of these were known Communists, and they were deported to Buchenwald or Oranienburg. The same day, the first convoy of women left for Auschwitz extermination camp: they included Danielle Casanova and Marie-Claude Vaillant-Couturier, of the P.C.F. Central Committee, following so many thousands of militants to a living death.

"Le parti des martyrs" had earned de Gaulle's grudging admiration; for all his anti-communism he knew that he could not exclude them from his plans, and realised the prestige their support would bring him. "I reckoned that their forces had great weight in the kind of war imposed by the occupation", he wrote later, but (as if to excuse himself), "I was decided not to let them ever gain the upper hand, by-pass me or take the lead."[16] It was in this frame of mind that he accepted the P.C.F. offer to send a delegate to the Free French Committee in London. Whatever his reservations and however half-heartedly, he thus included the millions-strong membership and following of the Communist Party, along with the anti-fascists of North Africa, in the official organisation of Fighting France.

NOTES

1. A. Moine, *Déportation et Résistance en Afrique du Nord* p. 239
2. ibid. pp. 245–249
3. G. Esquier, *8 Novembre 1942* (Paris, 1946) pp. 331–332
4. A. de Sérigny, *L'Enigme d'Alger* (Paris, 1947)
5. Moine, op. cit. p. 248
6. G. Warner, *Pierre Laval* (London, 1972) p. 322

7. ibid. p. 341
8. ibid. p. 346
9. *Les Documents* (F. F. Information Service, 1942), 15.12.42 p. 10
10. *Le P.C.F. dans la Résistance* p. 202
11. De Gaulle, *War Memoirs, Unity* pp. 55–59
12. Churchill, *Second World War*, II p. 509
13. ibid., p. 546
14. F. Bonte, *Le Chemin de l'Honneur* pp. 353–356
15. *Le P.C.F. dans la Résistance* p. 200
16. De Gaulle, *War Memoirs, The Call to Honour* p. 271

Chapter 11

FIGHTING FRANCE

Ne t'en va pas chez le tyran
Forger sa puissance toi-même
Et des fers pour ceux que tu aimes
Ne t'en va pas
Ne t'en va pas Prends ton fusil
Siffle ton chien chasse les ombres
Chasseur chasseur tu es le nombre
Ne t'en va pas
Prends ton fusil

Aragon, *La Diane française*

You must not go where you must serve
The tyrant for his evil ends
To forge his chains to bind your friends
You must not go!
You must not go. Fetch out your gun
Whistle your dog—Ah, you're the one!
Now chase the night! the game's begun
Fetch out your gun!

Trans. Frances Cornford

At the beginning of January 1943, as the Soviet offensive at Stalingrad tore into the Nazi ranks along the Volga, and the R.A.F. dropped its devastating loads on Germany, while the partisans in Yugoslavia and Greece redoubled their action with British help, and all over Europe the people silently starved and struggled, the arrival of an individual escaped prisoner in London might not have seemed of great importance. But the appearance of Fernand Grenier, former Deputy of St Denis, member of the E.C. of the French Communist Party, in the F.F.L. headquarters was of rather special significance. Pale and haggard after ten appalling months in the prison of Chateaubriant, where the horrors had culminated with the execution of twenty-seven comrades as hostages, Grenier brought a new element into the Free French scene. He was a symbol of working-class resistance, and determined that his Party should be given its share of credit for inspiring this resistance. At last de Gaulle had offered co-operation. In return the P.C.F. would give him loyal support. It was a big step towards French unity.

Simple in manner, straightforward in speech and extremely shrewd, Grenier was an excellent envoy and indefatigable propagandist for his cause. Left-wingers in England worked him off his feet touring, speaking, writing, being interviewed; and he seemed happier with them than he was in his efforts to win support from the Free French leadership, lunching in smart restaurants with the ministers-in-exile, politically so out of tune with him, or hobnobbing with the General, and with gaullist financiers and diplomats. However, he invariably maintained an impressive and relaxed front while never letting it be forgotten that he was a worker and a Communist. I remember a dinner at the Soustelles where conversation skirted carefully around the policy of the P.C.F., and the trades unions' future demands, till the hostess tactfully centred it on the subject of wartime cookery—though even this proved embarrassing, for while we were enjoying relatively lavish roast duck and peas, Grenier described how the French housewife was managing on half a pound of potatoes.

These flippancies aside, the presence of a real live member of the Communist E.C. was a great support to all on the Left of de Gaulle, and Grenier made a deep impression on his hearers whenever he spoke about occupied France and his experiences there. His pamphlet *Ceux de Chateaubriant* sold 5,000 copies almost overnight and would have sold more if funds had allowed further printing. The author complained privately that the Gaullists would not put up any money for its publication, and it had to be issued by private subscription.[1] This was the sort of indirect sabotage that was too often practised on Communists, though only to be expected when in partnership with such reactionaries as many in our London office.

When Grenier left London to join the Free French (from August 1942 known officially as *France Combattante*—Fighting France) Committee in North Africa his successor as P.C.F. representative in London was Waldeck Rochet, the Party specialist in agricultural problems who had served two years in the Maison Carrée in Algiers. The new delegate wrote later that all sorts of difficulties were put in the way of his broadcasts to France: "De Gaulle and his friends discriminated between the F.T.P. and the other resistance groups . . . I had managed to get a five-minute radio talk once a fortnight so as to put over the P.C.F. and Resistance programme, and I occasionally gave special broadcasts for peasants; these talks were censored both by the British and by the Gaullists. I had to fight every week to be allowed to express our policy of armed struggle."[2] The Communists were often to meet similar obstruction in more serious situations, sometimes with very tragic results. But during the spring of 1943, the time of the Red Army's stunning successes, the anti-communism of the media took merely a negative and muted form. Pro-Soviet feeling, strong and warm among British people and in the occupied countries, was important for the war effort and had to be officially supported and encouraged.

As 1943 wore on, all eyes were on Stalingrad. The Nazis were encircled, decimated, driven into the ground. The newsreels showed street fighting among blackened ruins, hundreds of terrified German infantrymen emerging out of holes in the ground, hands up over their heads, endless processions of utterly exhausted prisoners dragging their frozen feet through the snow. The Russians' victory was announced at the beginning of February 1943, and hope rose everywhere in downtrodden Europe, along with an overwhelming impatience.

The Nazis were far from finished, however. They continued to fight back doggedly in northern Russia, and every available German from fifteen to sixty-five, every woman between fourteen and forty-five, was called up for service. French railways were jammed with trainloads of unhappy soldiers going to the Eastern front. Sometimes they did not get far, for the F.T.P. derailed one or more trains almost daily: their underground press reported on 29 January 250 German soldiers killed and many wounded in a derailment at Chagny, and on 10 April it was claimed that 1,500 actions had been carried out against enemy transport between January and the end of March—including 150 derailings; 180 locomotives carrying material or troops destroyed; sabotage of 110 engines, 3 bridges, 14 barges, 8 canal locks; 800 Wehrmacht men killed or wounded.

We were told by new arrivals at Gaullist headquarters that these statistics were an underestimate. In every corner of France, they said, activity was being carried on indefatigably and with ever-increasing effect by the Resistance forces, which swelled rapidly as ever more Frenchmen were threatened with forced labour in Germany and escaped into hiding.

As already mentioned, Hitler's labour overseer, Sauckel, had since March 1942 been demanding manpower from France, but Laval had not been able to satisfy Sauckel either by his measures in March or by the Relève in June, nor by the new Labour Laws of September by which 250,000 workers were promised to Germany (while 250,000 P.O.W.s were to be released to work there—not much of a concession); some 17,000 left in the autumn of 1942.

As the tens of thousands were hauled off to Germany, more and more workers escaped into the countryside where peasants and labourers helped them with asylum and food. Great numbers, seeing the threat of deportation, joined the Resistance; Vichy reacted with panic measures of repression, arming its police and sending them against *réfractaires* and demonstrators of all classes in hitherto quiet areas. Civil strife broke out all over the southern zone. On 25 November 1942 after a public meeting, Strasbourg university (which had been evacuated to Clermont-Ferrand in 1940) was closed and many of its staff and students deported. On 5 December there were numerous arrests at Annecy, Grenoble, Sallanches. The working people were fighting back fiercely—while 30,000 miners struck in the north, 500 engineers came out at Durbec; German lorries came to take them away, but massive demonstrations forced their release. In Lyons a labour-recruiting office was attacked and burned down. In January and February 1943 the authorities were unable to cope with the hundreds of students who marched and demonstrated against Nazi repression in Marseilles.

By this time the Reich was so short of manpower that Sauckel insisted on extreme measures. In desperation the Vichy government decreed the *Service de Travail Obligatoire* (S.T.O.) in February 1943, calling up all Frenchmen of mobilisable age as if for compulsory military service. Before resistance to the decree had been organised, 250,000 men were forced to leave for Germany. Sauckel congratulated Laval on fulfilling the programme—and said he wanted another 100,000 from April onwards. Laval jibbed at this, pointing out that there were still a million prisoners in Germany and "new demands must relate to French capabilities"; he remarked that "one should not promote a policy which, while fighting Communism in the East, created it in the West".[3] Weygand had earlier said that "Anti-German workers were becoming Communists so as not to go and work in Germany".[4] Calling *réfractaires* Communists might render them more liable to punishment, but it did not alter the fact that almost all workers, whatever their politics, tried to evade the call-up. They joined the Resistance, not a party, although, once engaged, many did become militants.

The S.T.O. was possibly Laval's worst blunder, for it brought about the birth of the Maquis, the foundation of the "Secret Army", through the massing of great numbers of *réfractaires* all over France. Throughout 1943 the race was on, between the exodus of wanted men into safe hiding, and the capture of labour for the Reich by every possible means of military and police coercion.

In April, Sauckel demanded 220,000 more workers, to be sent off during May and June. By early July only 130,000 had been conscripted; Laval's excuse was that "he could not rely on the co-operation of the police and the lower ranks of the administration as much as he wished".[5] This was becoming more and more true, and in view of his unreliable underlings and his great personal unpopularity (he had a narrow escape when his car was blown up on 17 September) Laval began to oppose the more outrageous German demands presented in the late summer: 500,000 more workers, including women, to be sent by the end of the year, and 1 million more from civilian industry to be drafted for war work (for Hitler) inside France. Laval refused to agree to these figures, though he promised to try and complete the still unfulfilled programme of 220,000 for May and June 1943. Sauckel was furious and wrote that he had lost all faith in the prime minister's honesty and goodwill. "His refusal constitutes an outright sabotage of Germany's life-and-death struggle against Bolshevism." Facing the inevitable, however, the Germans thereafter modified some of their demands; one reason probably being that "there were totally insufficient German police and military available to carry out any large-scale actions against labour draft-dodgers", as one high Nazi official admitted to another. The unreliability of the French police was stressed in another German report: "Our experience shows . . . that the will to fight against the national Resistance movement is, in the main, lacking among the French police. . . . An effective action against the . . . organisations working for the enemy is not to be expected till the military situation has improved."[6]

By the autumn of 1943 Laval had clearly recognised the size of the problem he was up against. For all his cunning there was nothing he could do to win back support even from the Marshal's former faithful, no way to turn back the ever-encroaching tide of resistance. German bayonets and the hated Milice (Darnand's Militia) with their informers, were all that Vichy had to rely on. And though these could and did wreak hideous revenge on the patriots, the worse the slaughter the less the credibility of the government.

The Maquis, which by mid-1943 had evidently come to stay and from then on was an established factor in French life, of course had its own massive problems—but its members were fired with faith, determined to smash the enemy and confident of the Allies' support and eventual arrival, guarantee of final victory. The most urgent national task was to help them and to increase their numbers. Every section of society played a part in preventing their capture by the Germans: employers laid off their workers, housewives hid them, doctors issued sickness certificates to facilitate their evasion. When trains were due to leave for the Reich, women and children crowded on to the lines and squatted in front of the engine. While they were being hauled away the men on the trains jumped off and made their way into the woods.

The rural population welcomed the *réfractaires* and it was rarely that an informer betrayed them in the villages where they sheltered. Occasionally a confirmed local Pétainist or member of the Milice informed on the Maquis to the Germans, but the agent, usually known to the villagers, was sooner or later punished with summary execution. Aragon's short story *Le Mouton*[7] well describes such a situation in a small mountain community, and I have heard eye-witness accounts in Corrèze and Périgord of shameful betrayals; but by and large the Maquis was well protected by the country folk—it was the armed Milice from the towns who caused the worst damage, and from whom the patriots had most to fear. A friend of mine, daughter of a *petit propriétaire* in the Dordogne, very vividly described how she hid a *réfractaire* on the run, in her cellar. "*Le pauvre!* he couldn't bear the dark and the confinement, so we dressed him up as a woman and set him to work on the vines, keeping his back well turned to the road, until he could get away and join the Maquis." During 1943, she said, "F.T.P. would arrive at our home any time of the night. We never had a proper night's sleep during all the months, *ma chère*, waiting for a knock on the door in the small hours—it might be a maquisard, or—worse—the milice, or even the Gestapo. . . ." Mercifully, she was never betrayed—and the Resistance owed countless lives to women like her, unsung heroines of the Shadow army—the *armée des ombres*.[8]

In the spring of 1943, France entered the third phase of the Resistance—the building of the *Armée Secrète* (A.S.). The most important factors which led to this can be tabled as:

1. (*a*) The German pressures for labour, and (*b*) the large-scale escapes of men into the Maquis.

2. (*a*) The fury of German army and Vichy milice reprisals in attempting to capture escapers; (*b*) the lack of co-operation of the French *gendarmerie*, who indeed often actually helped the maqui-sards.

3. The organised working-class action—strikes, sabotage, go-slows particularly on the railways.

4. The co-ordination of the Resistance forces by the forming of the Conseil National de la Résistance (C.N.R.).

Up to May 1943 the movement was dispersed in many different groupings. Although the Communist organisations were always the most active (as admitted by Henri Michel, and by Jean Moulin in a report to de Gaulle in October 1941)[9] and the most numerous—with their F.T.P., their Women's Committees, the *Jeunesses communistes*, and urban and departmental committees all over the country— Gaullist, Christian and non-political groups had proliferated during the past few months. "Combat", "Libération", "Franc-tireur", "Action Chrétienne", "La France", among many more, had survived the blackest year; they had their own identities, their own *réseaux*, programmes and substantial membership among the middle classes.

The non-Communist organisations were largely inspired by de Gaulle and supported by the B.C.R.A. which kept information flowing by Radio London and sent its agents to form networks, arrange for material to be dropped and distributed, and generally keep in touch. The S.O.E. working from Baker Street headquarters, was sending its own agents to help French groups, encourage sabotage and anti-German activity, and deliver weapons—lamentably inadequate before 1944. One high-up "Baker Street Irregular" admitted later that "the potential secret army of 150,000 men" had received hardly anything in the way of arms from England: "This was true. For example, the French had asked for eighty supply-dropping operations in March (1943) of which only ten had been carried out."[10]

On one occasion the R.A.F. refused to fly sorties with supplies for a Maquis in Savoie. Baker Street offered instead to send "a small Anglo-American party" to the area. The French "might have been forgiven for sulking", says the writer, "for after all what they had really wanted was arms, not men". In fact, the Allied officers were made welcome.[11] But on other occasions things went less well and British agents met considerable difficulties: "Any British officer was suspect, as the (London) French seemed to see a political venture behind every bush," wrote Xavier, a highly experienced agent. He found that, even in the field, where men were united by a common destiny (in the Haute-Savoie, for instance) "it was difficult to bind the groups together, for they were all very suspicious of the British. 'Perfide Albion' was always in their minds."

Besides this distrust of the British, deep differences divided the resistants themselves. In Xavier's experience "there were Communist, Armée Secrète and Maquis groups, all squabbling politically and not liaising as well as they should have done". Xavier was asked in every camp he visited "about my political views and which party I supported for the rebuilding of France". He asked them to forget their political differences, but it was not so simple.[12]

The diversity of the unco-ordinated groups led to confusion and overlapping, if not to resentment and hostility between them, with grave consequent dangers. This was clear to Resistance leaders both in and outside France, particularly to the P.C.F. which had for many months been calling for unity. At last, at the end of 1942, thanks to the untiring efforts of Jean Moulin, de Gaulle's brave and broad-minded envoy, the heads of the main non-Communist movements were persuaded to meet for discussions; and after a series of secret meetings in Lyons in early 1943 they agreed to join with Communists and trades unionists in a joint Council of Resistance. On 26 March the para-military groups in the Z.O. had met and agreed to work together. On 15 May 1943, the *Conseil National* (C.N.R.) was formed, in Lyons, with representatives of all major groups and parties.

The Free French in Algiers and the *Conseil* promised to support each other. De Gaulle expressed his agreement and welcomed an organisation whose ultimate objective, as he saw it, was to form a Secret Army on regular military lines under his command. He instructed Moulin to see that "all resistance organisations other than Liberation, Combat and Franctireur [all Gaullist] should . . . affiliate to one of these and bring their units into the secret army now in course of formation".[3] This showed that the General was more than somewhat out of touch with the people of his country, and unaware of the motivation of the workers, who were actively resisting but who had no wish to be under de Gaulle's personal command.

Fortunately, Jean Moulin was more of a realist. He disregarded the instructions and, as a leading member of the *Conseil*, saw to it that the autonomy of all its constituent bodies was recognised. It would indeed have been useless to try to persuade the staunchly Communist F.T.P. or even left-wing Socialist members to give up their freedom of action. As it was, the C.N.R. worked together well and loyally towards the main aims of *France Combattante*: these were defined by Moulin at the first meeting as: (1) to carry on the war; (2) to give the French people back their freedom of speech and civil rights; (3) to restore republican liberty and social justice in a State *"qui aura le sens de la grandeur"* ("which will have the sense of greatness"); (4) to work with the Allies "for real international collaboration . . . in a world where France's prestige was acknowledged by all".

One recognises the General's touch in the above, and there was little to suggest that a more egalitarian future State might be envisaged. However, in the interests of unity the left-wing members supported Moulin and he was able to report to de Gaulle that "the Council decided to devote all its energies to bringing about throughout the country . . . the close union of the groups represented in the C.N.R."[14]

There were sixteen members (plus Moulin) present at the first meeting on 18 May: eight from the Resistance groups, one from the P.C.F., two from the trade union Federations, five from different political bodies active in the Resistance. It was too difficult and dangerous for seventeen persons to meet regularly, so an executive of five was elected to co-ordinate the work of the Resistance and prepare for the national rising, now seen as an attainable objective.

Moulin chaired the meetings from 26 May until the tragic day three weeks later when, in spite of all precautions, betrayed by one of his agents, he was caught by the Gestapo, questioned—uselessly—with the utmost brutality, and deported. As one of his colleagues wrote, "He was tortured, his body broken; but his lips remained sealed and he died on the way to Germany. . . ."[15] Moulin's death was a grievous blow and loss to the Resistance. But the invaluable service he had rendered and the bases of unity which he had helped to lay, were firm foundations for future success.

Georges Bidault, who had been working closely with Moulin, took over the direction of the C.N.R. and three months later was elected chairman. It is worth quoting Bidault's memories of this period. Egocentric though his accounts are they show how the work was carried out and do convey what it was like to be in that situation.

Dealing with de Gaulle's H.Q. was perhaps the most difficult of Bidault's problems. "I began sending coded telegrams to London in the name of the General Delegation in France", he writes. "We asked ourselves constantly what was going on in that remote place called 'Londres', and even those who had been there on a visit or stayed there for a time, found it hard to answer clearly. Who was doing what? What was de Gaulle like? Who had any influence on him? . . .

We faced a mystery." Immediately after 20 June 1943 he began sending coded messages to London regularly, using the transmitters he had at his disposal, and covering political and military affairs, questions of personnel, and technical information needed over there. He had to find the news, check it, code it and transmit it, all in Lyons where they had radio-detectors mounted on lorries which soon picked up the locations of illegal radio transmitters. The location had to be changed often, to prevent search parties from finding it. ". . . Radio sets had to be hidden close at hand in case of emergencies such as parachute drops of arms and people; we had to reach these as quickly as possible and we never solved the problem of transportation. . . .

"In spite of all these complications, I was able to bring out at least 250 roneo typed issues of the *Bulletin de la France Combattante* for the underground press. This bulletin was produced with the precious and tireless aid of several men. . . . To their names I want to add that of the kindly old Abbé Boursier who worked and hid our roneo press in his parish in a Lyons suburb. One day, men wearing swastika emblems suddenly appeared at his home and shot him down on the spot."

Bidault became very impatient as "the days passed, and I received no acknowledgement of my messages or even of Jean Moulin's arrest. . . ." Moulin himself "had found it very difficult to get the information he kept demanding. Sometimes, he had had the feeling that he was addressing himself to a deaf and distant god. Or was it that the Gaullists were so busy with their troops that they had no time left to deal with the organised Resistance? Perhaps the various ministers were quarrelling among themselves over allocations of power? Or were they naturally indifferent to the 'croakings' of distant men who besieged the Olympian sovereign with their suggestions, claims and protests . . .? We never found out, but I must admit that if we did croak . . . the frogs got a bit fed up with never having even a pebble tossed into their swamp."[16]

De Gaulle sent no representative, nor any word as to who should act for him in the C.N.R. He himself wrote later that "I needed someone who was a great administrator . . . capable, at the crucial moment, of rallying the kind of administration which the government would soon require. Months were to pass before I chose the man who answered all the qualifications."[17]

In the meantime, the lack of interest in Bidault's messages seemed to indicate a lamentable ignorance of the importance of the internal resistance, frustrating to those involved in the struggle at a time when they needed the utmost encouragement. Bidault wrote bitterly, "I can only say one thing for certain about my radio messages: there were a great many of them . . . I did get one answer and only one: the only reply that ever reached me was 'Reduce traffic'. That was all, but it certainly said enough."[18]

Eventually the C.N.R. acquired an envoy from de Gaulle—and was thus acknowledged as an integral part of the Free French Forces. Co-ordinating the different groups in both North and South, it could truly consider itself representative of all sections: the C.G.T. (Communist and Socialist) spokesman was Louis Saillant, that of the Northern Resistance movements was Maxime Blocq-Mascart, and there was a delegate of the Gaullist united movements of the southern Zone. With Bidault as Chairman, they met regularly, in the presence of the General's delegate, always in different houses. The full C.N.R. met only twice, in all-night sittings in a Paris suburb; but Bidault conscientiously kept in touch with the members, each of whom, like himself, faced immense risks. "Our life was dangerous and at the same time monotonous." Because of the threat of arrest, existence was a series of changes of address; nights spent in the open trying to snatch some sleep on the pavement; hairsbreadth escapes; problems over recuperating contacts lost through carelessness or mishap; tragedies when valuable colleagues disappeared.

Political opponents worked together in single-minded devotion to their cause. Bidault, a Catholic and Liberal, wrote of his trade unionist co-workers that "my friends were in charge of all the mail delivery, including printed matter between members of the C.N.R.— a very dangerous activity. The Communists kept a team of writers and printers in a safe hiding place and they were responsible for a lot of the documents that were sent out. They produced the most, and in certain ways the best material."[19]

The work of the C.N.R. was not always impeccable, its Chairman admitted. But even in normal conditions, centralisation is no guarantee against inefficiency, and under conditions of illegality and constant harassment it was impossible not to make mistakes. "When your liaison agents get arrested and your leaders move from house to house without trace," each echelon must work independently as best it can. A lot of superfluous matter got printed and distributed, some unjustifiable acts were committed. "But they are a small proportion of those heroic feats that Eisenhower said were worth fifteen divisions during the Allied landing; they do not compare with the untold number of anonymous sacrifices made to liberate our country."

The C.N.R. had a necessary and key function in the struggle for freedom. Its existence symbolised the unity of the French nation, and whatever the attitude of de Gaulle and the Allied Powers, without it the battle for France would have lasted far longer, and been won at much higher cost and even greater sacrifice.

NOTES

1. F. Grenier, *C'était ainsi* (Paris, 1955) p. 145
2. Waldeck Rochet, *Souvenirs d'un Militant, Humanité*, 30.3.56
3. Warner; *Pierre Laval* p. 365
4. ibid. p. 325
5. ibid. p. 272
6. ibid. pp. 372–373
7. Aragon, *Servitude et Grandeur des Français* (Paris, 1945) pp. 78–97
8. Mme E. Lagarde, Interview, 1974
9. L. Moulin, *Jean Moulin* (Paris, 1969) pp. 249 and 414
10. B. Sweet-Escott, *Baker Street Irregular* (London, 1965) pp. 183–184
11. ibid. pp. 185–186
12. Xavier, *Memoirs of an Agent* p. 209
13. *Le P.C.F. dans la Résistance* p. 240
14. Moulin, op. cit. p. 429
15. Bidault, *Memoirs* p. 30
16. ibid. pp. 32–33
17. De Gaulle, *Unity* pp. 168–169
18. Bidault, op. cit. p. 37
19. ibid. p. 41

Chapter 12

MEDITERRANEAN LIBERATION

... Sur le jungle et le désert
Sur les nids sur les genets
Sur l'écho de mon enfance
J'écris ton nom
Et par le pouvoir d'un mot
Je recommence ma vie
Je suis né pour te connaître
Pour te nommer
Liberté

      Paul Eluard, *Liberté*

... On the jungle, on the desert sands
On birds' nests and on heather
On the echo of my infancy
I write your name
And by the power of one word
I begin my life again
I was born to know and name you
Liberty

At this point we have to sacrifice exact chronology and go back to North Africa in the early spring of 1943. During those months when the French Resistance was finding and consolidating its unity, the Algerian situation was extremely confused. In spite of the so-called liberation, it took many weeks to sort out the tangle, owing to the American determination to keep control in the hands of the French colonialists. "The Vichyites stayed put and for several months braked, plotted and sabotaged", writes André Moine. There was evidence of dirty tricks directly inspired by pro-Nazi elements: on 1 February, for instance, an American journalist reported the light being cut off in Allied officers' quarters; somebody forbade flag-makers to produce Union Jacks; there were mysterious explosions on Allied munition trains and ships in Algiers port.[1] No attempt was made to restore confidence in the war effort or in democratic principles of government. Jewish property was not given back to its owners till after February, anti-semitic laws existed up to April.

The arrival of Marcel Peyrouton in mid-January caused much

concern among anti-fascists; this former governor of Tunis, sacked by Blum in 1936, had been Pétain's Home Secretary till he quarrelled with Darlan and was sent as Vichy ambassador to the Argentine. On his return to Algiers the Nazi press agency *Trans-ocean* recalled his words as minister: "I was the first Frenchman to introduce national-socialist measures into North Africa. I stopped Jewish influence; dismissed Freemasons from my offices; set up a State Police force on the German model."[2] (He might have added, "put well-known ultras into key positions where they would for the next two decades defend their racialist ideas tooth-and-nail against all comers and against the people of Algeria".)

As we have already noticed, Gaullists and resistants were arrested by the score after the November landings; they and the political prisoners breaking stones under the merciless sun of the Sahara, at Agda, Colomb-Bechar, etc., had in many cases to wait till April 1943 before being released, though they had immediately volunteered to join the Allies—they succeeded in one camp alone (Bou Denib) by staging a five-day hunger strike.[3]

An internee of Bossuet labour camp wrote that on 12 November the joyful hopes of liberation were dashed by their camp commandant who announced that "nothing has changed. Darlan has taken power in the name of the *Maréchal*". Following this cold douche, "discipline was reinforced—camp officials, all Pétainists, became more arrogant than ever, reduced camp rations, brought in over-zealous Foreign Legion men to guard us. . . . It was politically and morally the most difficult period of the whole war." Instead of letting out the anti-fascists, convoys of common criminals were brought into their camps, and in December 1943 nearly fifty pro-Nazi detainees added to the congestion—though in fact the latter, welcomed with open arms by the fascist officials, were lodged not four to a cell, but in individual bedrooms. "Tables which we had made for our own use were taken so that *they* could eat in comfort; they could go out to shop in the village; their families could visit them with provisions, clothes, newspapers; they talked about soon returning home. . . ."[11]

There was strong pressure from left-wing organisations in North Africa and Britain for the democrats' release. The International Brigade Association in London issued a list of prisoners held, and Anthony Eden (then Foreign Secretary) indicated his concern. Different figures were given of the numbers interned, the highest estimate being that of de Gaulle, who said on 10 February that there were 15,000 dossiers "which should be dealt with by incineration".

The Algiers authorities went through the motions at tortoise pace: American H.Q. announced that there would be an inter-allied commission of investigation; on 22 January Peyrouton disclaimed all responsibility, passing the buck to General Giraud; on 8 February the *Conseil d'Empire* decided on an examination of dossiers, at some future date.

Why all the delay? The deputy Florimond Bonte, jailed until 4 February, wrote: "We were kept in prison because it was known that on our release we would demand the punishment of traitors, and we would fight for the national and social liberation of France and Algeria. . . . We should be an obstacle to the domination of the Anglo-American Trusts in North Africa. U.S. Imperialism coveted the local resources of minerals and oil, which French colonialism had not fully exploited. . . . The only true defenders of national freedom were the Communists. So they were kept in camps and prisons."[5]

It was not till 4 May 1943 that a general amnesty of anti-fascists was announced and political internment ended. Those prisoners who still had the strength joined the Allied forces, to which they could have contributed so much all along had it not been for the political antagonism of the authorities. "For certain influential persons it was not a question of chasing the Germans off French territory, but of maintaining after Liberation a kind of fascism borrowed from the Nazi and Fascist regimes." It is almost unbelievable (but a fact) that in March 1943, four months after the landings, General Juin awarded the Légion d'Honneur to a M. Donic, former S.O.L., "for having in spite of severe losses succeeded in delaying the Americans' advance in North Africa". A U.S. journalist, John McVane, observed that "this is a testing ground for tomorrow's France . . . the real problem is to know what sort of France we are fighting for against the Germans".[6]

In spite of all the "attentisme", however, the war was being won in North Africa. Rommel's army and the Italians surrendered to General Montgomery and his Desert Rats in Tunis on 12 May, and in the comparative peace after the battles (in which French units had been engaged and fought with distinction) things began to settle down on the political front too. The question of who should represent France was decided after weeks of acrimonious bickerings. As Churchill puts it, "On May 30th de Gaulle arrived in Algiers and sharp and sulky negotiations were begun with the object of setting up a united Provisional Committee to administer the affairs of Free France. . . . Tension mounted in Algiers as these bitter discussions were prolonged. On the afternoon of June 3rd, however, agreement was reached and a Committee of National Liberation (C.F.L.N.) set up."[7] It consisted of most of the more prominent London Gaullists, two Communists, and a few ex-Vichyites who saw the time had come to turn their coats—Jacques Lacour Gayet, of the Bank of France, for instance, René Mayer (industrialist) and the financier Couve de Murville.

But the wrangling did not cease. De Gaulle would not accept Giraud as Supreme Commander, being well aware that the latter wanted to keep the French Army of North Africa intact and clear of Free French influences. De Gaulle's attitude exacerbated American dislike and distrust of him. Roosevelt cabled Eisenhower, "We will not tolerate the control of the French Army by any agency which is not subject to the Allied Supreme Commander's direction. We must have someone whom we completely and wholly trust."[8] The President's telegrams revealed such a mounting hostility to de Gaulle's actions in Algiers that Churchill feared "for the whole future of Allied relationships with the Free French".

Churchill tried hard to persuade Roosevelt to recognise the Gaullist Committee, as Britain and the U.S.S.R. wanted to do. In his memoirs he laments, "I could have made a good arrangement at Casablanca [between Giraud and de Gaulle] but . . . this was frustrated by the preposterous conduct of General de Gaulle. Since then the President has armed General Giraud's troops in North Africa on a very considerable scale and he is much concerned about the demeanour and control of this army." Roosevelt's great fear was that he would be committed to recognising de Gaulle's as the French government "as soon as we land on French soil", and he preferred to deal directly "with local French officials in the colonies whenever military advantage to the Allied cause so dictates",[9] however reactionary these officials might be. The President did, however, on 22 July suggest a joint formula based on "co-operation with" rather than "recognition" of the French National Committee.

"It was only after stubborn talks", says Churchill, "that I was able to persuade the Americans to make a declaration in general terms" supporting the political arrangements already in existence in North Africa. He asked Harold Macmillan to "tell his friends on the [French] Committee to welcome the American declaration in the most cordial terms. . . . If newspaper or radio polemics and reproaches are indulged in the only effect will be to rouse new flames of resentment in the State Department."[10]

At long last, on 26 August, the U.S.A. and Britain announced recognition of the C.F.L.N. as the provisional government; France thus became one of the Big Four, even if the most junior and least powerful, and the sense of belonging to the Great Powers Club was extremely important for de Gaulle and his adherents, both of Right and Left.

After the controversy and confusion of the first half of 1943 clarity and a sense of common purpose began to prevail. News of the Allied landings in Sicily on 10 July, of Mussolini's resignation on 25 July, and Italy's surrender to Eisenhower after the Salerno landings on 8 September, were all greeted with jubilation. Now, people felt, a united effort in support of the Allies and the Resistance was more important than ever, and would surely bear fruit. The Communist Party was in the lead in calling for unity in North Africa and inside France, and the declaration of the twenty-seven deputies, broadcast from Radio-Algiers, rang like a guarantee and promise: "We have always kept our faith in victory alive and unwavering. Today the triumph of freedom is on the way. The hopes of approaching liberation light up the famished faces ravaged by the cruel sufferings of foreign occupation. . . . We hold out our hands to French patriots of all opinions. We call on them to march shoulder to shoulder in the hard battles to win freedom, and to carry out the common task of destroying Fascist barbarism. . . . Victory can only be won by the union of all our forces."[11]

This call was heard all over France, and it was echoed to good effect in the island of Corsica, occupied since November 1942, and ripe for liberation. United action was to be spectacularly effective there throughout the summer of 1943.

Ever since the Italians had taken control of the island, concurrently with the Nazi occupation of Vichy France, acting as policeman with the help of a few German garrisons, the Corsican resistance fighters had been immensely active. Following the P.C.F. call for unity, the local Communists had welded the disparate groups into one organisation, the *Front National*, and had taken the lead in waging guerrilla war. By September 1943 the Corsican F.N. had 12,000 reliable men under arms.[12] When Italy's surrender was announced the F.N. called a great mass rally in Ajaccio and during the night of 8 September issued orders for the insurrection. At 10 a.m. next day,

15,000 people, many carrying weapons, went to the Préfecture where their leaders proclaimed Corsican freedom, dissociated the island from Vichy and declared their allegiance to Free France. All over the land the Vichyite councillors were thrown out and new councils elected. There was street fighting against the German garrison at Ajaccio, in Bastia and St Florent and in the countryside. 120,000 partisans came out into the open, and with 500 men sent by Giraud (still C. in C. in Algiers) drove the occupation forces back to the east coast where they had the choice of jumping into the sea or surrendering. On 3 October Corsica was declared free, predominantly through its own efforts, to the pride and delight of its people.[13]

During the following days, however, de Gaulle expressed great discontent and resentment at the Corsican liberation having been achieved without him—worse still, by his rival Giraud (who had not told him the advance plans of invasion) and, even more provoking, under Communist leadership. De Gaulle rebuked Giraud: "I don't approve of the monopoly you have given to the Communist leaders," and pushed the old general out of the C.F.L.N. He echoed the feelings of those ministers (including Mendés-France and Couve de Murville) who "at no price wished to see the Corsican precedent followed in metropolitan France".[14]

Alarmed at André Philip's report that Communists were installing town councils of their choosing and seizing control of all mass media, de Gaulle flew over to Ajaccio on 8 October to assert himself. He got a very friendly reception; but he could not put the clock back or squash the popular movement. Corsica had effectively proved that unity and self-liberation were no empty words.

Another word, *Maquis*, was also in everybody's minds. The Corsican undergrowth became the symbol of the protective colouring which French resistance was already adopting. The term *maquisard* featured more and more often in the weekly news sheets we were still putting out in London. (Notwithstanding the General's departure, our information office in Carlton Gardens continued to function.)

The thousands of young and middle-aged men who became maquisards by escaping from forced labour and gathering in the mountains and woods of France were clearly the nucleus of a great partisan army. They should have been immediately recognised as such, encouraged by the authorities abroad, and supplied with clothing, food and arms on a vast scale. Both the B.C.R.A. and S.O.E. gradually recognised this, but it was months before the full needs were known, and the fact that the Maquis was predominantly

Communist-led made the Gaullists unwilling to give them anything like adequate help.

None the less the organisation of the underground forces in France assumed major proportions in the autumn of 1943. The population, inspired by the Corsican example, by the purge of Vichyites at last witnessed in Algiers (Pucheu, for one, was tried and executed after being thoroughly humiliated in court by Grenier, now the Minister of Aviation in the National Committee),[15] by the restoration of many civil liberties, and by the resistance of the partisans in Italy—firmly believed in an Allied landing at any moment on the French coast. Resistants everywhere feverishly prepared themselves to support the Fighting French forces they thought were on the way.

But the Allies progressed all too slowly up the length of Italy, in spite of the invaluable guerrilla support. The "soft underbelly of Europe", as Churchill called it, was much more like the back of a porcupine. The Germans found the mountainous terrain well suited to defence, and fought a bitter rearguard action all the way. The prospect of a landing in France was still remote, and the slow pace of the Allied advance led the F.T.P. and other groups to believe that they would have to trust to their own efforts if they were ever to finish the nightmare of occupation and win their freedom.

NOTES

1. Moine, *Résistance et Déportation en Afrique du nord* p. 251
2. ibid. p. 252
3. ibid. p. 232
4. *France*, 10.2.43
5. Bonte, *Le Chemin de l'Honneur* p. 346
6. Moine, op. cit. p. 254
7. Churchill, *The Second World War*, vol. V p. 145
8. ibid. p. 147
9. ibid. pp. 148–151
10. ibid. p. 152
11. Bonte, op. cit. pp. 360–363
12. *Le P.C.F. dans la Résistance* p. 244
13. Michel, *Histoire de la Résistance* p. 31
14. De Gaulle, *Memoirs, Unity* pp. 146, 150
15. Grenier, *C'était ainsi* (Paris, 1970) pp. 220–223

Chapter 13

NACHT UND NEBEL

J'écris dans cette nuit profonde et criminelle
Ou j'entends respirer les soldats étrangers
Et les trains s'étrangler au loin dans les tunnels
Dont Dieu sait si jamais ils pourront déplonger

Aragon, *Le Musée Grévin*, p. 70

I write in this night, deep and criminal,
Hearing the foreign soldiers breathe
And the trains choking in tunnels far away
From which God knows if they'll ever emerge

The winter of 1943 was extremely cold and hard for the French people, who were suffering acutely from lack of heating and from malnutrition. The British agent, Yeo-Thomas, reported that "while the rich could resort to the black market, where a meal cost 800 francs and a pair of shoes 450, ordinary men and women earning from 1,800 to 2,500 francs a month suffered terrible privations". Meat had all but disappeared, bread was a tiny ration of coarse brown maize, and milk unobtainable; clothing was inadequate, shoes wooden and wine beyond price.[1]

A friend told André Gide, "You see women weeping in the streets of Nice because they have nothing to give their children." But women did not only weep—they protested in their underground women's press, and they demonstrated outside the empty bakeries and groceries in the Paris suburbs. Five hundred assembled at the St-Etienne Préfecture, shouting "Bread for our kids!" and the Aubervilliers authorities tried (in vain) to persuade people to leave the city that autumn because in view of the food shortage they feared popular unrest. Anger was indeed great at the sight of bare shelves in shops, while railwaymen reported on recent waggonloads leaving for Germany—93,000 head of cattle, 340 tons of leather, 40,000 tons of wheat, 500 of pharmaceutical products, 10,000 of vegetables, it was said in a widely distributed leaflet. Another underground paper, *La Ménagère parisienne*, quoted Professor Richet of the Académie de Médecine, who was arrested for writing in a medical journal that "in our cities, thousands of French people are being slowly famished and two million more are likely to die of hunger, either directly or indirectly, following the development of infectious diseases. . . ."[2]

The situation increased the longing for a Second Front. Every day the landings were delayed meant more victims of illness and starvation. It also meant more husbands and sons, brothers and comrades being sent to slave labour in Hitler's death camps and factories alongside French prisoners of war, "released" (according to Laval's agreement with Sauckel) from P.O.W. camps to work in conditions appalling beyond words. There have been many accounts of life in the Krupp arms works and other industrial centres, but here it is enough to quote just one example—the description of existence in the Dora factory, near Buchenwald, producing V2 rockets, given by Charles Sadon, a professor of engineering who was deported to Germany in early 1944, after the Nazis closed Strasbourg University (then in Clermont-Ferrand), and was put to work as a "technician" in Dora.

There were 10,000 workers employed in shifts in the immense underground caverns, many of them French and Russians. They slept in groups of 2,500 in cave-dormitories. "This mass of humanity who never went outside the factory, sick and dying men heaped up among a few healthy ones—verminous, struggling, crying, dying—lived, worked and slept in a stinking stifling atmosphere, forbidden to wash, surrounded by an aura of sweat, death, excrement hard to imagine. . . . At night we slept $4\frac{1}{2}$ hours, assailed by constant noise as shift followed shift. We were woken sporadically by explosions as rock was dynamited, and by pneumatic drilling. Powdered stone fell on workers and sleepers alike, penetrating skin and lungs. . . . 2,500 men had to get out of the 'dormitory' at 4 a.m. and were beaten if they didn't move fast enough, beaten unconscious if they stopped to tie up a slipper, beaten to death for not saluting. . . . Much later, the S.S. were forbidden to kill the badly-needed technical workers, but the infernal conditions continued. . . ."

The slaves' one consolation was that they could sabotage the production of V2s, which they did with might and main. "The Russians sabotaged by peeing on the tail of torpedo shells. To be caught in the act meant certain hanging but . . . the risk didn't matter much as we had no hope of surviving anyway. . . . In the wet shells, short circuits occurred which the Germans could not check." Professor Sadon found other ways of spoiling the weapons, and when questioned blamed the defects on poor materials and unskilled labour. 1,200 V2s were produced monthly; out of 72,000 turned out in six months probably 60 per cent were faulty. Thanks to this, large numbers never reached their targets—London, Antwerp, Paris—because they failed to take off, or fell short.[3]

This was a form of French resistance, carried on outside France. It was matched inside the country by similar sabotage in factories working for Germany, even more effective because this was organised by the trade union movement and carried out almost as a military operation in every group. The engineering unions called for action against the Nazis inside Renault, Citroën, Matford, Simca and other firms. "We must not allow one machine tool to cut, not one machine to function, not one brain to think", said an illegal C.G.T. leaflet; "nothing of ours must serve Hitler and his band of murderers." The response was devastating. At Citroën's the workers blew up a roller track and damaged thousands of components; at Gnome-et-Rhône they set fire to a conveyor belt and ruined scores of engines destined for German planes; in the Matford factory at Poissy, a pylon was dynamited. The order was carried out by industrial workers in many fields: "Chacun sabotait ce qu'il pouvait." ("Everyone sabotaged what he could.") In the P.T.T., telephone engineers cut wires, stole German plans; the Metro men arranged breakdowns, robbing the enemy of precious hours of work; navvies on the T.O.D.T. site pushed fifteen German lorries over the cliffs; even the slaughter-house workers did their bit, making carcasses bound for Germany unfit for consumption.[4]

*   *   *

While the trade unions improved their methods of propaganda and sabotage, the Resistance as a whole became better organised and co-ordinated, thanks to the C.N.R., and there was a general expectation of large-scale Allied assistance—if not a landing, at least massive arms drops by parachute. There seemed no good reason why greatly increased supplies could not be sent, as delivery and reception methods improved.

In the early days the inexperienced patriots had had all sorts of difficulties, well outlined by Henri Michel in his account of Allied operations. "Preparations needed extreme care; the grounds chosen by reception committees had to be well sited outside towns, not too near a road, on a treeless place hidden from the public but easily visible from the sky and accessible to vehicles taking away supplies after the drop." When the site was chosen, a message went to London by radio and a reconnaissance plane was sent to take photographs, on which the R.A.F. made a final decision; following this, a message from the B.B.C. informed the people on the spot of the time for reception.

In 1942 there were not a great number of drops but a high percentage of successes. Up to the late summer of 1943 the operations increased; the R.A.F. carried out ninety-nine in August alone, dropping 977 containers of supplies. That year, in fact, fifty-three agents were sent over and the average monthly drop was ten at least. But winter brought great difficulties, and in fog, cloud or high wind, operations had to be cancelled; it was only on full moon nights that planes could land. The Germans became more vigilant, and the 1942 record of 75 per cent success fell to 40 per cent in 1943. (In 1944, with new and more sophisticated communications, successes rose again, to 80 per cent.) By any standards, however, 18 Lysander planes landed in 1943 was a not inconsiderable number, and the total parachuted by Buckmaster's network—366 agents, 4,000 drops made to some 50 *réseaux*—reflects an immense effort. It is sad to have to admit that too often something went wrong. "Unfortunately the liaison with the Internal Resistance was not always perfect", Michel writes, "and sometimes the Forces Françaises de l'Intérieur (F.F.I.) were left with no arms, while nearby dépôts were left unused."[5] As we shall see later, the inadequacy of the weaponry provided was a cause of friction and heartbreak among those involved in building the Secret Army's battalions.

During 1943 the need for large-scale supplies was not properly understood. The S.O.E. was concerned mainly with providing for its own *réseaux*, and even these could not receive adequate help as there were such a very great number of them. It is extremely moving to see, in retrospect, how each, however small and whether helped by the Allies or not, did sterling work sending information gathered at great risk on enemy troop dispositions, supplying details on all sorts of different matters, from positions of ships and submarines to the tendencies prevailing in the French *gendarmerie* and Vichy *Milice*. All this was coded and sent to London—by carrier pigeon or fishing-boat in the early period, later by agents via Spain or Switzerland, and of course also by the quicker but much more dangerous method of radio transmission.

The Germans had developed means of intercepting messages, decoding them, tracing the transmitters by "goniophone"—as the terrible story of Rémy's *Affaire de Trahison* relates. After an agent had been seven minutes on the air it became dangerous to transmit messages; but owing to delays or blocked reception in London, transmissions sometimes took up to 45 minutes, and the Nazis were able to pick up the signals. They obtained nearly all their information on the Resistance by catching the cipher, tracing the centres and seizing codes, material and agents, with tragic human results. A few agents were bought over and worked for the Germans, causing catastrophe in the networks; some succumbed under the unspeakable tortures of the Gestapo. But the great majority refused heroically to speak, even if it meant death or deportation, rather than give anything or anybody away. On the whole, the traitors were pro-Nazis from the start and early on became double agents, intercepting messages, distorting replies, sometimes even attempting to get parachuted in the guise of agents in and out of England.

The French or Belgians who worked for the Nazis were probably the most contemptible of all the rotten elements thrown up in the war. They were highly paid by the Germans and they often also made huge profits on the side by procuring, blackmailing, and buying and selling on the Black Market.

Henry Masuy, the Belgian responsible for "interrogating" scores of patriots at Avenue Henri Martin, ran a *"Service économique français"* which provided the Wehrmacht with vast quantities of textiles, wool and coffee (robbed from the French people). "He pocketed commissions from every sort of speculator. . . . He disdained any *affaire* of less than a million. . . . His profits in less than four years amounted to hundreds of millions of francs. . . . He had at his disposal a horde of *agents rabatteurs*, a huge network of commercial relations among 'French industrialists', teams of smugglers operating on the Spanish frontier and in the vast warehouses of the Saint-Ouen. . . . His men had all the right papers, and any French policeman caught trying to investigate them would meet trouble."

A businessman visiting Masuy at his "bureau d'achat" in the Avenue Henri Martin reported that "he had come through an office full of German soldiers and plainsclothes Gestapo men. Among them, three men covered with blood and wounds, handcuffed, kneeling in the middle of the room." Another time, "going through the room I saw women in tears. . . ." This visitor declared himself stupefied when he was later told that Masuy "spent a good part of his time on other things than looking for coupons of material, blankets or hospital bed-tables". The torture chambers, the ice-cold baths and electric equipment were well disguised, and the cries of the victims drowned by loud radio music. "Two or three times a week,

Masuy went over to the Otto bureaux . . . at every visit he received ten million francs for what he had supplied to the Germans, after which he went back to deal with the patriots."[6]

Masuy and his friends would do anything for money; the black market in which they operated was of such importance in the Nazi-dominated society of wartime France that we will return to it. But for the moment we must take a look at the Nazis' other activities, their apparatus for repression and their use of collaborators, which will show something of the appalling dangers faced by the *résistants*.

The chief German police organisation was the Abwehr, based at the Hotel Lutétia, which included control of the Geheime Feld-polizei and Feldgendarmerie. These were army services, more professionally decent and less sinister than the Nazi Party services which were their rivals in repression. The latter consisted of the Sicherheitsdienst (Security) and Sicherheitspolizei (Police Security); the Kriminalpolizei, which dealt with ordinary crooks; and, most important, the Geheime Staatspolizei, or Gestapo. All were under the orders of Kaltenbrunner. There were also an anti-Jewish police (Avenue Foche) and the Secret Societies' Police (Square Rapp). The French police in the Northern zone were not an important part of the repressive machine, for they were not fully trusted by the Nazis although they were expected to carry out German orders (which they tended to do less and less as time went on). Far nastier and more useful to the Germans were the collaborators, such as Masuy's team who investigated 2,000 people, seized 54 radios, 20 tons of parachuted supplies and a great deal of money and personal property from their compatriots.

No less horrible, if less efficient because not directly under Nazi control, were the French fascist special police. Vichy, in its efforts to keep repression in its own hands, had set up many different kinds: to the usual *gendarmerie* and *sécurité*, Pucheu, when Minister of the Interior, had added a Police for Jewish Questions, and an Anti-communist Police service (S.P.A.C.) which operated all over France. A law of August 1943 introduced into every Court of Appeal a *section spéciale* which judged all crimes committed "with communist or anarchist intent"; in 1944 Laval and Darnand had set up court-martials which executed patriots out of hand.

The most detested of the French security forces was Darnand's Milice, described by a British agent as "scum of the jails, brutalised of the most brutal, cream of the offal, they worked for money and food for their carnal appetites; they worked for German money".[7]

From January 1943 on, these thugs hunted the *réfractaires* mercilessly and carried out countless summary executions of maquisards. One of the Prefecture's special brigades alone, under Commissaire David, made 2,071 arrests in 1944, handed 495 people to the Germans, and executed 125. There is no doubt that the French system greatly helped the Nazis, and the O.V.R.A. (Italian police) also collaborated loyally, and indiscriminately—shooting quite inoffensive mayors of small towns in Mussolini's Alpine zone.

It can be seen, then, how terrible were the risks of working against the Germans, and one need only use one's imagination or read some of the books and memoirs of the period to envisage the appalling life that faced the active *résistant*. If he became known, even if he escaped the police net, the least risk was the pillage of his belongings, the holding of his family as hostages; if caught, there was the prospect of torture, terror of succumbing, of deportation, slow death or execution. In spite of the dreadful dangers of being or helping an agent the number of individuals involved in activity continued to grow—in one month for example, 2,622 telegrams were sent from France, and 3,700 reports delivered to Allied H.Q., every one an act of courage and personal commitment.

But in late 1943 there was a qualitative change in the character of the Resistance. The system of depending on secret agents, dear to the I.S. and the *Deuxième Bureau*, gave way to the participation of the people *en masse*. Everybody who could, wanted to play a part in preparing the coming Liberation, and a whole population shared the underground life of camouflage and espionage. This had many failings, but it was an inevitable result of the spread of the movement. Michel reckons that about 18,000 French men and women suffered fatally from their patriotism—8,230 died, 2,578 disappeared in internment, and 7,381 returned from deportation in ruined health.[7]

These thousands of individuals were, however, only a tiny proportion of the working people who daily risked their lives in anti-Nazi activity, sabotage or propaganda, and by some miracle of organisation or solidarity, or chance, escaped. The factory workers who constantly interfered with production and damaged machines used for German industry, those who ruined the communications system, cutting cables, blowing up pylons and bridges, and the railwaymen who disrupted the train services, never knowingly harming French passengers, but derailing countless German convoys of men and goods. "It is impossible to estimate the cost to the Germans of their efforts", writes Michel. "To measure the effect it is enough to note that the S.N.C.F. in three weeks sabotaged more locomotives than the Allied airforces did with vastly greater raids in $4\frac{1}{2}$ months."

They would have done even better, had there been more supplies of explosives to the saboteurs. Agents such as Yeo-Thomas and Xavier saw this and bitterly complained to London of the "paltry parachuting". "The load of one Halifax bomber dropped to a reception committee and handled by the right men could ... have done more damage to the German war machine than the loads of 240 bombers dropped in a raid. Repeated air bombardments had failed seriously to hinder the work of a ball-bearing factory at Annecy; three saboteurs ... so damaged the machinery that the factory never produced another ball-bearing during the rest of the occupation."[8]

The story was much the same at the Peugeot car works near Besançon (then producing tank parts for Germany), only with the advantage that the pro-British director co-operated with the S.O.E. agent Harry Rée in organising the sabotage. With Peugeot's agreement and under Rée's instructions, firemen and workers set plastic explosives in key points, timed to blow up just after midnight when the factory was empty and maximum damage could be inflicted on equipment. The factory was put out of production for most of the rest of the war, and the saboteurs escaped and carried on the good work elsewhere.

A post-war report gave the number of acts of industrial sabotage effected in France with S.O.E. help in 1943 and 1944 as 122. Though impressive, when one bears in mind the risks and effort involved in every case, the extent of anti-German sabotage might have been vastly increased had more supplies been made available to the French. According to Yeo-Thomas of S.O.E., in mid-winter 1943 the scarcity of sabotage materials as well as of arms, was affecting morale among the partisans. They knew that scientific equipment which would have been invaluable for sabotage—time bombs with magnets, altimeter switches, explosive coal, electronic devices, etc.— was not reaching them because of London's insistence on using the R.A.F. for massive but often unsuccessful bombing raids, rather than for dropping arms and explosives. "The amount of arms that was being dropped in a month could equip only a hundred men of the Secret Army", complained British agent Yeo-Thomas who understood the potential of the growing Maquis and found this infuriating. All the groups of volunteers he visited were short of weapons. In one case "there were no grenades at all. The available arms were used by all in turn for instructional purposes. . . . Lack of ammunition prevented target practice". In another case, there were "thirty men whose sole armament consisted of one rifle and ten rounds of ammunition",[9] and so on.

Yeo-Thomas complained loud and long to his superior officers in London and by anger and tenacity succeeded in getting an interview with Churchill, in the course of which he described the Secret Army and the Maquis, "their appalling lack of arms and equipment", the need for aircraft to drop supplies, "the brave men and women risking torture and death carrying messages through the crowded police-ridden streets of Paris and waiting for agents in the darkness in the windy wilderness of central France". It seems strange that Churchill had not known all this until January 1944. For some reason, Yeo-Thomas's reports had not reached him. Churchill brusquely asked his secretary, "Why have they not been passed to me, Morton?—See that I have them immediately." Following which, the P.M. signed an order to the Air Ministry to make a hundred aircraft available for the French resistance and promised at least 250 sorties in every moon period. The result: "Within 48 hours, 22 Halifaxes, 12 Liberators, 36 Stirlings, 6 Albemarles and a number of small aircraft for pick-up operations, also some planes to operate from North Africa."[10]

Besides Yeo-Thomas, pressure was put on Churchill by Emmanuel d'Astier (the "lean mercurial left-wing poet") who claimed that resisters were currently killing two Germans for every man they lost, and were in acute danger for lack of arms. Another advocate was Michel Brault who ran a clandestine relief organisation supplying many Maquis with food, medical stores and clothing, and well understood their needs. An official meeting of British ministers on 27 January agreed that after Bomber Command's operations on Germany, "drops to the Maquis were to have first priority."[11]

Although things improved, thanks to Churchill's intervention, the high hopes placed by Yeo-Thomas on Allied aid to the Maquis were not by any means realised: ". . . air effort amounted, by the middle of May (1944), to the arming of about 75,000 men by F section and 50,000 by RF, at the most optimistic estimates. . . . Moreover, there were no adequate supplies of ammunition: Brault's opinion was that by the end of April hardly 10,000 maquisards had ammunition for more than a single day's fighting. . . ." But Yeo-Thomas would be unaware of this till after the end of the war. The valiant British agent was betrayed while making a too risky bid to rescue Brossolette from captivity in Rennes gaol, and he was arrested on 21 March outside

Passy Metro Station in Paris, mercilessly beaten up in Fresnes Prison, then deported to Buchenwald. He survived, astonishingly, thirteen months of torment and several hellish experiences of failed escape, and emerged sick and emaciated, but unbroken in spirit, to win the George Cross in February 1946. A much greater reward was the knowledge that he had contributed more than any single Englishman to the victory of the French resistance—because he was one of the very few English who understood and appreciated its needs.

NOTES

1. B. Marshall, *The White Rabbit* (London, 1952) p. 35
2. A. Tollet, *La Classe ouvrière dans la Résistance* (Paris, 1969) pp. 118, 137
3. Resistance, *Indre et Vallée du Cher* (Paris, 1972) II pp. 280–28
4. Tollet, op. cit. p. 182
5. Michel, *Histoire de la Résistance* p. 69
6. Rémy, *Une Affaire de Trahison* (Paris, 1947) pp. 20–26
7. Michel, op. cit. p. 80
8. *Private information*, November, 1974
9. Marshall, op. cit. p. 64
10. ibid. pp. 84–86
11. Foot, *S.O.E. in France* pp. 353–354

Chapter 14

CULTURE IN THE RESISTANCE

Ce cœur qui haïssait la guerre, voilà qu'il bat
   pour le combat et la bataille!
Et qu'il mène un tel bruit dans la cervelle que
   les oreilles en sifflent
Et qu'il n'est pas possible que ce bruit ne se
   répande pas dans la ville et la campagne
Comme le son d'une cloche appelant à l'emeute et au combat.

Pierre Andier, *L'Honneur des Poètes*

This heart which hated war, see how it beats
   for combat and battle!
And how its beating in the brain
   makes the ears sing
And how impossible it is that this noise
   should not spread through town and country
Like the sound of a bell calling to rebellion and to battle.

In the battle for freedom, the partisans with arms in their hands, the agents with their radio sets, the saboteurs in factories and on railways, were in the vanguard, risked life and limb in almost every action, and deserve the highest honour. But hardly less important, and nearly equally dangerous was the work on the cultural front—the spreading of information in countless newspapers and journals, the encouragement and confidence disseminated by the underground press, books, poems, pictures, which multiplied as time went on and flooded the whole country after the 1942 total occupation by the Germans. This involved a tremendous effort from thousands of people, and a considerable risk in writing, printing, distributing and even in reading the myriad sheets in circulation.

In the early days there were a few newspapers, brought out by the most energetic groups; the Communist Party never failed to publish its own propaganda, and *Humanité*, which appeared at least once every week of the Occupation, totalled 316 numbers in 15,300,000 copies by 1944. There were also several Party women's papers, and youth bulletins, besides countless Communist oriented trade union journals.[1] As André Tollet says, "this activity took a heavy toll of prisoners, deportees and executions", and the material cost was high—"very many secret offices, machines, stocks of paper fell into the hands of the police". At the end of 1943 the illegal C.G.T. worked hard to reduce risks, increase efficiency, and treble the trade unions' publishing capacity, building up dozens of small independent branches less liable to discovery and disaster. The difficulties were enormous—machines had to be stolen from employers or from German offices, transported and installed in secret places where the noise of printing was inaudible.[2] But the results were astonishing indeed. Gradually the non-Communist press became organised too, with *Combat, Libération* and other papers mentioned earlier. Georges Bidault ran a sort of underground press agency for eighteen months, producing some 250 numbers of an information bulletin which was useful to the movement in France and also to Carlton Gardens. But the editors of the illegal press gradually came to collect and use their own information, and eventually nearly every group published its own particular views and news.

In late 1942 *Marseillaises, Libérations, Patriots, Populaires* sprang up everywhere. In 1943 in Provence alone there were five regional newspapers—*L'Espoir* (Socialist), *Rouge-midi* (C.P.), *La Marseillaise* (Front national), *Le Marseillais* (M.V.R.), and *Provence libérée*, alongside departmental organs. Fighting groups had their own papers, such as *Ceux du Maquis*. Prisoners' families brought out *Victoire* and *Aide*, peasants produced a variety voicing their opinions and needs, from *La Terre*, and *Le Paysan patriote* to *La Résistance paysanne*.

As a result of the efforts already mentioned, the trade union publications were immensely prolific; *La Vie ouvrière* came out in 2,400 roneoed, and 15,000 printed copies every month, and in June 1944 printed a record 243,000 texts. Tollet puts their publications at over a million per month.[3] There were also *Le Peuple syndicat* and the *Mouvement ouvrier français*, besides more specialised papers such as *l'Usine français*, and *La Voix du Mineur*.

Professional groups had their particular mouthpieces: *Le Médecin français, Palais libre* (for lawyers), *Le Guide des Infirmiers* (for nurses) and *Les Enseignants* (for teachers). For most of these people were patriotic and responsible, and even if not 100 per cent militant they formed a solid bloc of resistant opinion, and helped the movement in many ways. Scientists manufactured explosives in their laboratories and showed workers how to make Molotov cocktails and hand grenades. Doctors signed false certificates to get youngsters out of S.T.O. Lawyers slowed down the processes of "justice". Welfare and health workers spoke or wrote, with the authority of their experience, of the effects of the Nazi starvation regime.

The teachers, a section of French society very varied in views, and earlier split into mutually distrustful political factions, became gradually drawn into resistance and also published their own press early on. In the North they had seen the effects of Nazi occupation on education, and many had helped the militants to reorganise their union within the C.G.T., to produce newspapers (*L'école laïque*, and *L'Université libre*) and to carry on propaganda for the Resistance. In the provinces there had for some time been *"le brouillard"* (fog) owing to the disappearance of many left-wing teachers; at the beginning of 1942 Paul Delanoue, trying to organise trade union activity in the *zone non-occupée* "found a most depressing atmosphere there". But after German occupation of the Vichy zone "the situation had changed . . . the climate was far more militant".[4] A national committee was formed and began to produce its newspapers in all parts of France—*l'Ecole de Bara* and *Université libre* came out in the South to match the publications in the North. From Lyons an appeal went out, "Teachers are working in their regional organisations which have been reborn while Vichy's are dying. . . . Teachers in higher and secondary education, it is up to you to join in the battle!"[5] And teachers, too, began sabotage—but in reverse—against the go-slow of Vichy's orders, against the misuse of their time, against the disorganisation of schooling by stupid activities and against the "French Nazis" programme which was "to limit the instruction given to children to the minimum necessary for workers and peasants, to P.T. so as to stifle ambition, and discipline the young". Instead of attending lessons, children had to "collect paper, search for colorado beetles, sell Pétain's portrait, collect for the *Secours national*, help with the harvest". Unlike other trade unionists, the teachers did not call for strikes, but on the contrary asked their colleagues "to work, and to denounce overlong holidays, official ceremonies, agricultural labour. . . . The teacher should not be a maid of all work, serving the mayor or the priest according to Vichy's ideas, but should defend the best traditions of French education."[6] Teachers' newspapers began to come out; *Ecole et Liberté, l'Ecole et la Libération, l'Ecole Laïque* joined the others of the underground press in calling for resistance to deportation, opposition to Vichy, and for support for the Maquis.

Elsewhere in the cultural field, actors, musicians, artists helped to preserve France's true traditions. There were a few who collaborated, but far more played an honourable part. Many film stars and well known actors refused to appear on the Vichy-controlled stage, but took a role in plays by Giraudoux or Sartre where the anti-fascist message was thinly disguised in a classical setting. Distinguished musicians commissioned to appear before the Germans somehow managed to avoid doing so by pleading illness or accident. Composers wrote music to words by the Communist poets Eluard and Aragon, and the songs were duplicated and circulated among the people; concerts were carefully programmed to include works by Jewish or Russian composers and songs with a patriotic flavour.

In the art world, resistance took many forms. The fifty-two guardians of the Louvre wore F.T.P. badges at the Liberation, and long before that had proved their devotion by protecting precious paintings from possible German desecration or robbery. During 1940, 4,000 canvasses were packed into sixty-five vans, crossed the Loire and were safely lodged at Montauban; when the Nazis invaded the Z.N.O. they were divided between four castles in the Lot department. The Mona Lisa went from Chambord to Louvigny, then to Rochile and finally back to Montauban for safekeeping. As Louis Parrot wrote, in 1947, "the Louvre took to the Maquis, with its H.Q. in the Château of Montal".[7]

I remember visiting the Musée Rodin in Paris, in late 1940, and being told as a great secret that the best bronzes were hidden underground for fear of confiscation by the Germans, who badly needed metal for their war effort. The Director of the *Musées nationaux*, M. Jaujard, refused to allow paintings to go to the East, as Abel Bonnard demanded in the name of security. He also delayed negotiations over the purchase of treasures coveted by the Germans, so that, as one example, Goering never got the valuable Boucher painting he wanted to have delivered to him in Berlin.

The resistants in charge of the dispersed paintings in the South took good care that the Allied bombings did not touch them—by sending messages such as "Van Dyck thanks Fragonard" and "the Gioconda is still smiling", to indicate the location of these treasures.

The post-liberation *Salon d'automne* of 1944, which had been organised in the "underground", proved that France's artists had gone on working during the war and had kept alive the great French painting tradition. Three names must have special mention: Picasso (who showed eighty paintings at the 1944 exhibition), Matisse and Lurçat, who all did much to maintain the national spirit during those terrible years. Picasso refused to budge from his Paris studio in spite of pressing invitations to flee to America. Working unceasingly, he became a centre for young artists and "illuminated Paris in her humiliation with a lustre which no might on earth could dim", as Louis Parrot put it. There are a legion of Picasso stories: one was his defiant answer to the Germans coming upon *Guernica* during a search of his studio and asking "Did you do this?" "No, YOU did!"; another, his refusal to let his bronzes be taken away: "These could never be used for big weapons", insisted the Nazi intruder; "No, but they might for small ones," said Picasso.

Henri Matisse, too, was something of a legend. Like Picasso he was offered a visa for America, but refused to go. He had nearly left for Brazil in 1940, but "simply as a way of turning the phoney war period to good account," says Aragon. He never had any intention of leaving France, and turned down the offer of a post at Mills College, California. He retired to his Provençal village and throughout the dark years painted glorious life-enhancing canvasses and frescoes. Though fully aware of the evil around him, though his daughter Marguerite was arrested for helping the Maquis, and though he "was very worried about his son Jean, knowing that Jean had dynamite hidden under his sculptures", the septuagenarian Matisse never gave way to pessimism. He wrote to Aragon, "Haven't you the support of Hope and the approach of Spring?"[8] He made drawings for the underground review *Poésie 41*, and sketched his "little girl" after her return from detention—"Those eyes have seen prison and its horrors", Aragon commented—but on the whole his work throughout the war years was basically optimistic, full of joy in life. To quote Aragon again, "I am deeply convinced that . . . today in the struggle for good, Matisse is like a great banner unfurled . . ." and "assuredly the whole achievement of Henri Matisse is a powerful assertion of our right to happiness, to the happiness of the young, who are all too liable to this century's anguish." The work of this great artist was, like Picasso's, an encouragement and message of hope: "In those days, people will say, they did at least have Matisse in France. . . . At the darkest point of our night, they'll say, he made those luminous drawings."[9]

Another artist, and also a very great man, was Jean Lurçat. Of a younger generation, he was a former surrealist, and an active Communist who found a way of combining art and action in the service of the Resistance. He left Paris in 1942 to join the F.F.I. in the Dordogne, and while in the south he set up a studio where he designed tapestry with the object of reviving the old French industry which had fallen on bad times in Aubusson. Lurçat had an indomitable optimism, never doubted victory, and foresaw a future French socialist state which would encourage culture in every corner of life, restore the traditional crafts and use works of art to decorate civic buildings, public monuments, schools, hospitals, railway stations. Several famous artists including Picasso, Dufy and Marc Saint-Saëns shared his confidence and joined him in making designs for the tapestry factories. Their work was inspired by socialist idealism, and Lurçat most of all was able to convey a pervasive warmth and fervour in his huge panels. The sun rising over his beloved Dordogne, with its trees, flowers, foliage; his butterflies, stars and fishes; above all his cocks, resplendent in blue, white and crimson plumage, express his deep love of France; his *Poet* and his *Man* proclaim his belief in humanity and faith in the future. Unfortunately the great hopes that the new tapestry would be available for all to enjoy, in public buildings and galleries everywhere, came to nothing—and it is now difficult to find Lurçat's tapestries even in the national Paris museums, while his ideas for rehabilitating the industry, with young artists designing for Aubusson's benefit and the world's enjoyment, have disappeared in the clouds of economic depression and the State's professed need to cut down on culture.

One unusual feature of Lurçat's work was the incorporation of poetry, or of a poet's idea, in his creations. The words of Paul Eluard's "Liberté" are woven into one of the most beautiful tapestries, and there are many single lines in other works. Literature and art went hand in hand during the resistance, and this is strongly and dramatically conveyed.

In its own right, literature of course played a vitally important part in the struggle. The writers of France managed in spite of the Nazi and Vichy censorship to bring out journals, broadsheets and books by the hundred. The most important vehicles for underground literature—*Les Lettres françaises* and *Les Etoiles*—were widely read and introduced many "clandestine" authors to the public. There was also the *Editions de minuit*, the writer Vercors' illegal publishing house, which produced some fifteen volumes during the Occupation, including several collections of poems by Aragon and Eluard, and *Le Cahier Noir* by the distinguished Catholic novelist François Mauriac. The *Cahier*, written in 1940–41, is a short but extremely moving outburst of concentrated bitterness over the defeat and disgrace of France, lambasting the collaborators, exalting the martyrs "who bear witness to the people's heroism".

"The working class alone in its entirety has been faithful to France in her hours of desecration," Mauriac declared. He refused to follow Goethe's example in detaching himself from the political *"brouillamini* of errors and violence. . . ." "This *brouillamini* is our affair; it concerns us and we should be cowards if we gave way to detachment. . . ."[10] His sombre protest against tyranny and torture ends on a note of defiance: "We have made our choice. . . . We believe that Man not only can escape the law of mutual destruction but that all his dignity lies in Resistance to that law, with his whole heart and soul. . . ."[11]

The "clandestine" writers, of whom Mauriac was the oldest and most eminent, had a far wider readership than the collaborationists who had the use of Vichy's press and publicity—Céline, Maurras, Henri Béraud—and Vercors' *Silence de la mer*, Aragon's *La Diane française*, Eluard's *Au rendezvous allemand* became classics almost overnight. They struck an immediate chord in the population, and travelled to the remotest areas of France, raising the spirits of refugees and maquisards, and to countries overseas, where exiles and foreign friends alike learned how poetry was serving and speaking for the Resistance.

Of all the underground literary ventures, the most ambitious and successful was *Les Lettres françaises*. This was started by the young philosopher Jacques Decour, in early 1942, and after the tragedy of his arrest and execution seemed doomed to disappear; but it was taken up by Claude Morgan the novelist, and Louis Parrot, poet and editor who worked in the Louvre,[12] and after a few months it became the organ of the newly formed *Comité des Ecrivains français* (French Writers' Committee: C.E.F.) which grouped an impressive number of names, including Mauriac, Jean Guéhenno, Sartre, Camus, as active members, and others—Paul Valéry, Georges Duhamel, Paul Hazard—who supported and wrote for it.

The *Lettres* came out regularly, twenty issues in about as many months, with special numbers on occasions of national or tragic importance, such as the Oradour massacre. Producing the paper was a dangerous operation, which has been vividly described in Parrot's *L'Intelligence en Guerre*. Twelve thousand copies were usually printed, 1,500 of which had to be sent out by post; the three people responsible, M. and Mme Rossi and "the cyclist Poudens", had the arduous job every month of folding and putting 1,500 newspapers into as many envelopes, which had to be addressed, stuck down, stamped, and (for safety) pushed into a hundred different letter boxes. The remaining 10,500 were given out to members of various groups—teachers, doctors, students—who distributed them. "What with the newspaper and all sorts of additional leaflets and supplements, our distributors were always in the throes of work . . . there was never any end to it. . . ."[13] The files of the *Lettres françaises* testify to the spirit of the journal's workers, and show how regular and professional was its production by the devoted team.

The risks involved at every stage were high: whether it was collecting the material for every number, which was Paul Eluard's job (and entailed pestering his friends for articles, visiting houses under supervision, prolifically distributing leaflets), or whether doing type-setting and printing. The *Lettres'* valiant printers took extra risks in stealing type from the Nazi-controlled *Paris-Soir* and transporting it to their secret workshop. "One day," writes Parrot, "George Adam, the printer, with his inside jacket pockets full of lead, was searched by the police at the exit of a Metro station. By merciful chance they only felt his *outer* pockets—but it was a nasty moment for our friend."[13] Many of the editors and printers of the underground press were, alas, not so lucky—Peclet, of *Franc-Tireur*, and his Lyons colleagues Orsini and Vacher, *Combat*'s André Bollier, Jean Rochon of *Libération*, among many others—joined the roll of martyrs, arrested, tortured, deported or shot.

Writers, too, faced grave dangers—no ivory tower for the resistant author or poet. Jean Cassou, eminent writer and art historian, was imprisoned for eighteen months for anti-Vichy propaganda in Toulouse jail.

When I visited his relatives in that town in 1941, his wife was just going out with food to supplement the miserable prison meal. I asked how he passed the time in solitary confinement, and she said simply, "He writes poetry". The result was Cassou's *Thirty-three Sonnets* (published under the name Jean Noir) composed without one word written down, and carried in his head for months on end— an astonishing feat of intellect and memory.[14] A conversation with Cassou thirty years later revealed that he considered this contribution to the Resistance far less important than his work helping railwaymen with sabotage and other communal activity which had resulted in his arrest. "Les intellectuels c'est la m . . .!" declared the poet. "What counted was our secret action, our solidarity with the people . . ." and he gave me a vivid account of underground meetings, rendezvous with unknown colleagues, hairbreadth escapes, which had nothing whatever to do with literature.

None the less, the writers were front-line fighters, and their work added up at least to the equivalent of several parachute drops of arms. Poetry and short stories were weapons of lasting deadliness, especially in the hands of men like Eluard, who used his art to flay the Nazis and exalt the French patriots in unforgettable verses.

Aragon was another equally formidable warrior: former Surrealist, novelist, Communist, he was immensely active in the Z.N.O. during 1942 and 1943; with his wife Elsa Triolet, author of several short novels on resistance themes, he travelled from place to place, continually changing address, organising, editing, writing. The police were on his trail many times, in Nice, Avignon, Dieu-le-Fit, Paris, but miraculously he escaped their net and never flagged in his activity of encouraging and stimulating his fellow writers, as well as producing an immense number of poems, eventually published in the collections *La Diane française, Le Musée Grévin, Le Crêve-Cœur, Les Yeux d'Elsa*. The importance of these poems, technically superb, moving in the extreme, was for Aragon their militancy. "For him, there is no poetry except militant poetry. A successful poem, is for him an act of war—a war in which the poet is ever-present, because it contains his liberty, his life itself."[15] Aragon's own comment was in "Contre la poésie pure", where he defends himself "pour avoir préférant la vie à la feintise, préféré le sang à l'encens" ("in having preferred life to fantasy preferred blood to incense").

Like a poet-laureate, Aragon, marked every national occasion with a poem. The occasions were mainly tragic—the defeat of France ("O mois de floraisons mois des métamorphoses"),[17] the Occupation ("Complainte pour l'Orgue de la nouvelle Barbarie")[18] the execution of Gabriel Péri, the German attack on Strasbourg University. But there followed the victories of the Maquis ("Gloire"), the Liberation of Paris. His output was extraordinary, in view of his other activity. He wrote prolifically in the *Lettres françaises*, kept in contact with all his surviving friends, and attended regularly the meetings of the Writers' Committee in Paris. The C.N.E. owed a great deal to Aragon and to Eluard; but due homage must also be paid to all the others who shared the dangers and the work involved in membership: to Edith Thomas, Charles Vildrac, Pierre Seghers, Pierre Leyris (editor of *Cahiers de la Libération*) so active in organising; to Mauriac, Sartre and Camus, not in illegality but invaluable "above ground" in their staunch attitude; to Valéry, Duhamel, Pierre Bost, who did not attend meetings but kept in close touch. Every one of them played an important part in the Resistance, both in spreading hope and truth as an antidote to the fascist "culture" on the market, and in keeping alive the great tradition of French literature, criticism, thought.

These writers, and their collaborators, might well be proud of their achievement during the four years of illegal existence. In no other occupied country, nor indeed in Britain or America, was there such an output of poetry, stories, essays, autobiography in such a limited period. It was largely literature *engagée*, "committed" writing, but all the better for that, and it added up to the extraordinary phenomenon of a kind of cultural renaissance in the darkness, unmatched at the time or since.

NOTES

1. L. Parrot, *L'Intelligence en Guerre* (Paris, 1945) p. 216
2. Tollet, *La Classe ouvrière dans la Résistance* p. 186
3. ibid. p. 187
4. P. Delanoue, *Les Enseignants* p. 227
5. ibid. p. 239
6. ibid. p. 268
7. Parrot, op. cit. p. 173
8. Aragon, *Matisse, a novel* (trans. Collins, 1972) p. 183
9. ibid. pp. 143–144
10. F. Mauriac, *Le Cahier noir* (Paris 1945 ed.) p. 37
11. ibid. p. 46
12. R. Penrose, *In the Service of the People* (London, 1945)
13. Parrot, op. cit. p. 275
14. ibid. pp. 91–100
15. Parrot, op. cit. p. 152
16. Aragon, *Crêve cœur* (London, 1944) p. 36
17. ibid. p. 41
18. *La Diane française* (Paris, 1945)

Chapter 15

1943–1944

MAQUIS

Frères, ayons du courage!
Nous qui ne sommes pas casqués,
Ni bottés, ni gantés, ni bien élevés,
Un rayon s'allume en nos veines,
Notre lumière nous revient . . .

Maurice Hervent, *L'Honneur des poètes*

Brothers, let's take courage!
We who have no helmets,
Nor boots, nor gloves, nor education,
Have a flame burning in our veins
Giving us back our light . . .

Looking ahead into 1944 was like peering down a dark tunnel murky with *Nacht und Nebel*—but at last there was a glimmer of daylight ahead. Along a 4,000-mile front the Red Army was counter-attacking in ten mighty offensives; from Norway to Greece, in Denmark, Holland, Yugoslavia, the underground patriots were harassing the Nazis and pinning down whole divisions; while in Italy, although the Allied advance was slow, the Italian partisans were up in arms, the workers striking, the Germans in retreat. The Resistance in France took heart from the anti-fascist offensive everywhere and the conviction that the Allied armies would surely arrive soon.

Sabotage assumed major proportions as more and more *réfractaires* joined one or other group. Differences of political opinion seemed less important now that so many people were in the struggle together, and the C.N.R. worked loyally as a co-ordinating body. Drops of arms were far more frequent than hitherto, thanks perhaps to Yeo-Thomas and to repeated representations from France. Unfortunately, the main concern of the Allied authorities and of de Gaulle's provisional government was to keep control of the Resistance movement, suspected of being too much in the hands of the Communists.

The limited amounts of material and arms from abroad were directed wherever possible to the "safe" organisations rather than to the F.T.P. who might use them for their own possibly revolutionary ends. Although in February 1943 de Gaulle had declared to the P.C.F. that "an effective co-ordination of Resistance organisations is indispensable to our common goal—the liberation of France as soon as possible", he hoped that the Gaullist leadership would be unquestioned. As Tillon writes, "the F.T.P.s gallantry was admitted by the General but he disputed their rights to benefit by the material support given to organisations controlled by Passy".[1]

By agreement with General Delestraint in 1943, the activities of the F.T.P.s and de Gaulle's Secret Army were to be co-ordinated, each organisation forming a liaison committee to ensure the distribution of arms in proportion to the respective membership, and to give priority to those actually fighting. But now that France was becoming a battlefield again, with thousands of untrained, enthusiastic volunteers wanting to take up arms, the questions arose "Under whose direction?", and "With what strategy?"

For months the F.T.P. leaders warned the C.N.R. that British and American agents, and those of Passy and Soustelle, "were making every effort to direct the volunteers into large formations within the structure of the professional army", and to abandon the spontaneous guerrilla warfare so suitable to the present conditions. The F.T.P. national committee in May 1944 declared that France's war would never be won without the help of the patriots who were now not trusted or armed by the B.C.R.A.: "France is a battle ground, bombed by the Allies, scene of hundreds of skirmishes and ambushes where our martyrs are avenged. . . . Frenchmen are surprised to be getting so little encouragement and help in playing their decisive role. As if there could be any other aim in France than that of combining as a great nation to win freedom from Fascism, now that everybody knows what Fascism is!"[2]

There were two opposing conceptions offered to those entering the Resistance: (1) to join massive units, guaranteed arms, allied aid, even money, controlled by unknown strategists in London; (2) to group as and when the situation arose, with the manpower required for a particular action, and never in numbers which would be a security risk.

These two positions were manifest at all the resistance groups' meetings; one was dominated by *attentisme*, the other by a concern for efficiency and awareness of the recent qualitative change in the nature of the Resistance. The underground press on the whole was against the idea of massive groupings and urged the need to

have the Maquis integrated in the guerrilla army right up to the
moment when insurrection would be needed for the final liberation
of the country. *France d'abord*, for instance, wrote:

"Thousands of 'réfractaires' have become soldiers and these
soldiers are one with millions of civilians. An army of citizen-
soldiers is ready to rise up. . . . In spite of long out-dated calculations
nobody will prevent a people of 15 million patriots, inspired by their
passion for freedom, from sharing in their own liberation."

"The Corrèze peasants know that non-intervention means death
to them, because they see the Milice setting fire to their farms and
murdering their families in isolated places, under the pretext that
there are patriots hidden there. Those patriots are their brothers or
their sons, helping them in the fields! So the peasant burns down his
barns himself, drives his cattle towards the Maquis, and puts his
family under the protection of the citizen-soldiers whom he joins so
that he too can carry a gun."

"That's what the war in France is about, though the *attentistes*
won't recognise it. . . . There would be no national uprising if it were
only to consist of battles of maquisards and partisans. It would only
be the limited action of parachute divisions, not the mass rising of a
third front taking the *boches* in the rear, paralysing their supplies, ·
overwhelming their occupation."[3]

However, instead of listening to the underground press and encouraging the citizen-soldiers in guerrilla tactics (which might lead
to a national insurrection beyond official remote control) the
Gaullists and "Anglo-Saxon" military people insisted on regiment-
ing their followers into regular army formations; they provided them
with arms at the expense of the F.T.P. irregulars, and massed them
in certain areas where, alas, they were to be easy targets for the
Germans. Subsequently the mistake of building up massive legions
for defence, instead of numbers of small units able to attack whenever the chance came, was recognised—too late to save countless
valuable French lives.

On the insistence of the Allied authorities, then, young Frenchmen were persuaded to leave the towns and villages in or near which
they had found refuge with the local Maquis, and to assemble in big
formations in several remote areas, to wait for supplies and air
support which would (it was said) accompany the Allied landings.

In mid-January 1944 Radio London called on the *réfractaires* to
make their way to the plateau of Glières in Haute-Savoie, regardless
of the arctic conditions of the high Alps at that time of year. By

March there were 457 volunteers on the plateau, cold, hungry, isolated, kept going only by their belief that they would soon be taking part in the longed-for liberation. The Vichy police surrounded the "citadel" area, and supplies could only be brought in by arrangement with them. Naturally this led to many disasters through treachery and inefficiency; one officer, Morel, who tried to negotiate with the G.M.R. (Mobile Reserve Group) was murdered by a fascist policeman. The maquisards were reduced to most inadequate rations, and pitiful appeals were made by Morel's successor, Captain Anjot, for food, medical supplies, clothing, radios and arms. Anjot wrote to the Lyons F.F.I. command, that "the parachute supplies asked for several times were never sent, so since 25 March the men have been on a ration of 100 grammes of bread a day."

Arms were dropped late, and were mainly light weapons. Anjot appealed for more of everything, radioing to London in desperation, "On our side we will do our duty, *but we must have help!*"

Help was not forthcoming, and as Henri Michel writes, "The Germans took over, using nearly 12,000 men, supported by heavy artillery and aeroplanes. The attack began on 18 March. The maquisards held out for a fortnight. Most of them were killed, either in the battles, or executed (nearly 200) after capture; some were deported after being tortured."

Those in favour of the Glières operations bore a heavy responsibility, whether British, American or Gaullist; the B.C.R.A. encouraged the volunteers to think they were holding an impregnable position and would be supported by the "Anglo-Saxon armed forces"; the Anglo-Saxons did not deny this.

Worse, the same mistake, of assembling large forces in exposed positions, immobilised and lacking arms, was repeated a few months later, just before D-Day, with even more disastrous results. This time, several thousand volunteers were assembled in the Vercors area in Haute-Savoie, "with the idea, which proved unfortunate", says Henri Michel, "of forming a sort of fortress in the centre of France. . . . Poorly equipped with artillery and deprived of all air support, they were attacked in the centre of the plateau by S.S. divisions dropped from gliders, at the end of July."[4]

In the operation as originally conceived by General Delestraint and his colleagues Yves Farge and Pierre Dalloz, the plateau was to be used as a base for aerial landing by the Allies; several airborne divisions would act from this base in co-operation with the coastal landings. But when D-Day came there was no joint action—the Vercors was abandoned, left without enough arms, so that the plateau was merely a trap for the patriots. Dalloz reported to the B.C.R.A. in Algiers that "there is no question of settling in the Vercors but merely of taking up positions there, so as to come out and attack the enemy. . . ." But the orders from Passy and Soustelle were exactly the opposite. The Vercors volunteers who believed they were acting in liaison with the Allies ". . . saw no airborne forces except those of the S.S."[5]

The story has been told, vividly and in detail, by Tillon and others, and we need only mention the most essential features.

The Vercors (according to my guidebook) "is a pastoral and wooded plateau (of some 30 by 12 miles) broken by mountain ridges and deep valleys. . . . Thanks to its inaccessibility it became a rallying-ground for the resistance to the Germans in 1942–43, and by 1944 some 4,000 maquisards here constituted a well-trained and well-armed force, harassing the enemy communications."[6]

Tillon in his account contradicts the term "well-armed". He says "there were about 3,000 men on the plateau, placed at strategic points supplied with small arms, but no artillery nor mortars in spite of repeated requests to Algiers". The Germans surrounding the area had "as many infantry troops as they needed . . . provided with heavy armaments": they had artillery, tanks and planes based near Valence.[7]

The small villages dotting the plateau—La Chapelle, St Agnan, Les Baraques-en-Vercors (all "destroyed" or "badly damaged" according to the guide) were frequently bombed, with heavy French casualties; on 11 July, the F.C.N.L.'s military delegate in London, General Koenig, wired congratulations to the Vercors commandant —"a few cannons or mortars would have been more welcome", comments Tillon. Cables had been sent to London and Algiers on 23 June: "Make haste, we are having a tough time. Even limited parachute units would be valuable . . ." and "After heroic resistance St Nizier fell on 15th. No parachute drop as hoped. . . . Feel lack of mortars severely. Parachute troops badly needed." Help came too late to be of use on 14 July, and indeed made matters worse. A massive parachute drop by eighty-two American bombers was carried out in broad daylight with a striking display of national colours and tricolor flares. German planes, amply notified, at once machine-gunned the area, making it impossible to pick up the dropped supplies. On 21 July the Germans surrounded the Maquis, simultaneously dropping airborne troops in the central area. Two days later they had attained all their objectives. They used the landing ground at Vassieux, carefully prepared for the Allied planes so ardently expected, to drop 400 S.S. men for attacks on the Maquis at chosen spots.

Protected by their fighter planes, six in the air continually, the S.S. took up positions in local houses and with their superior weapons decimated the maquisards who threw themselves valiantly but uselessly against them—without anti-tank weapons or mortars it was hopeless to try to dislodge the Nazis from their positions. The French troops were smashed, the inhabitants of the village of Vassieux massacred. The local hospital, with its patients and medical staff, was the victim of unspeakable atrocities.

˙ The disaster of Vercors, like that of Glières, and of Mont-Mouchet, les Manisses (Ardennes), Saint Marcel (Morbihan) and other places where large formations of Maquis were ordered to wait in the expectation of supplies which never arrived, was mainly due to certain politicians' dislike of the Communist-led partisans. Tillon writes bitterly that "after having engaged the Maquis on an extremely dangerous course, London and Algiers abandoned them to the fury of the Nazis".[8]

The last telegram from the Vercors summed up the drama: "La Chapelle, Vassieux, St Martin, bombed by German planes. Enemy troops parachuted on to Vassieux. We demand immediate Allied bombardment. Promised to hold out for three weeks; have waited six weeks. Morale excellent but men's opinion will turn against you if help not sent at once. And we will agree with them in saying that London and Algiers have failed to understand our situation and must be considered criminals and cowards!"[9]

The Communist Commissaire for Air of the Provisional Government, Fernand Grenier, was not shown any of the Vercors telegrams which were intercepted by Soustelle's secret service department. It seemed as though someone highly placed wanted the blame for the inaction and catastrophe to fall on Grenier. The latter had, in fact, weeks before urged de Gaulle to authorise the formation and dispatch of an air squadron to help the F.F.I. of *Zone sud*. This was to be under the order of Colonel Morlaix, a hero in the 1940 Battle of Britain. Grenier planned to recuperate bombers standing idle in Syria, and to put all available training planes in Morocco into use. Three times the number of pilots needed had already volunteered to serve; French and Algerian Communists were working day and night to produce containers to be parachuted to the Maquis. Grenier, impatient at the General's delay in discussing his proposals, went to him on 26 June pointing out the urgent need to send arms and parachutists. On 28 June the Committee for National Defence approved the proposals and two decrees were immediately prepared for de Gaulle's signature. But he ignored them, went off to America for nearly a week (while 30,000 Nazis attacked 3,500 maquisards in Vercors) came back and returned the decrees to Grenier with a curt note "Organisation insufficiently prepared". New plans were put before him on 15 July and turned down on 22 July with the terse comment, "On ne peut créer un corps aérien."

On 24 July, hearing the news of the terrible happenings at Vercors, Grenier, deeply shocked and angry, called a press conference and described what he had tried to do. "Despite my efforts, aerial help to the F.F.I. was made impossible. . . . Like all Communists I disso-ciate myself from this *attentisme* [delaying tactics] which we consider a crime against France." Later that day, on learning of the final disaster, he wrote a furious letter to de Gaulle, which led to a flaming row between them. In front of the assembled Provisional Govern-ment, the General read out the letter and ordered Grenier to retract or give up his post. The Minister defended himself at length and with vigour: "I described the birth of the first F.T.P. groups, their heroism, their military importance, my struggle in London to get them arms, my suffering at seeing them always underestimated, in-deed abandoned by Fighting France. . . . Here in Algiers when I wanted to help the F.F.I. I came up against a blank wall; and when I learned of the Vercors tragedy my indignation burst out. . . ."

Apart from Billoux and one or two more, the other ministers, Gaullists to a man, opposed Grenier. Believing his duty to the Resistance required him to stay in the government, he agreed, with considerable bitterness, to retract what he had said in his letter. This did not prevent de Gaulle dismissing him two months later, with the excuse that since his letter the General could no longer trust him.[10] It is interesting to read in de Gaulle's memoirs the comment that "Fernand Grenier was induced by a manœuvre of his party during the battles of the Vercors, publicly to adopt an attitude contrary to the government's solidarity."[11] Two years later, a defamatory article appeared in the Gaullist periodical *Carrefour*, written by Rémy, and purporting to show that Grenier had sabotaged aid to Vercors. The former Minister had no difficulty in refuting the slander, by documents and eye-witness reports; but it was a nasty example of anti-Communism posing as history. The truth was that responsibility for the disaster lay squarely on those who had allowed the Vercors operation to proceed without full co-operation from the Allies; the Allied Command had made no provision for carrying out the "Montagnard" plan, which was lost or forgotten somewhere in Whitehall during the preparations for the Normandy landings.

From April 1944 on, General Koenig issued orders to the F.F.I. Unfortunately he knew nothing at all about guerrilla war, and was only interested in official military procedure, as soon became clear to the Maquis leaders (who certainly did not need a rigid hierarchy in London). Furthermore, Koenig was a screen for the B.C.R.A. operational office manned by Passy's anti-communists; on their side they were, first, unwilling to help the F.T.P. and, secondly, unable to act except by agreement with the Allied High Command; and the latter, in their turn, were not interested in helping the maquisards who had been stuck away in remote parts of France by the tiresome Free French government. Responsibility was disclaimed by de Gaulle, who threw the blame on the Anglo-Americans. The B.C.R.A. office continued to intervene in all affairs touching the Liberation in the same spirit of *attentisme*, with the same procedures as before—while the British and U.S. Secret Services continued to interfere in de Gaulle's affairs. Yet, if there had been co-operation, if the armed forces of the Alpine Maquis had been organised as part of the Allied operations, correlated with the landings in Provence, and acting as part of the guerrilla forces of the interior, their units would have played an important and victorious role in the Liberation.

* * *

At the same time that the Vercors tragedy was being enacted, the F.T.P. were fighting guerrilla actions all over France involving far fewer patriots but with striking results. In the Aube department, for instance, in mid-June 1944 the Maquis of the Lisière des Bois, a group of 320 men based in a wood, attacked by some 3,000 Germans, kept the latter at bay for eight hours and finally drove them off leaving 252 dead and many wounded. The maquisards lost twenty-seven men. "After the battle, the patriots divided into groups of ten men who went back into the woods or to hospitable farms to carry on the struggle. . . ."[12]

The picture was the same everywhere in the country during the early summer of 1944. As the leader of a Maquis in central France put it: "In the plains and marshes of Berry, the undulating country-side of the Limousin, in the bright valleys of Périgord and the deep forests of Creuse and Corrèze, young men from all over France—new men—helped by a bitter, iron-hard peasantry, carried on an exhausting, unending war against the enemy and his mercenaries . . . R 5 was their name and that of their battlefield. Their orders were 'strike and disappear'; although they did not wage battles defending tragically costly fortresses, they carried out thousands of ambushes, and armed strikes by the hundred. . . ."[13]

Out of countless stories, here is just one, typical of the heroism, tragedy, initiative, of that time. The young men of the Maquis at Argenton-sur-Creuse decided to seize a German arms train on the Toulouse–Paris line, take off its load of petrol, and drive it into a siding to explode the ammunition on board. To do this they had to overcome the local police. Entering the Garde Mobile barracks, they managed by a mixture of force and persuasion to disarm the police-men and to get them into the Maquis ranks. With the police on one side of the ammunition train and the F.T.P. on the other, the twenty-three Germans guarding it were soon overpowered and the operation appeared to be highly successful. Unfortunately, several Germans managed to escape and to let the Wehrmacht at Limoges know what had happened. In the afternoon a punitive Nazi expedition arrived in Argenton, with ten lorries, two armoured cars and at least 400 S.S. men. The Maquis told the local people to take refuge, and began to defend the village, fighting till their reserves were exhausted, then making their escape into the nearby woods. "Then the carnage began in the street that had resisted the Germans. They broke into houses, seized the inhabitants and shot them on their doorsteps, women, girls, children. Blood ran down the pavements. Marching down the street the Nazis picked up 200 hostages and forced them into a yard where they were kept all night, being told at intervals that they would be shot in ten minutes. Thanks to the intervention of a German-speaking teacher most were released next morning, but ten were taken to Limoges and executed. At last, the Nazi howls stopped. While the S.S. got drunk in the cafés, the people of Argen-ton counted their dead, fifty-four civilians and ten soldiers, and the hostages. The same day, other S.S. men took the road to Oradour. . . ."[14]

*　　*　　*

The background to the story of Oradour, which we now, painfully, have to look at, is the whole area of Southern France between Bordeaux and Limoges—the wild shrubby slopes of the Lot, the green and golden Dordogne, and the friendly small towns settled by the rivers and streams of the fertile Limousin valleys.

The Nazis marched into and over this peaceful country in November 1942 and made their base at Bordeaux, with a sub-Kommandantur at Limoges. During 1943 they concerned themselves with military matters, and left the job of policing the interior mainly to Vichy. But by 1944 the Maquis had grown to such proportions in the area that the German Command ordered widespread operations to "eradicate" them—an almost impossible task, as one sees, reading and hearing accounts of the partisans' universal presence in these parts, and the strong local support they enjoyed.

One of the German divisions most actively engaged in these operations was the S.S. *Das Reich*, a formation of fanatic Nazis. Their movements can be traced from a marked map, dropped by a soldier and found later near Oradour: they roamed the countryside, staying odd nights at Barsa and Langon, three weeks at St Médard, where there is a large gunpowder factory, going on via Agen and Valence, and reaching the Cahors region on 8 April. They stayed nearly a month in the Lot and Aveyron departments. Ostensibly they were fighting the Maquis; in fact, faced with the dangers of guerrilla-hunting they preferred to take on the unarmed villagers. The tablets beside the roads today testify to the shootings of hostages, singly or in groups, or atrocities like the murders at Carlux, where the Nazis threw incendiary bombs into a living-room, killing all the children at a birthday party, and at Frayssinet, a tiny village south of Gourdon, where twelve hostages were shot and houses burned down, on the pretext that they were helping the Maquis. Wherever the S.S. went they brought terror and death, and after D-Day their bestialities reached a climax of dreadfulness, so far unknown to Western (so-called) civilisation.

As soon as the news of the 6 June landings reached them the Germans' main objective became the blocking of the Allies' advance in Normandy. Company after company headed northward. Journeys were a nightmare for them, with railways sabotaged— trains derailed, men and munitions blown sky high—roads blocked and ambushed. They travelled in a state of extreme nervousness, shooting and burning en route, but many of the atrocities could not be explained by soldiers losing their heads and killing out of panic. In the case of *Das Reich*, repression was cold-blooded and systematic, and the operation at Oradour was an example of methodical brutality, made to terrify the populations of the area into submission. Oradour, 13 miles from Limoges, 15 from St Junien, where the S.S. were quartered for two nights, was a quiet little town, where families from the north had taken refuge, not at all a centre for the Maquis. The S.S. company *Der Führer* (splinter of the *Das Reich* division) sent from St Junien on 10 June had orders which they conscientiously carried out to the last drop of blood. This has been proved by documents found after the event, and published.[15] The most telling proof, however, is the village itself, every one of its 400 houses burned out, gaunt skeletons where the clock on the wall, the rusty sewing machine, the baby's buckled pram are mute accusers of the monstrous crime. Of the 700 inhabitants, nearly 500, mostly women and children, were burned alive in the church, 200 men were shot down inside their sheds and barns which were then set alight: 642 people were accounted for. About twenty escaped alive, one woman alone from the church. The S.S. having done their "duty" retired to Nieul, a hamlet 20 miles to the north, bearing much loot from the houses which they had sacked before setting them on fire. Taking over Nieul school they proceeded to eat up the stolen food and to drink large quantities of Oradour's wine. Shouting and bawling, they kept the population in a state of terror all night, before setting off north on the 11th, killing and burning on their way.

The people of the region were at first incredulous, then shocked, horrified, and—far from being cowed—resolute in anger. The terrible task of clearing up Oradour, burying its victims and livestock, was undertaken by neighbouring villagers under a medical officer, the Red Cross and local health services. An enormous crowd attended the funeral service, held in Limoges Cathedral in spite of efforts to prevent it by the German police with the connivance of the regional Préfet. The Bishop, Monseigneur Roustouil, also spoke in the cathedral on 16 June, letting his flock know that he had expressed his grief and indignation to the German general "that the church of Oradour had been soiled by the execution of hundreds of women, young girls and children, and profaned by the destruction of the Tabernacle and the removal of the Eucharist"; he prayed for the souls of the victims and for God's pardon for the sacrilege committed.[16] As a friend of Vichy, he could hardly have been expected to make a political speech condemning the Germans, but many must have thought that stronger words might have been in order.

The protestant Pastor Chaudier spoke rather more forcefully: "The terror spread over a small Limousin town dictates a duty not only to honour and mourn the victims. The human conscience and the Christian conscience must join in protest against such murders. . . ."[17]

It was left to the underground press to express popular sorrow and indignation, and this it did in hundreds of newspapers and leaflets, the most telling expression being that of *Les Lettres françaises* which published a special issue, "Sur le ruines de la morale" in 20,000 copies. It was based on an account given by a railwayman who came home from work to Oradour to find his house a smoking ruin, his family vanished in the holocaust, and an elegant German officer complacently surveying the desolate scene. The text of this account had been given to the *Lettres françaises* by Georges Duhamel (an author honoured for his help to struggling young Resistance writers) and printed without comment but with a passage from Victor Hugo, calling the French people in 1870 to take up arms:

"Now, at once, without losing a day or an hour, let everyone—rich, poor, worker, bourgeois, labourer—pick up, at home or on the ground outside, anything and everything like a weapon or a projectile. Roll rocks, pile up paving stones, turn furrows into graves. . . . Into battle, you stones of our holy soil, smash the invaders with mother France's bones. O citizens, what you are flinging at them, those pebbles, they are France, our Country."[18]

And whether or not this was read, whether the pebbles would have availed much or little against the Wehrmacht, the spirit of the message was widespread, and the masses of French people were ready to respond. Their response came, electrifying and dramatic, in the historic days and weeks following the news of the Allied armies' arrival in France.

NOTES

1. C. Tillon, *Les F.T.P.* p. 258
2. ibid. p. 284
3. *France d'abord*, 1.6.1944
4. H. Michel, *Histoire de la Résistance* p. 100
5. Tillon, op. cit. p. 311
6. Muirhead, *Southern France* p. 59
7. Tillon, op. cit. pp. 305–306
8. ibid. pp. 307–309

9. F. Grenier, *C'était ainsi* p. 251
10. ibid. pp. 252, 255
11. C. de Gaulle, *Memoirs: Salvation* p. 11
12. Tillon, op. cit. p. 330
13. *Résistance, Indre et Vallée du Cher*, I p. 9
14. ibid. pp. 13–18
15. *Oradour-sur-Glane*, Official Report (Limoges, 1970)
16. ibid. p. 128
17. ibid. p. 130
18. Parrot, *L'Intelligence en guerre* p. 274

Chapter 16

D-DAY AND AFTER

Au quatrième été de notre apocalypse
Une étrange paleur parait sur l'horizon
Est-ce qu'on toucherait à la fin d l'éclipse
L'espoir palpite dans la paille des prisons
Entendez-vous gémir la nuit comme une porte
C'est l'aurore qui fait les bourreaux blémissants.

Aragon, *Le Musée Grevin*, p. 47

In the fourth summer of our apocalypse
A strange pallor appears on the horizon
Can we be reaching the end of the eclipse?
Hope throbs in the straw of the prisons.
Do you hear the night groaning like a door?
It is the dawn, which makes the tyrants blench.

On Friday, 5 June 1944, U.S. and British armed forces under General Ike Eisenhower embarked from somewhere on the Hampshire coast in a fleet of 5,000 ships, dragging Mulberry harbours and landing craft with them over a choppy sea, in Operation Overlord. Hidden by deepest secrecy and the darkness of a cloudy night, protected by the powerful support of 2,000 planes, they crossed the Channel, reaching France at 9 a.m. on the 6th and landing 156,000 men and 20,000 vehicles at different points of the Normandy coast. Many more followed—totalling eventually some 875,000 men.[1]

De Gaulle's *France Combattante* contributed 90 vessels and 7 groups of aircraft to Overlord. At a conference in December 1943 de Gaulle had threatened to withdraw French troops from Italy if the Allies did not guarantee "that a French division will be transported to Britain to participate in Operation Overlord and to liberate Paris".

When news broke of the extraordinary achievement of organisation, teamwork and bravery, bringing the longed-for allies to their shores, the spirits of the French people rose to a pinnacle of exultation; people celebrated the landings with bottles of champagne saved up for this occasion over the years, and dancing to homemade music. "Everyone began talking to everyone else in an uncontrollable explosion of joy", according to one British witness in the countryside,[2] while in Paris, said Simone de Beauvoir, "the days following were one long fête. Everybody greeted each other laughing out loud. How the sun shone, how the streets radiated gaiety!"[3]

But there were terrible tribulations too, during the next few days and weeks: Oradour, Vercors, Tulle martyred by the Germans, and Norman towns and villages mercilessly bombed by the Allied planes. Owing to bad weather conditions Montgomery's plan to take Caen immediately could not be carried out, and to prevent the Germans consolidating their forces in and around the city Allied Command ordered air-raids almost as cruel as those on Germany. Wave after wave of Lancasters and Halifaxes went over Caen throughout 6 June, sowing systematic destruction; "the rescuers fought desperately in smoke, flames, dust, rubble, ruins, against death, while Caen blazed, blazed, blazed!!!" wrote one horror-stricken eye-witness.[4] An enormous pillar of smoke was visible from fifty miles away. Hundreds died and thousands lost their homes. The bombings went on day after day for a month—the last being on 9 July when 460 aircraft each dropped five tons of bombs (i.e. 2,300 tons) and among other targets totally destroyed the university then being used as refugee centre and storehouse. Local resistance was diverted to rescue work—on a massive and impressive scale—and to sending brave volunteers with messages across the battle lines imploring the Allies to spare certain parts of the city.

When the Canadian division finally entered and "liberated" Caen there was little left of the town. "The population had declined from 32,000 to 12,000." Other places suffered proportionately: "Avranches had no more than 35 left out of 6,000; Saint Lo, which the Americans called the 'capital of ruins' sheltered no more than ten inhabitants. Both there and elsewhere whole families were buried under the rubble." In Le Havre, the last Norman town to be freed, where 1,500 tons of high explosives were dropped in two hours, "thousands were killed in an inferno, burned alive by whole families at a time"; there were between 2,000 and 3,000 dead, while 35,000 were completely bombed out of 10,500 houses.

If I have given space to these bombings out of proportion to the subject matter of this book, it is because they are too often forgotten or accepted as a normal part of modern war; also because it is now recognised but not always admitted that had the Allies understood the role of the French Resistance and incorporated its forces into their plans there would have been no need for the raids with their toll of tragedy and harvest of bitterness. The writer Julien Guillemord asked, "How could these people, mourning their many thousand dead, most of them burnt alive as a result of useless bombing, welcome their liberators? . . . British soldiers were seen in tears by the graves . . . for they too could not accept this devastation for which there was no military necessity whatever."[5] At a conference in April 1944 when bombing of French towns was discussed Churchill opposed it with all his authority, saying "Post-war France must be our friend". Eisenhower's "strategic necessities" however won the day.

Yet in spite of this treatment by the U.S.A.F. and R.A.F., the people of north-west France stood staunchly by the Allied forces, fighting against the Germans however and whenever they could. D-Day had been the signal for the Resistance to go into action, to which the F.F.I. volunteers responded as energetically and courageously as the soldiers in uniform; they multiplied attacks on every German post and stronghold, blowing up even more pylons and sabotaging more trains, obtaining and bringing much valuable information to Allied H.Q.

There were in June an estimated half million men in the F.F.I. which had grown as if by spontaneous generation from about 100,000 in January. The Allied authorities had little idea of the potential of the underground forces, and saw the F.F.I.'s role as one of support with intelligence and some activity in the rear; Gaullist Headquarters recognised the possibilities of the volunteer formations but were not keen to give them unqualified support—strongly disliking the idea of a popular mass army impatient for action and possibly inclined to "reckless adventures". All the top brass outside France would have preferred the soldiers within it to be a tidy disciplined body under a conventional command. But there they were—in Normandy and Brittany alone, 80,000 partisans, waiting only for the word to fight for the freedom of their country, if possible in the front line.

Here let us take a brief look at the make-up of the F.F.I. There had been up to February 1944 broadly speaking three forms of military organisation in France: first, that favoured by the Gaullists who believed in putting the *Armée Secrète* (A.S.) into the hands of career soldiers, in formations of a professional nature well armed by the Allies and linked by the S.O.E. and B.C.R.A. networks to London; secondly there were the groupings on the F.T.P. model, led by units of six men with subsidiary groups of thirty, working along guerrilla lines from the basis of the hundreds of local Maquis.[6] This was the overwhelming tendency of the A.S., and according to the German general Kaltenbrunner, 80,000 volunteers were already mobilised in such formations as early as June 1943. These men did not believe in *attentisme* and the partisans were the leaders in spectacular activities which weekly attracted hundreds of new recruits. They were full of enthusiasm but always short of weapons, and apart from the arms daringly seized from the enemy, their arsenals consisted mainly of home-made Molotov cocktails, hand-grenades and supplies of explosives made in local workshops and in the laboratories of friendly scientists.

A third type of military organisation was the re-formed "Armistice army", consisting predominantly of former regular officers with a good many weapons at their disposal. But although there were not nearly enough ranks to make full use of these arms their leaders did not dare let the "irregulars" have them, and after the Germans invaded the Z.S. in November 1942 most of the arms depots had fallen into enemy hands. When the French army was officially dissolved by the occupying Germans the O.R.A. (*Organisation de Résistance Armée*) was formed; it kept its "regular" character, hung on to what arms were left to it and refused to engage in any action before D-Day. As one British observer remarked, "in June 1943 very few former French officers were prepared to share the hard life of the maquisards. A year later, officers emerged in droves, donning freshly pressed uniforms smelling strongly of mothballs." Hence their nickname, "naphthalards".[7]

The F.F.I. organisation was created in February 1944 by agreement between de Gaulle and the C.N.R. to include all these military groups under a plan which divided France into twelve regions each with a leader acceptable to all sections. London-based General Koenig had the tough job of co-ordinating internal activity in France with the Allied plans. The "Anglo-Americans" accepted this, (Roosevelt at long last having agreed to let the F.P.G. take responsibility in France instead of his intended Allied Military Government, A.M.G.O.T.), though having little faith in the military efficacity of the Resistance: "They had to see it in action to believe in it", as the historian, Michel, says.

In April 1944 a plan was worked out jointly for using the F.F.I. on D-Day and during the following weeks. The main battle zones were to be left to the Allies and the Maquis relegated chiefly to the "non-operational" zone in remote parts of the country where they would paralyse the Germans' communications and blow up petrol and munition dumps. Their potential was so far underestimated that the arms and planes they needed to carry out this allotted role were not supplied to them; the Allies sent over only missions of a few parachutists with far too little equipment to fight the Wehrmacht. "The F.F.I. should have had 60 tons a day, but in March 1944 only 20 tons were dropped in France. So only half the F.F.I. were armed on D-Day; they had no artillery, tanks, anti-aircraft, anti-tank guns or air support of any kind."[8] The gradual stream of recruits to the F.F.I. none the less swelled to a flood after 6 June, news of the "débarquement" acting as a catalyst. To their astonishment, on 10 June an order came from Koenig in London, *"Freiner au maximum activité guérilla"* (put the brake on the guerrillas); the reason given being that it was impossible to supply enough arms and ammunition. In face of amazed disbelief this order was repeated on 14 June, the day de Gaulle landed in France. The F.T.P. took no notice and went into action wherever the possibility presented itself—and that was all over the north-west.

Owing to varying numbers of German troops, conditions differed from area to area. In Normandy there were seventeen Wehrmacht divisions and as most of the local population had been evacuated inland or were pinned down by the bombing raids, there were relatively few French to do battle; so activity there was limited to sabotage and harassment by small teams of daring men with very limited means, outside the areas being strafed by the Allied planes. But in Brittany the F.F.I. volunteers waged pitched battles of considerable scale. From mid-June on there were 50,000 men in small groups all over the four Breton departments, day and night worrying the enemy with ambushes and skirmishes, and stopping trains over the whole region. The Germans did their utmost to dislodge them in fierce fighting at Malestroit, in the Morbihan on 18 June (where 2,000 F.F.I. were involved and lost 200 men) and on 27 June in the forest of Vioreau, north of Nantes (where the partisans had to retreat after killing about 100 of the Wehrmacht).

By the end of July the F.F.I. virtually controlled the north-west region. Their bulletins give some idea of the spectacular sabotage: "In July the Côtes du Nord F.F.I. caused 200 rail 'accidents', 40 derailments, made 300 breaks in telecommunications, 50 ambushes, 30 attacks on enemy posts, and captured a big petrol depot" and so on. The Breton troops worked with the Allies in freeing many towns and villages, often forging ahead of the armies, and in fact entering Nantes and Chateaudun on 18/19 August, well before them.[9]

It was the Bretons of the F.F.I. who were left in charge of mopping-up operations in the area, and their achievements included freeing a large part of the coast, besieging Brest, Lorient and Saint Nazaire, and taking some 20,000 prisoners. They held up the German divisions trying to reach Normandy from Nantes for a whole fortnight, so that these only arrived after the fighting was finished, and ended up as captives of the F.T.P. As Michel says, "What would the Allies' position have been had they had to fight alone to free the towns and villages of France? How much more devastation and ruin?"[10]

All too often, even after the June and July raids, the Americans decided to "liberate" without the help of the F.F.I. by bombing towns still occupied by the Germans. The results were tragic, as in the case (3 September) of the village of Telgruc, where some of the enemy were ensconced in forts. Colonel Eon, the French commander of the S.A.S. mission Aloes, wrote to the U.S. general responsible that "German contingents, comfortably sheltered from your bombing in the fortifications of which my 2me Bureau have given you details, will be delighted to witness the massacre of patriots who have till now been their most redoubtable enemies", and who deserved "some other reward from you than to be massacred". The heavy bombers came over three times, and killed 800 civilians as well as F.F.I. men and even some U.S. soldiers. General Earnest continued to send bombers in attempts to destroy German-held forts in spite of urgent appeals from Eon to attack these from the sea. "The absence of co-operation from the fleet," said Eon, "has gravely prejudiced operations against these forts. . . . The massive air and artillery action has caused immense damage to the civilian populations without effective results."[11]

There were to be many similar complaints from F.F.I. leaders during the following weeks and in spite of enthusiasm for the Allied cause a good deal of disillusion among the volunteers who felt they were regarded as second class soldiers. Some also complained bitterly of their treatment by the G.I.s: "We have seen American units systematically destroying guns captured from the enemy, and preventing our men, who are very short of footwear, from acquiring boots from prisoners; while the Americans cram the German prisoners with food and give them new boots, our men die of hunger and go barefoot through the gorse."[12] But the main grievance was always the lack of weapons which had been promised to the Maquis and never materialised, or had fallen into the hands of reactionary militarists who made no secret of their antipathy to partisans and franc-tireurs. De Gaulle's Military Regional Delegates (D.M.R.) had been sent to France from Algiers with the ostensible task of receiving arms and distributing them to the F.F.I. But there were repeated protests that the D.M.R. were boycotting the Resistance forces; for instance, from Seine-et-Oise, in June: "This department has received no arms in spite of dire need. The D.M.R. blackmail us for weapons and money. . . ." Rol-Tanguy, commander for the Ile-de-France, wrote on 10 July that to his pressing demands for cash and arms, the D.M.R. answer was, "systematically and briefly", "nothing available". Later it turned out that the F.T.P. of the Pas-de-Calais had just 100 revolvers and 12 submachine-guns between them; the Maquis of Spezet in Brittany had four pistols, (two non-functioning) between them; in the south, Marseilles' partisans boasted about 100 weapons, in Lyons, 150 volunteers out of 4,000 had guns. All over France, the F.F.I. armed themselves as best they could: "the peasants at Douarnenez fell on the Germans *à coups de sabots*, to tear the guns out of their hands". Ambushes, raids on Pétainist police posts, attacks on German sentries yielded hard-won gains but nothing like enough. In June the Maquis in Ain had to refuse a thousand recruits for want of arms. And it was the same everywhere, to the fury and frustration of the volunteers, panting to go into the attack.

Where, they asked, were all the weapons going? There were plenty being parachuted:"They were literally pouring down in some areas," says Tillon. The truth was that "the H.Q.s in London were sending them only to their trusted agents, who were stocking them up. . . ." Why? and what for? Pétain's minister of propaganda, Philippe Henriot, gave a cynical answer on Vichy radio on 15 February 1944: "The British have become the source of supply for arms to Darnand"; the Milice was amply equipped with British Sten guns; and radio transmitters were seized by the Nazis because the B.C.R.A. reception committees did not give them to the partisans. Thirty tons of arms in the Nièvre region fell into Nazi hands, one example among many, causing a F.T.P. leader to lament, "up to now our depots have supplied the enemy. . . ."

It all dated back to the "Armistice Army's" refusal to co-operate with the underground movement, which they found politically suspect. In fact the attitude of the top people was that of General Frère, who said in February 1943, "I am prepared to deal with the Germans and . . . if need be to take up arms with them against the Bolsheviks." Raymond Aubrac, of Combat, was refused arms by

Vichyist officers who "preferred to keep their arms for mobilisation after the Liberation. . . . They had political reservations about the Resistance movements."[13]

"Political reservations" accounted for much of the lack of co-operation within the wider resistance, especially from the British and Gaullist side. The Americans, Tillon remarks, "aimed at economising U.S. lives at the expense of everything else", had far more material than their cadres required, and still nursed a liking for Vichy, but at least they did not systematically practise discrimination between the different forces of the Resistance as did de Gaulle's henchmen or the British co-operating with the B.C.R.A.

In the north-west, "leaders" well equipped with arms and material, were sometimes brought in and assumed command, or formed a force apart from the F.F.I.; there was, for instance, Commandant Bourgoin, the indomitable one-armed French officer who had a price of a million francs on his head. (When his presence in the area was known the Gestapo arrested all the one-armed men in the department including an old man of seventy-five). He landed in Morbihan in June 1944 with an S.A.S. unit of 400 selected French parachutists, officially under orders of the British general MacLeod, but at the same time claiming authority from Koenig over the F.F.I. in three departments of Brittany: he ordered 7,000 maquisards—mostly unarmed—to assemble in a wood north of Vannes, to be graded and put into "correct" formations. During this lengthy process the Germans not unnaturally got wind of something and attacked the outskirts of the wood. "Fortunately they did not penetrate it", wrote one of the partisans, "for we had practically no weapons and couldn't have resisted."[14]

The self-appointed commander repeated the mistake on 13 June, assembling 3,000 maquisards at nearby St Marcel, and exposing them to a heavy German assault. The enemy lost 560 men, but 150 F.F.I. and 50 parachutists were killed, and terrible reprisals followed against the local population. A similar disaster occurred at Saffre (Loire-Inférieure) where 1,500 S.S. attacked a large Maquis and massacred the people of the village. Little, it seems, had been learned from the tragic lessons of Haute-Savoie, although a British observer noted that "it is fatal for S.A.S. to assemble a large concentration of men, particularly of half-armed Maquis; it is bound to draw down on the area heavier forces than it can repel. . . ." There seems no doubt that the casualties, reported by the F.F.I. leader Morice, were severe, in spite of the comment in *S.O.E. in France* that Bourgoin "gave the order to disperse overnight and there was no foretaste in Brittany of the blood-baths of Montmouchet and the Vercors".[15]

Colonel Eon, S.A.S. parachutist, and unbiased witness, commented that Bourgoin's "large and visible Maquis led to the destruction of the whole local organisation, and made work thereafter very difficult in the Morbihan. Many supplies of parachuted weapons fell into enemy hands." Moreover, the manoeuvres to disrupt the F.F.I. and build a separate army under Gaullist control made it possible for the Nazis to hang on in Lorient for several more months.

Tillon does not deny that there were some officers from London who loyally co-operated with the F.F.I. "unlike the B.C.R.A. men who used the bogey of a Communist plot to divert the Resistance into the hands of the most reactionary Gaullists". Such was Eon, who appreciated the partisans and wrote later that "most of the F.T.P. were determined militants, devoted body and soul to a cause for which they were prepared to make any sacrifice. . . ." He found their fighting spirit and hatred of the Nazis far more pronounced than in any other units.[16]

Eisenhower himself paid the F.T.P. and F.F.I. the tribute of calling them "the equivalent of fifteen divisions" when they cleared the way for the Allied armies through Normandy and Brittany, and he wrote later of "the great assistance given us by the F.F.I. in the task of reducing Brittany", commending the "overt resistance forces which had been built up since June around a core of S.A.S. troops. . . . When our armor had swept past them they were given the task of clearing up the localities where pockets of Germans remained, and of keeping open the Allied lines of communication. . . . Not least in importance, they had, by their ceaseless harassing activities, surrounded the Germans with a terrible atmosphere of danger and hatred, which ate into the confidence of the leaders and the courage of the soldiers."[17]

It had only taken a few weeks to turn the Breton workers and peasants into seasoned soldiers. "The Breton F.F.I. proved when they cleared the Paimpol zone or took Menez-Hom that they were rapidly becoming capable of using heavy arms and waging classical warfare just as well as professionals," as their leader, Charles Tillon insisted later, in the face of Gaullist unwillingness fully to recognise the fighting merits of these patriots.

The General and his highly placed supporters were in fact less impressed by the military prowess of the F.F.I. than disturbed by some of their political actions, such as the execution of German prisoners in Vannes, the punishment of collaborators in Rennes and Nantes—where rough justice was administered by the F.T.P. to various pro-Nazi police chiefs—and the election by popular acclaim at Dinan of a Communist Mayor. (In view of the appalling atrocities committed by the Germans and the Breton collaborators, described by the pro-Gaullist Robert Aron, it was hardly surprising that the Breton maquisards took reprisals; they "committed fewer cruelties than those they had had to endure".[18])

The Gaullists wanted at all costs to ensure a future regime on their preconceived lines. Colonel de Chevigné, emissary of de Gaulle, travelled with the Allied forces, in the words of the historian Robert Aron, "to see that after the Germans' departure there should be no revolutionary disorder". M. de Chevigné was accompanied by a bevy of police officers and administrators from Algiers ("Personnel to help restore order") with a Pretorian guard of Senegalese soldiers, and a military tribunal attached to his person. In each village the head of this caravanserai summoned the mayor pre-appointed by the B.C.R.A. and invested him with administrative power. A police inspector was left behind to see that this was put into effect and "to prevent certain abuses practised by the F.F.I. and the F.T.P." It must have seemed odd to the local inhabitants that certain other "abuses", which had been practised by the men of Vichy on their side, were ignored by the liberators. As early as 8 June, when the Allies entered Bayeux we know from M. Aron that "there was no resistance from the Vichyites . . . their aims being to restore France as a Great Power and . . . to prevent a coup by the Communists either at Bayeux or at Cherbourg (liberated on 24 June)." At Bayeux, the former town council was summoned, and a new *sous-préfet* named by the Gaullist representative. As the new man had no uniform, he asked the former *sous-préfet* to give him his "Of course", said the Marshal's man, "but don't forget to change the buttons, mine are stamped with the *francisque*."[19]

The incident highlights de Gaulle's problem: how to restore the old order to which he was at heart deeply committed, and at the same time to satisfy the French people, expecting and waiting for a radical change? His long-term solution of the problem was revealed later. In the meantime, the makeshift measures of placing his (or Pétain's) men in temporary positions prevented the Resistance "reds" from taking office; most of them were anyway too busy fighting and clearing a passage for the armies bringing freedom, as they thought. But a great many French were surprised at the cool assumption that

the Algiers government was entitled to appoint administrators, with
no democratic procedure whatever. The assumption was explained
by Aron: The great danger feared equally by Algiers and Vichy
was "a hiatus in the administration of the liberated territories. . . .
Any lapse might well be taken advantage of either by the Communist
Party or the Allies to endanger French independence." M. Aron saw
the possibility of Communism as serious: "the political situation in
France on D-Day was such as to justify the worst prognostications.
The government in power had completely collapsed. . . ." The great
merit of Gaullism ". . . is that before it actually came to power it had
planned in minute detail the institutions necessary for the avoidance,
or at least the limitation, of disaster".[20]

The Gaullists' political preoccupations might well have had the
unfortunate effect of dividing the Resistance and damping down its
fighting spirit. In fact, the F.F.I. and their supporters refused to be
affected by the *attentisme* of Algiers, and in the main firmly backed
the Resistance leaders in their line, which was that of the P.C.F.s
statement of June 1944: "In France today the problem over-riding
all other preoccupations is that of unflagging struggle. It is disturbing that the preoccupations of the C.F.L.N. in Algiers seem to be
rather different, and concentrated more on post-Liberation problems
than on the paramount need of the moment: to carry on the war."[21]
This was echoed by the leadership of the F.T.P. on 18 July, which
dealt with "the preoccupation of many F.T.P. officers and men who
fear that (*attentiste*) propaganda will make a general rising seem
premature." Concern with post-war politics was waste of time when
action was so urgently needed and every volunteer had to be drawn
into battle. The matter of military grades was unimportant: "The
difference between the patriots organised in the F.F.I. and those
outside is that the former have some arms and experience and the
latter have no weapons. . . . One wonders why arms have not been
provided for those thousands of other patriots? . . . Abandoning
guerrilla action under pretext of military operations has sometimes
served political interests more than military considerations. For us
what matters is that guerrilla actions should be organised, so as to
smash the enemy and to build workers and peasants' formations
(*milices patriotiques*) suited to armed struggle."

This message reached the resistants all over the country. Wherever
they might have felt confused by conflicting orders and frustrated by
the lack of arms, it gave them new heart to face difficulties, shortages,
reprisals. The workers and peasants in the Maquis only needed the

assurance that they were needed, to put their whole strength into the final battles for freedom. And though there were still many occasions when "political considerations" divided the Resistance it was unity in the struggle which won the day.

NOTES

1. H. Pelling, *Britain and the Second World War*, London, 1970 p. 197
2. J. Teissier du Cros, *Divided Loyalties* (London, 1962)
3. S. de Beauvoir, *La Force de l'Age* p. 597
4. A. Gosset, *Caen pendant la bataille* (Caen, 1946) p. 22
5. R. Aron, *De Gaulle before Paris* (trans. London, 1962) p. 149
6. H. Michel, *Histoire de la Résistance* p. 104
7. E. Cookridge, *They came from the Sky* (London, 1964) p. 47
8. Michel, op. cit. pp. 106–107
9. C. Tillon, *Les F.T.P.* p. 377
10. Michel, op. cit. pp. 111–112
11. Aron, op. cit. pp. 188–189
12. ibid. p. 189
13. Tillon, op. cit. pp. 346–348
14. ibid. pp. 385–387
15. M. R. D. Foot, *S.O.E. in France* (London, 1966) pp. 407–408
16. Aron, op. cit. p. 97
17. Foot, op. cit. p. 408
18. Aron, op. cit. pp. 192–193
19. ibid. p. 84
20. ibid. p. 122
21. *France nouvelle*, June–July 1944 p. 37

Chapter 17

FRANCE AFLAME

. . . Tous les bergers les marins et les mages
Les charretiers les savants les bouchers
Les jongleurs de mots les faiseurs d'images
Et le troupeau des femmes aux marchés

Les gens de négoce et ceux du trafic
Ceux qui font l'acier ceux qui font le drap
Les grimpeurs de poteaux télégraphiques
Et les mineurs noirs chacun l'entendra

Tous les Français ressemblent à Blondel
Quel que soit le nom dont nous l'appelions
La liberté comme un bruissement d'ailes
Répond au chant de Richard Cœur-de-Lion

Aragon, *Les Yeux d'Elsa*

All shepherds, wise men, butchers, bakers,
Accountants, carters, scholars, all
Jugglers with words and image-makers
And women round the market stall

The men in ships and railway tracks,
The men who weave and weld and steer
The merchants and the steeplejacks
And the black miners—all must hear.

To all in France of every name
This new name Blondel must belong
And freedom like a whispering flame
Answer to Cœur-de-Lion's song.

Trans. Frances Cornford

While the battles between the F.F.I. and the Wehrmacht raged in the north-west the rest of France was like the crater of a volcano— seething, bubbling and sporadically erupting into violent activity, now here, now there. Although much fiercer in June and July, this had been the picture since the early spring of 1944 when the F.F.I. was formed; following which, groups had rapidly become better organised, had acquired more experience, well-trained leaders and arms (though never enough) dropped from Britain or acquired by daring coups on arsenals and enemy units. The majority of the population was now openly anti-German and tacitly against Vichy, and (to use Mao Tse-tung's famous phrase) the partisans moved about among the people like fish in water.

If one looks at the map of France alongside an account of the growth of resistance such as Michel's *Histoire* or de Benouville's *Sacrifice du Matin*, one realises the phenomenal changes brought about since 1940. Then, the only organised activity was by small scattered groups of anti-fascists, most of them members of the illegal P.C.F. (disbanded but still very much alive), who set up printing presses in Bordeaux, carried on sabotage in central France, formed the O.S. (Organisations spéciales) and *Bataillons de Jeunesse* for action against Vichy and the Germans in Dijon, Lyons, Marseilles, with no funds and little popular support. By 1944 Resistance had become a mass movement, divided only by the labels of the groups; their networks—Combat, Libération, Franc-tireur, S.O.E. and the rest—covered almost every region, while the Communists worked among the people everywhere preaching and practising united struggle. At D-Day there were few indeed who still believed in Nazi victory or whole-heartedly supported Pétain—even inside the Vichy administration the police and civil service were tending to switch their allegiance, and though they were not always to be trusted they were extremely useful to the Resistance activists, who obtained information, passes, food tickets, pardons for suspects, far more easily than before, from compliant officials with an eye to the future.

Apart from the turncoats there were hundreds of thousands of patriotic French who were only too glad to join in open rather than tacit defiance of the hated Occupation, and more than ready to help the Allies and the F.F.I., putting politics aside at least temporarily as soon as liberation became a real prospect.

Reading the personal testimony of some of the 1944 survivors, one senses the prevailing enthusiasm for united action. There are dozens of accounts which describe the efforts to achieve this. Typical is one from Chateauroux where, on 5 March, there was a meeting of the Indre Department Liberation Committee attended by fifteen members of the different Resistance organisations and Maquis leaders. "The M.U.R., A.S., F.T.P., P.C.F., the Radical Party, the illegal trades unions and the local community were represented. The meeting was held one Sunday morning in the home of the chairman, Dr Roger Cazala, where friends, ignorant of each other's activities in the Resistance organisations, discovered with amazement and joy that they belonged to the same movement, had the same aims. . . ."[1] Further on we read that "Roger Cazala (a respected local chemist) was arrested and deported on 30 May 1944".

There were spies and traitors still around, Lacombe Luciens who did not meet their fate till much later; and whatever their eventual punishment, it could not bring back the men they had betrayed to the Gestapo—some 500 patriots in the Indre Region, imprisoned in France or deportéd to Germany from where most of them never returned. These tragedies did not damp down the movement for French liberation, but perhaps spurred it on.

To give an idea of popular feeling in France's countryside during the hectic weeks after the landings, one cannot do better than quote one or two of the reports from witnesses of the guerrilla war in regions far from the front but still very important to the Allied armies. These show how close the co-operation had become between *résistants* of different political opinions, and also how vivid was the realisation that they were now a part of the wider war effort, thanks to the British parachute drops which at last began to reach the Maquis; these are often described in enthusiastic vernacular (not easily translatable).

A maquisard, Roland 2, of Saint Gaultier, Indre, wrote of his first experience on a "reception committee":

"The arms we needed could only come from the sky, and the lads in the woods certainly welcomed the 'drops' whatever the risks and the wear and tear of getting them.... We listened-in for nights on end for the message addressed to us. One night it came through at last! What excitement to hear that it was for that night! We had Alex (British agent) with us, so we knew we were OK. *Quand le patron vient tout va bien* (When the boss comes along things go well). And *he* was lucky to have *us*. It wasn't a kid glove affair, but we went in with all our hearts. . . .

"As soon as we heard the plane coming we lit the fires to guide it. The plane came down to 200 metres, then on went all its lights. You were there, ready, waiting for the manna from heaven. You saw the containers swinging up in the sky on the tip of the parachutes; then there was a metallic noise as they hit the ground. Every container had a label with the total number of cylinders. You had to find every single one of them even if you hunted all night till morning. Sometimes the aeroplane didn't come and we had to wait four nights for nothing, and it came on the fifth. But we were getting weapons to drive out the Boche and no amount of waiting or effort was too much for us."[2] Before this, the F.T.P. had been restricted in its actions, as it had had to rely for its arms on dangerous raids on the stocks of the local regular army regiment, which had always been refused them.

With the parachuted supplies the partisans became more daring in their exploits.

One example is their "liberation" of the commune of Saint Amand, on 6 June, inspired by the news of the Normandy landings: if somewhat premature, it shows their spirit and their reaction to the situation. Deciding to eliminate the local enemy stronghold, they attacked the *Milice* headquarters of the little town, where they annexed all incriminating documents, wounded and captured several of Darnand's men and kidnapped Mme Bout de l'Ann, wife of the chief's secretary. She was removed, protesting vigorously, to the forest hideout of the Maquis. Elated by their success the F.T.P. took control of Saint Amand, occupied the *Mairie*, the *Sous-préfecture* and the Post-office and called a public meeting at which almost the whole population turned up and volunteered to form resistance teams. Arms which had been kept back by the Regiment and other groups were sent along "in lorry loads from the neighbouring communes", we are told. "Hundreds of boys wanting to fight enthusiastically responded to the call and were handed a weapon. The number of volunteers was 200 one day and 600 the next!"

Furious at the damage to the Milice, the Germans retaliated by sending swastika-emblazoned aeroplanes low over the town, followed by Nazi troops from Orléans in full battle dress; "their faces blacked, branches stuck on their helmets, they inspired general terror. They fired on sight at everything that moved. . . ." After shooting ten young men, setting fire to a number of shops and houses, and threatening a hundred men, women and children, chosen at random, with execution (for some reason not carried out), the Germans returned to base. The Milice then took over and arrested 61 townspeople, 54 of whom they took to Vichy as hostages for the kidnapped Mme Bout de l'Ann. Negotiations began for the exchange of prisoners on each side, and eventually, thanks to a letter from the lady to her husband testifying to her humane treatment by the maquisards, and owing to much pressure on both her husband and her captors by the F.F.I. chief in Saint Amand, she was handed back, and the hostages released. There was little doubt that Darnand would have ordered their execution as he had threatened to do if his secretary's wife had not been released.

The incident was closed, and Saint Amand at last freed from Nazi supervision which it had endured for two weeks. Although its premature occupation by the Maquis had not resulted in liberation, it had in fact succeeded in immobilising a great number of Wehrmacht men and material. "To hold Saint Amand, the Germans had to keep the equivalent of 3,000 armed men in the area, and to parachute 800 into the town itself," pinning down these forces for over a fortnight—two weeks crucial in the timetable of Allied advance. The local population and partisans were proud of themselves. To have achieved this by a kidnapping, with little loss of life, showed their potential strength and bargaining power—though it was with considerable relief that they welcomed back the fifty-four victims from Darnand's clutches and the Vichy gaol.[3]

Everywhere in occupied France the release of hostages and captives was high on the F.T.P. agenda. There were literally thousands of political prisoners and Jews in French prisons, living under execrable conditions and threatened with deportation to Germany or Poland. Throughout the war years attempts had often been made to succour individuals, rarely with any success—if not always as complicated as the case of Saint Amand, it was never easy and usually extremely dangerous. Many rescues were planned by members of *réseaux* whose leaders had been arrested, but too often failed disastrously (such as Yeo-Thomas' efforts to get Brossolette out of Rennes prison, or *Combat*'s to save Berthy Albrecht from the Gestapo in Lyons).[4]

However, with determination and luck occasional escapes were made by individuals, and I have heard many stories of successful rescues by audacious partisans in the Southern countryside. It is worth re-telling at least one of them as an example of Maquis life in the department of Corrèze, in 1944.

This department was a stronghold of the F.T.P. and had a striking record of resistance. An area with many Communist councils in the 1930s (the Préfet reported 15,000 P.C.F. votes in 1938), its antifascist mayors and councillors had been purged by Daladier in 1939, and many militants arrested and deported at the beginning of the war. A P.O.W. escaping from Germany in 1943 and returning to his home town, Tulle, in 1943, described it as "difficult to recognise—a dead dark town under the heel of the enemy . . . thousands of absentees—prisoner; thousands of new inhabitants—refugees from Alsace and Lorraine, and Jews; and a youthful population haunting the woods and isolated farms, who were not much seen but much talked about—the Maquis of Corrèze, led by the F.T.P."[5] The latter's organisation was remarkable, their relations with the local people good, their list of ambushes and sabotages impressive; the number of arrests was high, but the rate of growth was higher. The condemned prisoner, as Eluard wrote in the moving poem *Avis*, "had, he knew, not *one* comrade but millions and millions to avenge him"; this, written in 1942, was even more true two years later.

In mid-1944, according to the collection of eye-witness accounts entitled *Maquis de Corrèze*, "a lot of patriots were shut up in Tulle prison, including three F.T.P. leaders arrested on the way back from a parachute operation". The local underground Military Committee decided they must be rescued before the Nazis executed or deported them, the certain fate for active partisans. For a fortnight a commando of twenty-four maquisards met secretly to study the plan of the prison and to learn their tasks. Equipment was assembled: rope-ladders, guns, knives, a van big enough to take everyone away after the rescue. One problem was how to deal with the prison guard dog should it begin to bark; someone volunteered to approach it with a "bifteck" in one hand and axe in the other. A local policeman known to be anti-Vichy agreed to take a message in to the prisoners to prepare them.

On the chosen night the commandos made their way in to the gaol and, dropping from the roof (reached by their ladders), silenced the guards and frightened the Vichy police inspectors by bawling "Down arms! there are 250 of us, the building's mined and will blow up at the first shot. . . ." The guards' guns were taken off them for the F.T.P. arsenal, and the police were locked up, fourteen *résistants* freed (it was decided to leave the criminal elements in gaol) and the captives— sick, haggard, verminous but jubilant—piled into the van and taken off to friends' homes to the singing of the Internationale and the Marseillaise. Everything had gone smoothly: the dog had not barked and had been given the steak in reward;[6] the guards had been more docile than in some cases where the partisans had had to apply chloroform.

Possibly the Vichy police were already beginning to feel respect for the Maquis and trying to move over to the winning side. They were sadly torn between the devil (the F.T.P.) and the deep blue sea (their still-powerful German masters). Many during that summer tried to help rather than hinder the Resistance and themselves suffered as a result.

We have barely glanced at what was happening in a few parts of France—the North, the Loire valley, Vercors, the south-west and the centre—and can here hardly mention the many other regions where guerrilla war went on throughout the summer. Readers will find vivid and detailed descriptions of resistance in Savoy, in the Auvergne, Bordeaux, Provence (among others) in accounts by British agents, and in the group *témoignages* (testimonies) available in French, listed in the Bibliography. The scene in the departments to the East is neatly summed up in *S.O.E. in France*:

"The whole of Eastern France was so thick with ambushes that the German 11th Panzer Division, which took a week to reach the Rhine from the eastern front, took three weeks more to struggle from the Rhine to Caen."[7] By and large, F.F.I. activities throughout the country followed the same pattern: attacks on the enemy, sabotage, ambushes, according to the nature of the terrain, the positions of the German or Milice forces, of supplies available. There were differences which arose between political groups, but these were largely sunk during the feverish summer months when British and B.C.R.A. agents worked alongside Communists and Gaullists alike, with both the A.S. and the F.T.P., in the cause of French victory over the Nazis.

All this is too vast a subject to attempt to cover in one short chapter, but there is one element of the resistance which must be mentioned in some detail, for its activity was identical all over France, unaffected by locality, and it was perhaps the most important of all for Allied success at this crucial time. This was "Résistance Fer" the railwaymen's war. The network of French Railways (the S.N.C.F.), which was spread equally across the whole country, was eventually a web of death for the Germans and destruction of their goods (property looted from the French, of course, and loaded on German-bound trains, which the patriots preferred to see destroyed rather than going to the Reich).

At every stage of the four years' Occupation the *cheminots*, the railwaymen, had been a basic part of the Resistance. Through their illegal trade union and political organisations they were able to keep in constant touch with each other, and they also worked in close co-operation with the F.F.I., the guerrillas and the underground *réseaux* of S.O.E. and Gaullist groups. Thanks to their good offices, special couriers came and went between the two zones, hundreds of prisoners managed to escape, important information was conveyed to the Allies about enemy troop transports and material on the move. They held up the dispatch of munitions and arms to the Germans; they sabotaged the enemy postal services, opening parcels, removing documents, taking note of economic programmes, and became highly qualified propagandists against Nazi lies. They told the

people, through leaflets and the underground newspaper *La Vie
ouvrière*, just how much food and material was being sent to
Germany; without their reports the extent of the pillage would have
been unknown. They caused extensive damage in stations and
sidings. Under the direction of the central sabotage service in Paris
(*Groupes de sabotage et de destruction*—G.S.D.) led by Joseph
Epstein, a Polish ex-International Brigader, railwaymen practised a
variety of tricks to stop trains running—pouring sand or steel filings
into grease-boxes, cutting rubber vacuum brake tubes, and so on.
Trains and waggons were sent off to places far from their intended
destinations by a simple change of label. A Paris arms factory would
wait in vain for a delivery of tank or gun parts which had been
switched to Lille, or vice versa; soldiers heading for Marseilles would
find themselves at Bordeaux—or more likely stuck somewhere on
the way.[8]

Setting fire to locomotives and derailing trains was one of the
railwaymen's most important functions. When trains with supplies
of German-bound food were derailed the local Maquis were there to
help retrieve the precious provisions and deal them out to the local
people. F.T.P. and *cheminots* worked hand in glove; it was the
former who altered points and caused accidents on the main lines,
the latter who told them when and where a train was due and
whether it should be attacked—the railwaymen were careful to see
that no French passengers suffered from their activities. The S.N.C.F.
workers on the line helped in the sabotage.

Engine drivers risked their lives travelling on doomed trains, which
they leapt out of at the last moment before derailment; they also
risked capture and death by the Nazis, as the station master of
Chateauroux, a member of the *Front national* reminded readers of
Liberté, in April 1945; "The price that the French railway workers
paid for their patriotism was fearful: 17,141 prisoners, 300 shot,
2,102 deported, 8,000 sent to Germany by S.T.O. This is why the
cheminots will never forget."[9]

As already mentioned in this book, derailings and attacks on
enemy troop trains were frequent throughout the war years, with the
numbers of lost waggons and engines mounting rapidly in 1943 to a
climax in June and July 1944. "The entire French railway system was
so shot through and through with subversion that the Germans had
practically to abandon its use over much of the land they were
supposed to hold," writes Professor Foot. What made the railways
unworkable was "the permanent attitude of non-co-operation and

go-slow of the railway staff, even when they were not on strike, that made it impracticable to clear up enough of the mess for trains to run".[10] After 6 June trains and engines were destroyed daily, and the railwaymen happily recalled the *Pariser Zeitung* dictum that "every waggon is one more step to victory, 100,000 machine-gun bullets, steel for a hundred shells"—as they saw the valuable stock disappearing in a cloud of smoke and dust down an embankment, or inside a tunnel.

After D-Day the *"bataille du rail"* held up almost all trains, preventing thousands of German troops from reaching the North to fight the Allied armies. General Koenig, for all his mistrust of guerrilla war, paid a handsome tribute to the *cheminots* at a mass meeting in Paris on 19 November 1944: "In the defensive battles that the Germans fought against the liberating armies, one of the most certain reasons for their defeat was the paralysis of transport, achieved by you railwaymen."[11]

Koenig might have added that another reason for German defeat, and the key to the railwaymen's success was their basic attitude—one might say, ideology. It was their single-minded militancy and their solidarity with the other workers, free of factional disputes, that guaranteed success. Unity was a reality in the *bataille du rail*. It was a reality too, in another battle—the battle for the liberation of Paris, to which we now come.

NOTES

1. Guéguen-Dreyfus, G., *Résistance Indre et Vallée du Cher*, Paris, 1970, Vol. 1 p. 124
2. ibid. pp. 94–95
3. ibid. pp. 211–220
4. De Bénouville, G., *Le Sacrifice du Matin* p. 390
5. *Maquis de Corrèze* p. 198
6. ibid. pp. 245–250
7. Foot, M. R. D., *S.O.E. in France* p. 411
8. Tollet, A., *La Classe Ouvrière dans la Résistance* pp. 178–179
9. *Liberté*, 28.4.1945
10. Foot, op. cit. p. 411
11. Guéguen-Dreyfus, op. cit., Vol. 2 p. 47

Chapter 18

PARIS INSURGENT

En plein mois d'aôut notre pays aux barricades
Paris osant montrer ses yeux
Paris osant crier victoire
En plein mois d'aôut un lundi soir

Paul Eluard, *Au Rendezvous allemand*

In mid-August, our country at the barricades,
Paris daring to look up,
Paris daring to cry Victory,
In mid-August one Monday night.

Paris was perhaps the only big city where the problems of a divided control hardly affected the course of events. True to its long revolutionary tradition, the capital was to show the world that whatever plots in high places, the Parisians would determine their own destiny.

On 14 July 1944 Paris celebrated its national day with massive demonstrations, for the first time in four years, in spite of the presence of the occupying forces. There was an all-pervading sense that freedom was not far off. Tens of thousands came out on the streets and milled around for hours. André Tollet estimates at 100,000 the demonstrators in the Paris region, despite the terror, police, German army, Darnand Milice, Gestapo—"Something has changed—We are going into battle" (Tollet, *La Classe Ouvrière dans la Résistance*, p. 217). Tricolor badges and tiny flags were sold to enthusiastic buyers, and in rue de Belleville and the Place de la Republique people waved blue-white-and-red banners. The police drove into the crowd and vainly tried to grab the flags; in fact, seeing the mood, many gendarmes desisted and even joined the demonstrators.[1] Tricolors could be seen hoisted over factories, on pylons, and flying for two days from church towers.

From the eve of the Allied landings, the ferment in Paris had set in and it grew with the awareness that liberation was now near. Economic disruption increased the problems of the Nazis, who had to deal with strikes and demonstrations in many suburbs, including women's committees and noisy protests against hunger.

Under F.T.P. orders acts of sabotage multiplied. Extracts from a few of their reports show how railways and roads around the city were paralysed: 9 June—sabotage on the Longueville–Paris and Coulommière–Paris lines; a train of German tanks derailed and stuck for 24 hours near Persan; 10 June—derailment between Flambouin and Montereau, traffic stopped for 12 hours; two cranes blown up at the German depot at Chambly; 4,000 enemy soldiers immobilised at La Ferté Gaucher for 3 days; 47 acts of sabotage by F.T.P., including blocking of the Maison Rouge Tunnel.[2]

Official S.N.C.F. documents refer to 296 actions against the railways, adding up to 1,193 hours of travel lost.[3]

At the same time, a great popular movement spread through the capital, and as the Allies advanced from the West, without any declared intention of freeing Paris, the city began to organise its own liberation. Plans for total war against the occupying Germans included the disruption of the economy by strikes in all sectors, organised by the illegal C.G.T. in conjunction with the Paris Committee of Liberation (C.L.P.). The main slogans were "co-ordinate action", and "prepare for national insurrection"; they called for the building of a patriotic militia, and support for economic and insurrectional strikes. While seeking to protect French factories and public buildings from damage and to keep essential services going, the C.L.P. stressed the need to hamper the Germans by stopping transport and other services, thus leaving the workers free to take their place on the battle front.

On 3 August the railwaymen struck and three days later presented their demands: the release of prisoners, 500 grammes of bread a day, and three months' advance in wages. Not surprisingly, these were refused, and a week later the strike was 100 per cent in seventeen depots. On 14 August seven hostages seized by the Nazis at Villen-neuve were released as a concession, but the railwaymen continued the strike, entrenched in their positions and sabotaging without respite. Recognising that they were bearing the whole brunt of industrial action and of German reprisals, the Paris C.G.T. called a general strike in support of the *cheminots*. The postal workers were the first out, on 16 August, the Metro men on the 17th. With the telecommunication workers (P.T.T.) they marched, 4,000 strong, headed by three girls wearing red, blue and white frocks, to the Hotel de Ville, where they demonstrated, shouting "Du Pain!" (bread!) and singing the *Marseillaise*.

On 18 August, the postal services, Underground, railways, engineering and textile works had closed down almost completely. André Tollet and a C.G.T. comrade toured the suburbs on their bicycles and found all the big factories, construction sites and markets in the grip of the strike. In the cafés "everybody's in it and in complete accord, except for the joker who tells us that he is working for the Boches, and enjoying it. It turns out that he is the grave-digger at the Petit Montrouge cemetery!" Elsewhere, however, we are told that "on several occasions the workers of the city's funeral services had to be relieved as they were disappointed at not taking part in the strike".

The personnel of the great Paris stores all came out—Aux Galéries Lafayette, the Printemps and Samaritaine shops all closed down, along with banks and insurance offices. The majority of strikers volunteered to help the F.F.I., and railwaymen and building workers particularly played an important part in securing arms from German depots and transport centres. A group of volunteers raided the hospital de la Pitié, which was under German control, and took a large stock of weapons. The 250 sick and wounded Germans in the hospital served as hostages, a few days later, to save the lives of many French patriots in German hands.[4]

On 10 August the joint command of the Front National, F.F.I. and F.T.P. issued an order that was obeyed throughout the region:

"Franctireurs and Partisans of Paris, glorious among the soldiers of the F.F.I. FORWARD INTO BATTLE!

1. Cut all communications—trains, roads, lanes. Set up ambushes and booby traps, cut down trees, stretch tripwires, scatter nails. . . .

2. Block, attack and destroy enemy headquarters. . . .

3. Attack all enemy forces, disarm fugitives, exterminate pockets of resistance. . . . Besiege, harass . . . co-ordinate guerrilla action with that of the Allied troops. . . .

4. Halt all factories useful to the enemy; call on workers to enrol with the F.T.P. . . . Organise a disciplined mass rising for battle; smash the repressive apparatus of the enemy and traitors, wipe out the Gestapo agents, the spies and informers, Darnand's *Milice*, the S.S. . . .

Attack and disperse the police and Feldgendarmes' controls. . . . Block the food depots; defend goods and persons against enemy sabotage and destruction. . . .

With the patriotic militia, under the control and authority of the Liberation Committees, set up the law of French justice against the enemy's illegality. . . .

TO ARMS—and set Paris once again on the road to Freedom as in France's finest hours.

Make de Gaulle's order *'Tous au Combat'* the war-cry of Paris resurgent!

Long live the F.F.I.! Long live France! Long live the Allies!"[5]

De Gaulle's order, mentioned here, had been given before the question of insurrection arose. Now that he realised what his call to arms implied, and that he was under Eisenhower's command, he changed his tune. On 12 August, his words addressed to "Paris and the other large cities still occupied" were merely: "Resume work immediately and in a disciplined manner on the arrival of the Allied forces."[6] But words from Algiers were to have little effect on the historical events taking place in the cauldron of insurrectionary Paris.

*   *   *

The Allied plans for driving the Germans out of France gave little importance to Paris. Although to the G.I.s "Paris beckoned with a greater allure than any other objective in Europe", as Omar Bradley put it with brutal frankness: "tactically the city had become meaningless. For all its past glories, Paris represented nothing more than an inkspot on our maps to be by-passed as we headed towards the Rhine." A liberated Paris would complicate the provisioning of the armies: "Logistically it could cause untold trouble, for behind its handsome façades there lived 4 million hungry Frenchmen. Food for the people of Paris meant less gasoline for the front."[7] The U.S. needed the Normandy dairy and wheat granaries to feed its men, and Paris would just have to wait till late September for relief. By then the Allies would have reached Germany, and having encircled Paris would return to clear up the pocket of Germans left in the city. "Paris-Sandwich!" as Tillon exclaims. The F.F.I. soon saw that this would mean Paris becoming a battlefield, attacked by the Allied air forces, possibly blown to bits by the Nazis.

The French Resistance had no interest in stopping the Germans from leaving, and set to work to hasten the enemy's defeat by every possible means. Its conviction was that, the position in Paris being what it was, the best way was to turn the capital into a huge trap where the people, masters of the streets, would join in and add enormously to the fighting efficiency of weapons and F.F.I. Nobody knew what Von Choltitz, Stulpnagel's successor, would do—his orders were to destroy every town he left, as he had done in Warsaw, where he had "liquidated" 277,000 people, and as he had tried to do in Russia. Hitler's orders on 23 August were: "Destroy Greater Paris as completely as possible, and specifically the 62 bridges. . . . Take widespread and severe reprisals if German troops are fired on. Evacuate Paris after this destruction and even at the price of 30 per cent German losses." Paris was not evacuated nor destroyed by Von Choltitz. Why? Simply because Paris did not allow him to carry out Hitler's order.

This Nazi general was no different from the others and certainly no philanthropist. But events in August 1944 made it impossible to practise time-honoured Nazi methods, and the fear of insurrectionary revenge no doubt contributed to his desire to gain favour with the advancing Allies by sparing Europe's most popular city. None the less, he ordered the crushing of local resistance by all the military force at his disposal, and the Germans carried out shootings and reprisals in a desperate effort to keep control up to the bitter end. On 16 August, as the Allies landed on the Mediterranean coast, thirty-four young people were executed in the Bois de Boulogne; prisoners from Frésnes and other jails were hastily bundled into vans and taken off to Germany; many were shot in last-minute revenge.

But it was no use—the rising and the victory of the Parisians were by the third week of August almost a *fait accompli*. The response to the C.G.T.s call for a general strike was impressive: almost all transport and postal employees and factory, service, and white-collar workers were out, and 99 per cent of the Paris police had come over *en bloc* with their arms to the F.F.I. The city was gradually grinding to a halt, while simultaneously the excitement in the streets was reaching fever pitch.

On 19 August the F.F.I. occupied the Préfecture de Police and the Hôtel de Ville, tearing down the swastika and hoisting the tricolor there. The Germans brought tanks up to attack these buildings but the occupying partisans, besieged all day, emerged victorious late at night. There were pitched battles around the Panthéon, in Boulevard Saint-Germain and in the Tuileries, besides skirmishes all over the suburbs. Overnight, barricades in most streets, made of paving-stones, overturned cars and buses, sandbags, railings, old furniture, were hastily piled up at the call of the F.F.I. Flags appeared every-where; every Parisian who could find one wore a badge, or blue, white and red flowers. Groups of jittery Germans drove tanks hither and thither, guns in hand, nervously shooting into café terraces or at the beflagged windows. A cannonade by a group of panic-stricken S.S. men brought down the wing of the Villemin hospital, causing many casualties. By and large, the German infantry, threatened by partisans with revolvers or grenades, after a half-hearted show of self-defence gave themselves up. They were disarmed and individuals sometimes allowed to go free, though big groups (sometimes nearly 100) were proudly surrounded by the F.F.I. delighted at their haul, and taken into detention.

During the day of 19 August, Commandant Dufresne, driving round inspecting his forces (and narrowly missing arrest and shoot-ing by the Nazis), saw "violent combats" in the streets, "rude assaults" on several municipal offices, the liberation of Drancy camp where 3,000 Jewish and political prisoners suddenly saw freedom after two years, the taking over by the F.F.I. of *Paris-Soir*'s offices, where the underground press teams immediately installed themselves, and many other public buildings seized from the Ger-mans. "By the evening of this first day of the insurrection . . . German troops are posted in five centres: Gare du Nord and Gare de l'Est, Magenta, République, Hôtel de Ville, Senal. Their patrols outside these are constantly harassed by the F.F.I. . . . By nightfall we are in complete control of 43 out of 80 quartiers, and our patrols with F.F.I. armbands line most of the main streets, exchanging brisk fire with the enemy. . . ."[8] The position was alarming for the Germans, and also for their collaborator friends, who were being dealt with by the F.F.I. M. Bouffet, for instance, the well-known pro-Nazi Préfet, was taken by a band of partisans straight from the occupation of the Préfecture to police Headquarters, to be detained and later judged by a people's tribunal. The next few days were to see energetic attempts to save fascist skins by getting some sort of truce between the F.F.I. and the Germans and delay the final reckoning until the Americans could arrive and take over command, "saving Paris" from the "mob rule" which threatened it. We will have a look at these frantic, but vain, efforts in a moment.

*   *   *

On 19 August, Paris in its state of siege, strikes and turmoil, must have appeared as chaos in the minds of those outside. In fact, the organisation of the city under these strange conditions was highly efficient. The F.F.I. saw to it that nobody went hungry or lacked medical attention, looked after sanitation, electricity and gas. The food supply was in the hands of the F.T.P., under Commandant Raynal who had for months been planning it in co-operation with the trades unions of the transport and *ravitaillement* services.

It was known that the Halles, Paris's main market, with their refrigerators and their stocks, were on the list for destruction by the Nazis. The F.F.I. moved into the vast buildings on 19 August and on Sunday 20th turned them into a fortress which was defended against German tanks by partisans within and volunteers outside, armed with a few rifles and grenades. The battle went on all Sunday and Monday, and eventually the tenacious defenders drove back the Germans, losing several valiant fighters but saving the Halles for Paris.

By Monday 21st, evening, meat was being distributed from the central market and stocks were being taken to butchers in every part of the city by brave drivers accompanied by riflemen, who made their way past German troop units in vans marked with a Red Cross. One important source of supply was the food depots of the Germans in Fontenoy, the Ecole Militaire and elsewhere; these were ferociously attacked by the F.F.I. and equally fiercely defended by the Wehrmacht, which finally gave way and left the doors open to their larders, stocked with "tons and tons of provisions of all sorts. . . . Impossible to enumerate, but including every thinkable delicacy, things that we had forgotten but which the enemy had seized and was hoarding for German consumption."[9]

Reports came in continually to Raynal from all over Paris of new hauls: a train-load of flour bound for Germany, held up at St-Denis; meat from the slaughter-houses of La Villette and from Ivry, Vaugirard, Louis Blanc; masses of food from the docks of Austerlitz and supply dumps of rue Petit. After two days all the stocks were under F.F.I. control. Bread was still in short supply, so vans went off to the outlying mills and loaded up with flour which they drove back often under sporadic fire; others went to fetch fruit and vegetables thirty miles off, with *"Ravitaillement"* painted on the car roofs, under escort of armed volunteers. Some were stopped and their drivers arrested; a few were shot out of hand and others were kept standing against walls, hands above their heads, for several hours but finally released, by German soldiers who no doubt realised what their own fate might be when the tide turned. In spite of incidents, 60 tons of goods were brought back in the evening, to be divided specifically between hospitals and the fighting units.

Within a few days, things at the Halles were back to normal, with supplies coming in and regular distributions being made. Commandant Raynal turned his attention to the black market: "I'm going to fight it with all my power and in every field", he told a reporter. "We'll seize the black marketeers red-handed, by investigations, and by controls on the roads where they chiefly operate." One place where the F.F.I. were able to deal with black marketeers and Nazis simultaneously was the Palace of the Senate, part of which had been occupied since 1940 by Marshal Sperrle, the bloated head of the Luftwaffe, Western Division. The Marshal had stuffed his quarters with stolen furniture and vast quantities of provisions, and installed huge refrigerators, a bakery, and an enormous steam bath. The reporter from the journal *Libération*, who visited the Senate shortly after Sperrle had fled, found it transformed into something between a luxury hotel and a fortress, with explosives and concrete defences dug in deep under the ground. The masses of dynamite were clearly intended, if need be, to blow up the Senate.

The Chambre des Députés which had been the German seat of military administration for Greater Paris was heavily fortified too; most of its rooms were taken intact by the F.F.I. on 21 August, though the library had suffered grievously from a fire which consumed about 60,000 books. There was broken glass everywhere, and the shattered remains of a gun emplacement facing the Concorde.

This was bad enough, but the Senate building was far worse: the Nazis had in their hasty exit left an unholy litter of old firearms, ammunition, helmets, uniforms, all over the state rooms and the chapel; doors and windows had been blown in, leaving a trail of ruin. But the worst damage had been done by the S.S. after the regular soldiers had left; these vandals destroyed everything they didn't want and looted the rest. Paintings, clocks, cabinets and precious volumes had disappeared in a caravan of lorries, leaving a shambles of lacerated pictures and tapestries splashed with ink and paint. The reporter "shuddered to think what would have happened in Versailles or the Louvre if the defenders of Europe had had their way there. . . ."[10]

Fortunately the Germans were too busy to trouble with the defence of the Louvre. They put their energies into defending their remaining strongpoints at the Gare de l'Est and on several boulevards, and attacking the Préfecture buildings again. But everywhere they were forced to retreat. On the evening of 21 August, the Paris

Committee issued an appeal to the population:

"PARISIANS! your insurrection has already freed many public buildings . . . and the first great victory has been won. The struggle goes on and must continue till the enemy is driven out of the Paris region. More than ever, all into battle! Join the F.F.I. The whole population must combine to stop the enemy's movements. Cut down trees, dig anti-tank ditches, throw up barricades. The Allies shall be received by a victorious people!"[11]

The people victorious was something which, whatever lip-service they might pay, neither the Allies nor the "neutrals" nor a fair section of the French bourgeoisie wanted to see. In spite of a general wish to get rid of Hitler and clear the Nazis out of France there was a price they were not keen to pay. The spectre of revolution haunted them as persistently as it always had, and Paris up in arms was all too reminiscent of 1848 and of 1871.

NOTES

1. *Documents* (Free French Information Service), October 1944
2. C. Tillon, *Les F.T.P.* p. 445
3. A. Tollet, *La Class ouvrière dans la Résistance* p 213
4. ibid. pp. 232–234
5. R. Massiet (Dufresne) *Préparation de l'Insurrection et la Bataille de Paris* (Paris, 1945) pp. 64–65. Tillon, op. cit. pp. 453–454
6. ibid. p. 455
7. O. Bradley, *A Soldier's Story* (U.S., 1951) p. 386
8. Massiet, op. cit. p. 133
9. *Cahiers Français* (Free French Information Service) October 1944 p. 43
10. ibid. pp. 44–45
11. Massiet, op. cit. p. 252

Chapter 19

PARIS LIBERATED

Rien ne m'a fait jamais battre le cœur
Rien ne m'a fait ainsi rire et pleurer
Comme ce cri de mon peuple vainqueur
Rien n'est si grand qu'un linceul déchiré
Paris, Paris soi-même libéré

Aragon, *Paris*

Nothing has ever made my heart beat so
Nothing has made me so laugh and weep
As this shout from my victorious people
Nothing's so great as a torn winding-sheet
Paris, Paris, by her own self freed.

As the full significance of the insurrection dawned, in mid-August, a frenzied political and diplomatic activity began, conducted through the Swedish Consul Nordling, with the aim of ensuring "order" in Paris until the arrival of the Allies. This suited the Gaullists and it was also infinitely preferable to the Germans and Pétainists (if they had to surrender) to plead for mercy from the generals of a regular army rather than risk the rough justice of the angry Resistance.

In Bayeux and Caen the takeover by de Gaulle's representatives in the wake of the Allies had been comparatively easy. But the situation in Paris was very different. The anti-Communists of Vichy, London, Sweden and the Wehrmacht entered into the most elaborate intrigues to stave off the storm breaking about them.

First there were the endeavours of Laval and his cronies to save something from the wreck of the Vichy regime; the Premier travelled hot-foot to Paris at the beginning of August to talk to Abetz and Taittinger (in charge of French affairs under the Nazis in the capital). Someone had the idea of bringing Herriot back from his house arrest near Nancy on 8 August, to give an air of republican respectability to the Franco-German deals—but the former President would not play and was taken back to captivity, while Pétain's cook, brought hopefully from Vichy, waited in vain beside his empty oven.[1] Prevented from coming himself, the Maréchal sent a repre-

193

sentative, M. Rueger, who pleaded with Commandant Dufresne to be allowed to fly to London to meet de Gaulle and arrange a life-saving operation for the Marshal ("the feebleness of these people's imagination and political sense was quite incredible", remarked Dufresne). Another visitor was one General Brécard who asked to be given a guard of honour of F.F.I. men to the Hotel de Ville, in order to proclaim that de Gaulle was on the way and that, until he arrived, Brécard must be entrusted with the sovereignty of France! ("This intrigue showed how individuals tried to play their own game, as always happens in a revolutionary situation", was Dufresne's comment.)[2]

On the morning of 20 August, Taittinger sent for Dufresne very urgently and greeted him with the advice "Drop the Insurrection!" "You must know", said he, "that General von Choltitz has threatened to bomb Paris and 20,000 S.S. men will go into action if the attack on the Germans continues. . . ." Seeing that this did not impress Dufresne, Taittinger declared that he was ready to work with the Liberation Committee and would open the Hôtel de Ville to them; he added that "he and his City council" had decided to receive de Gaulle when he arrived in Paris. The F.F.I. leader "replied coldly and contemptuously that there was no question of this. 'The C.L.P. will carry out your former functions. Vichy's representatives have been dismissed from office.' "[3]

Taittinger, still clinging to hopes of appeasement, went off to discuss matters with Von Choltitz. The latter said with brutal frankness that if the F.F.I. attacked his key positions in certain streets he would burn down the whole neighbourhood. He intended to hold up the Allies' advance and had plans for mining the capital, should he choose to destroy it. But he had three more divisions with which to hold the city. In view of this he demanded an assurance that he could treat with the Allies according to "military honour". He also talked to Nordling about a possible exchange of captives: five German soldiers to be released for one French political prisoner. What Von Choltitz wanted, of course, was to gain time by paralysing the popular rising—later, his excuse, to a German military tribunal, for not executing Hitler's orders was that the insurrection "had broken out too soon", before the arrival of promised reinforcements.[4]

A commentator of Le Monde wrote in 1949 that "the insurrection saved Paris from the destruction that would most probably have ensued had the Allied and German plans been carried out".[5] To halt the rising, as some French politicians wished, would have saved

Choltitz—and left his divisions free to escape or to fight on.

In the meantime other conversations had been going on, also aimed at braking the insurrection, on 19 August, between de Gaulle's representative, J. Chaban-Delmas, and the Swedish Consul, Nordling. Chaban had just arrived, hoping to assume the leadership of the F.F.I. and thus to keep them in rein. With two other Gaullists, Le Trocquer and Parodi, some members of the C.N.R., a couple of German officers, and Nordling, it was agreed to send the following "order of the day" to the F.F.I. headquarters: "Because the German Command has promised not to attack public buildings occupied by French troops . . . the Provisional Government of the French Republic and the C.N.R. ask you to cease fire against the Occupation Forces until the promised evacuation of Paris."

The F.F.I. and their friends could hardly believe their eyes. How could de Gaulle allow such negotiations or such pronouncements? he would surely disavow them when he arrived! The cease-fire order shocked not only Communists but all those engaged in the battle; Dufresne said "it came just when we were masters of three-quarters of Paris", and recognised it as a manœuvre to prevent the insurrection from spreading. As Commandant Villatte wrote, "It was impossible to stop the fighting without playing into the enemy's hands. . . . To do so would have allowed them to regroup their forces."[6]

The F.F.I. ordered all its men to patrol Paris continuously, thus flatly contradicting the directives for a truce. A notice had also gone up announcing that "everyone who . . . has contributed to weakening the patriotic movement shall be considered as helping the enemy and punished as a traitor".[7] The spirit of insurrection was encouraged, grew and spread through the city.

In spite of this, or perhaps because of it, efforts to fix a truce were redoubled—although Choltitz's "good faith" was demonstrated by his men setting fire to the Paris flour mills to which the F.F.I. had just brought in supplies. The Gaullist group installed itself in the Hôtel de Ville at 5 a.m. on 20 August "to save it from extremist elements of the C.L.P.", and took Taittinger into custody, then spent the day in vain negotiations—first with the C.N.R., which was assured, on Abetz' and Nordling's word, that 4,200 prisoners would be released by the Nazis if the F.F.L. would stop fighting; then with Choltitz, who doubted that Nordling and his friends could influence the Resistance, swore that he "would not talk to *voyous*, terrorists, Communists", and incidentally passed a remark about "the common battle that his tanks would soon be waging with the Americans against the U.S.S.R."[8]

Then on 20 August there was a meeting between Chaban-Delmas and the six representatives of the E.C. of the C.N.R. which pushed through a resolution in favour of the truce, against strong opposition by Villon, Chairman of C.O.M.A.C. and André Tollet. As a result the police were ordered to put up posters announcing a cease-fire, thus leaving the Germans in control of the city's centre with un-hindered access for their troops, in or out. Tillon says, "while fierce fighting raged around the Préfecture, cars sent by Nordling, accompanied by German vehicles bearing white flags, called through loud-hailers for a stop to all fighting and aroused fury or consterna-tion wherever the insurgents were duped by the enemy's game".

Dufresne describes how the cease-fire was observed: "A quarter of an hour after the first announcement, a German motor-bicycle came along with two men carrying sub-machine guns, waving a white flag. The F.F.I. let them pass, but 20 yards further on the Germans fired several rounds, killing three and wounding four of our men. . . . Taking advantage of the depression caused by the truce orders, the Germans arrested many F.F.I. medical workers, shot prisoners in the Hotel Continental, mowed down passers-by in Avenue Ledru-Rollin, tried to recapture the Mairie of Saint-Ouen killing 90 patriots. . . ." This showed how far the enemy could be trusted, and the whole Resistance rallied to the call from Rol Tanguy and the central committee of the F.F.I., installed in the catacombs, "to avenge the heroes . . . hasten the end of the war by your action."

A poster went up calling the entire Paris population to build barri-cades, cut down trees on roads and avenues: "All little streets must be blocked by barricades. Organise by house and by lane to with-stand enemy attack, so that the Boche will be isolated and unable to take reprisals. ALL TO THE BARRICADES!" In fact, before their formal leadership had rejected the truce, the people's organisations had brushed it aside.

A meeting of the full C.N.R. of 21 August was stormy, and punctuated dramatically by the gunfire outside. Bidault, who presided, had hoped to reach a gentleman's agreement. His sup-porters in their defeatism quoted Koenig: "The situation was highly critical, the Allies wouldn't arrive for at least a week." Mutter, a Gaullist, forecast the "massacre of 50,000 Parisians"; "there are no weapons", said others, themselves responsible for withholding arms. "The Germans have orders to bomb the city." The F.F.I. answer was that the enemy's morale was shaken and the Nazis only wanted to save their skins. Was this the moment for a French general to negotiate with an enemy in full retreat?[9]

Chaban then proposed a truce for inner Paris, letting fighting continue in the suburbs. But he was defeated, and the meeting supported the C.L.P. in its opposition to a plan which would enable Choltitz to disarm the F.F.I., give his troops free passage out of Paris and control the bridges over the Seine.

Late on 21 August, Choltitz offered new proposals, equally un-acceptable; the Resistance fighters should confine themselves to an area of roughly one square mile in central Paris, leaving the roads out of the city available for a German withdrawal. It struck many as absurd to think that Choltitz would quietly leave Paris, just to please the truce-makers, disobeying Hitler for whom he was going to fight for another nine months.

The offer was turned down flat. It was obvious to most of the C.N.R. that certain politicians were seeking to connive at the Nazis' plans, in a devious attempt to muzzle the F.F.I. and allow Gaullist *préfets* and administrators to take power.[10]

*   *   *

Meanwhile the battle was raging on in every quarter of Paris. Throughout Sunday, 21 August, Franc-tireurs held the Place Saint-Michel against German lorries and a tank which they destroyed: several important buildings including *Paris Soir*'s offices and the telephone centre in rue de Grenelle were taken, with prisoners and a good haul of guns; in the 18th *arrondissement* thirty-three Germans surrendered after heavy fighting and a hundred in the 17th; at several Metro stations firing went on hour after hour. By the evening the municipal offices at Pantin, Lilas, Noisy and many more were in French hands.

Paris was full of burning lorries, dead Nazis, smoke, shouts, screams, and the rattle of machine-gun fire. People were poor—few workers were earning more than F.F.I. allowance, or strike pay—and food was short, life was nerve-racking but exhilarating, and faces were lit up with an intense joy and confidence. The C.L.P. Committee again called everyone to arms: "The simple and sacred duty of all Parisians is to fight!" At 6 p.m. in response, three detach-ments of F.T.P. launched a co-ordinated attack on a German garage at the Porte d'Orléans, seized all the army vehicles there and with-drew in good order at 7.30. By nightfall sixty-one out of eighty areas of Paris were completely free. Two symbolic events are worth mentioning: the seizure from Darnand's Milice of the P.C.F. offices, where Duclos and Frachon reinstalled their headquarters after four years;[11] and the appearance that evening of many Resistance newspapers (some printed in *Paris-Soir*'s offices) in the open, instead of illegally. *Combat, Franctireur*, and *Humanité* were snatched up by the news-hungry populace who for so long had been threatened with death for such self-indulgence. The message in all the papers was the same: Fight on till final victory.[12]

Tuesday, 22 August, was the day of German immobilisation, the day of the barricades. A journalist described "men, women and children tearing up paving-stones, filling sandbags, sticking spikes and railings on top of the barriers, adding a broken enemy car or even tank for good measure—young men dig anti-tank ditches, women bring food and medical supplies, everyone's laughing and singing the *Marseillaise* and revolutionary songs. . . . A Red Cross service functions, directed by Valléry Radot and other eminent doctors."

To go over to the offensive in force, Paris only needed ammunition. The F.F.I. had enough guns and the engineering workers had repaired large numbers of German armoured cars in a workshop at Issy: "We should have had three divisions of Tiger or Panther tanks by 27 August." But no ammunition. Rol sent demand after urgent demand to the Provisional Government in London: "Immediately request several tons of plastic; several thousand detonators; several thousand metres Bickford cord for making anti-tank bombs. 10,000 10,000 'Gammon' grenades would be decisive in the anti-tank battle." On the 24th, Rol noted, "We have had no satisfaction whatever to our request. . . ."[13]

On 23 August the Germans held only nine strongpoints in central Paris, including the Ecole Militaire, the Luxembourg and the Admiralty. The F.F.I. were hunting tanks with incendiary bottles made in Joliot-Curie's laboratories. At every corner there were hand-to-hand battles, grenade attacks, scared Germans surrendering. Flames rose from the Grand Palais, and from the St Ouen petrol depots set alight by the Nazis. Paris was feverishly fighting and impatiently waiting—where were the Allies? and where the promised supplies?

On 22 August in Normandy, General Patton was still saying "My orders are not concerned with Paris", when Rol's personal aide, Gallois-Cocteau, contacted the U.S. Command, asking for support, especially arms. Gallois went to Bradley, who consulted Eisenhower. Not till 6.30 p.m. did Leclerc get the order to leave for Paris with his second armoured division. "The Free French Forces inside the city forced my hand", Eisenhower wrote, months later, recognising that the insurrection had upset all his plans.

The American decision opened the way for de Gaulle, who flew in from Algiers (via Rome, where he visited the Pope) to the out-skirts of Paris. At Rambouillet Palace, on 23 August, while Leclerc forged forward from Argentan, de Gaulle met a delegation who came to him in the middle of the night to discuss the fate of revolu-tionary Paris. It included the Gaullists Parodi and St Phalle, an influential businessman and Red Cross representative; Nordling's brother Rolf, and Jean Laurent, director of the Bank of Indochina— a curious collection of high-ranking capitalists, hardly fitted, it might be thought, to speak for the French people. With them were an I.S. agent and Baron Poch Pastor, A.D.C. of Choltitz (and a double agent, as it later transpired). "They all came that night in order to secure the swift intervention of regular U.S. troops", wrote de Gaulle in his memoirs.[14] The Resistance, deeply involved in mortal struggle knew nothing about this secret meeting, nor indeed of de Gaulle's arrival on the scene. What would its members have thought of these agents and financiers anxiously seeking to turn events to their own advantage? The discussions with the Wehrmacht, while Paris fought its last battles with outworn rifles, were only too reminiscent of the 1870 Versailles intrigues which betrayed the Paris Commune. The leader of the F.T.P.'s comment, "By receiving this aristocracy of fear, de Gaulle had in his heart forever denied the Resistance", has, alas, been confirmed by history.

*   *   *

While the Rambouillet meeting worked out ways and means of keeping the people of Paris in their place, those people were saving Paris. The men fighting at the Batignolles station, in the rue des Martyres, between the Place d'Italie and rue de Tolbiac, on the cor-ners of bridges—wherever you see a plaque today honouring the name of a fallen patriot—had one thing only in mind: to drive out the Germans. On 24 August it was still touch and go around the Hôtel de Ville and in the Luxembourg, where German tanks were based and taking heavy toll of the F.F.I. At St Mende, a northern suburb, a detachment of Nazi armoured cars tried to force their way out, with French prisoners bound to the front of the vehicles, and there were ugly incidents before the Germans abandoned their positions, especially in the Poissy district where they were concen-trated to cover the retreat through Paris of Hitler's Seventh Army.

Fabien's plans for a final attack, ready on 23 August, were carried out on the 24th. They included the destruction after desperate resistance of the most important enemy position, the fortified Luxembourg, held by 600 men. During the day a message of encouragement reached the combatants: it was from Leclerc and was dropped from a plane on to the space in front of Notre-Dame, with the words "Tenez bon, nous arrivons" ("Hold fast, we are coming"); and sure enough, at 9 in the evening an advance section of the Chad army arrived at the Porte d'Orléans, and within an hour was driving triumphantly into the city centre.

As Commandant Dufresne sat down to supper, amid the sound of repeated explosions, there was a sudden clamour outside, and a cascade of coloured rockets lit up the sky. "We hurried to the window. Could it be possible?" wrote Dufresne. He soon found it was not only possible but reality. "The deep bass bell of Notre Dame begins to toll, sending out its appeal, sonorously, into the night, answered by all the bells of the capital, in an immense hosanna which seems to shake the reddening sky. 'Les Français! Les Français! they are at the Hôtel de Ville! . . .' Tears trickle down our cheeks . . . I have to stay at my post, and I listen, trembling, alone in my office to this splendid *Marseillaise* of the Liberation which rises from the barricades of Paris, still echoing from the noise of bombs and bullets, while the tricolor flag floats everywhere, proud symbol of freedom, confronting the enemy—who is still there, plotting his last blows."[15]

It was all true—the glory, the relief, the joy; and also the last-ditch stand of the trapped, panic-stricken, defeated Nazis.

*   *   *

On Friday, 25 August, at 11 a.m. Von Choltitz was taken under F.F.I. escort to the Préfecture and received by Leclerc, Valrimont of C.O.M.A.C. and Colonel Rol-Tanguy. There he signed the unconditional surrender of the German garrison, furious at being thus humiliated before the Resistance leaders (*"ces voyous"*). De Gaulle himself expressed his annoyance that the matter had not been handled by regular soldiers only. But even he could hardly suggest that the lion's share of the honour was not due to the Resistance commanders.

While the surrender was being signed, it was announced that the Germans were still holding the Champ de Mars and that the Ecole Militaire was being attacked. In the 7th *arrondissement* and at the

Etoile, fighting went on sporadically all day. Orders went out for barricades to be left up and reinforced, in case of a German come-back. But by the afternoon Leclerc's four columns had entered Paris and joined up at the Place de l'Etoile, where the soldiers attacked the Hotel Majestic, the last remaining German stronghold, and com-pelled its occupants to capitulate. At last at 5 p.m. white flags went up everywhere: the defeat of the Nazis was complete—Paris was free.

The exultant F.F.I. volunteers, who joined Leclerc's soldiers in the last of the fighting, were accepted that day as a vital part of the French army, regardless of their casual clothing and lack of ranks and badges. Dufresne wrote that they were given essential and responsible posts, guarding the city's gates, verifying identities and arresting suspects; and they supported Leclerc's men wherever man-power was needed. "So this great day, one of the finest in France's history, witnessed the formation on a battlefield of a people's army of volunteers, of an army of citizens which had forged itself thanks to the mass rising in illegality."

Colonel Lize declared in a broadcast that "in six days of hard fighting where your bravery and temerity made up for the lack of arms, you have alone completely liberated the capital. . . . The battle continues. You now have the honour of serving as infantry to the magnificent armoured troops of Patton and Leclerc.

"Forward, F.F.I. of the Seine. . . . Let us make the enemy pay dearly for the crime of desecrating the heart of France for four long years."[16]

The battle of Paris was almost over. Details of the last hours of fighting can be found in several histories. Here it is enough to mention the arrival of de Gaulle on 26 August, while the Wehrmacht held some of the northern suburbs and shooting was going on even in the centre. The Germans hung on desperately and a violent bombardment on the night of 26 August expressed their last frenzied attempts at revenge. The threat of reprisals against German hos-pitals alone may have saved Paris from blanket-bombing. However that may be, fierce rearguard actions, sniping and grenade throwing continued all the week-end. This in no way lessened the delirious welcome given to de Gaulle by several million Parisians, waving flags and flowers, shouting, singing, laughing, weeping, as the General and the members of the C.N.R. proceeded across Paris from the Arc de Triomphe to Notre Dame.

Snipers shooting from the rooftops and even inside the cathedral killed and wounded dozens of demonstrators, but it did not damp (rather increased) the popularity of the General. Even the extreme Left (who realised the implications of Gaullism, the dangers of having an idol, the anti-democratic procedures indulged in, under his name) were grateful that afternoon for the figure which could unify France just for a moment—and this role de Gaulle, as he ignored the snipers, and looked benignly around him, fulfilled with sincerity and dignity, earning the gratitude of many who earlier had reason to mistrust him, and later were to have to confront him and defend the ideals of the Resistance against betrayal.

It was only when the excitement and jubilation had died down that people saw that the war was not over after all, and that the F.F.I. realised what de Gaulle had in mind for them: to fight the Allies' battles in the east of France, and in Germany, regimented, graded and uniformed, as regulars in a Gaullist army; and eventually, after Germany's defeat, branded as "Irregulars" to disappear from the scene.

The Liberation had cost many lives. The Germans lost 3,200 dead, 4,911 wounded and 14,800 prisoners. The French Resistance suffered 2,357 dead and wounded, while civilian casualties were 2,408. The French people would say without reserve that though this was a heavy price it was worth paying for the result—Paris, liberated by its own hands, could be proud of its contribution to the cause of the world's freedom. It looked forward now to contributing to the building of a brave new France.

NOTES

1. Tillon, *Les F.T.P.* p. 480
2. Massiet, *Préparation de l'Insurrection et la Bataille de Paris* pp. 126–127
3. ibid. p. 128
4. Tillon, op. cit. pp. 473–474
5. *Le Monde*, 29 August 1949
6. Tillon, op. cit. pp. 486–487
7. Massiet, op. cit. pp. 140–141
8. Tillon, op. cit. p. 489
9. ibid. pp. 492–494
10. Dansette, *Histoire de la Libération* p. 363
11. Tollet, *La Classe ouvrière dans la Résistance* p. 266
12. Massiet, op. cit. p. 161
13. Tillon, op. cit. p. 502
14. De Gaulle, *Mémoirs: Salvation* pp. 368–369

15. Massiet, op. cit. p. 192
16. ibid. p. 205

Chapter 20

VICTORY AND ITS SEQUEL

Où sont les flammes et la sueur
Où sont les larmes et le sang
Où sont le regard et la voix
Où est le cri de ralliement
Paul Eluard, *Au Rendezvous allemand*

Where are the flames and the sweat,
Where are the tears and the blood
Where are the eyes and the voices
Where is the rallying cry?

While Paris was tearing off its shackles, the rest of France was also setting itself free. News of the Parisian insurrection, of the Allies' advance in the north and of the landings in Provence on 15 August increased both the fears of the Germans, who tried frenziedly to retreat north-eastwards, and the enthusiasm of the F.F.I. all over France who redoubled their harassment of the enemy. Fighting raged in every department.

In Savoie, the partisans avenged the massacres of Vercors by taking control of the region and threatening the rear of the German army in Isère, Drome and the Ardèche. By mid-August transport was totally disrupted, the canal system of central France was unusable, the Route Napoléon patrolled by the partisans and bridges blown up between Marseilles and Lyons, and between France and Italy. By 22 August, Valence and Grenoble had fallen to the F.T.P., fighting alongside the U.S. forces. Annemasse, Cluses, Annecy were freed between 21 and 28 August, and Lyons on 25 August, weeks before the Allied schedule. The F.F.I. captured 40,000 prisoners and took up positions on the Italo-French border, as they already had on the Spanish frontier. On 27 August they took Clermont-Ferrand, and on 28th Soisson, while the Germans surrendered at Marseilles to a combined force of Allied troops and F.T.P.

On 21 August Bordeaux, Gap and Limoges were also free. The First German Army, attempting to reach Dijon from the West was hopelessly stuck on 10 September at Issoudon, and only a quarter of its forces managed to get to Dijon. 20,000 men under General

Elstler were surrounded and captured at Issoudon; 18,000 prisoners were taken at Tours, 20,000 at Autun.[1]

The Nazis retaliated in out of the way villages, such as Maille, Indre et Loire, where they massacred 126 civilians; but their atrocities did not help them. By the end of August, 28 departments were completely liberated and two weeks later almost the whole of France was free though fighting continued in the Ardennes in the north-east, and at Lorient and Royan the Germans held out till the end of the year against groups of the *Armée Secrète*.

*   *   *

In the French countryside the weeks following the D-Day landings were the most hectic of the war, but the preceding months had also been militarily eventful and hostilities had taken their toll of young men and civilians, and caused much material shortage.

Ever since the beginnings of the Maquis in 1943, as we have seen, patriotic villagers had given their manpower to the F.F.I. rather than let Germany have it, and had supplied food, clothes, blankets and refuge to *réfractaires* on the run. A visit to the Dordogne region and talks with former resistants, in 1974, gave me a vivid impression of how the movement had developed over the eighteen months of Occupation from passive resistance to the Nazis and their puppets, to active militancy and self-liberation.

A look at the files in the village Mairie at St Julien was revealing. The 1942 Mayor was evidently anti-Vichy, for there are numerous complaints from the Préfecture: announcements of S.T.O. were not always displayed sufficiently visibly (17.2.1943) and "Why have food tickets not been accounted for? . . . Send by return of post a note of the measures you are taking to remedy the situation!" (The food tickets had of course been handed over to the Maquis, a common practice in the region.) Another note asks for information on "young people who try to avoid their obligations to join the *Chantiers de la Jeunesse*". A form dated 27.1.1943 requests lodgings for German army men: what rooms are available in the village for officers, what stables or sheds for soldiers, what space for horses? (Nobody, I was told, had offered accommodation in that village.)

Another communication of January 1943 notifies the Mayor that his secretary, M. Binet, has been sentenced to four months' prison for "outrages à la personne du Chef de l'Etat". The Mayor is asked to suspend him. Receiving no answer, the Préfet writes impatiently demanding an official statement of the secretary's suspension.

My friend Madame D. sighed when I reminded her of M. Binet. "Ah, he was a good fellow! That was how they treated decent people!" Madame's husband had himself been an active member of the Maquis. I found his name among those who had not given up their usable guns, but deposited an old "carbine à piston" and "boite de capsules" in a list of arms requisitioned in the village. Under the comment, "aucune bonne volonté", the Préfet complains of the difficulty of recovering guns: "Certain persons' lack of interest leads us to suppose that they have kept their good rifles, to deposit instead a rusty old pop-gun, disused and found in the garret or over the fireplace." Madame laughed heartily when I showed her this note, and remarked that of course people had kept their weapons, against D-Day.

Her husband, who had acted as Maquis agent, had had many adventures and hairsbreadth escapes from the Vichy Milice and the Germans. Once, picked up by a Nazi car when on a mission, and being driven between two soldiers to the nearest Gestapo office, he had escaped by jumping out of the car and rolling down a precipice overgrown with bushes; the Germans had machine-gunned the undergrowth but had not hit him, although, his wife told me, she had later been to the spot and filled a whole basket with used cartridge cases! They also escaped narrowly from the *Das Reich* column on its way to Oradour, which burned down some houses, but found not one inhabitant in the village—the entire population having been warned and taken to the woods.

After D-Day the whole region became embroiled in the fighting between demoralised Germans and enthusiastic partisans. Almost every family had some member engaged in the battles; many lost a husband or son. The Technical College of La Boétie at Sarlat mourned nine students or former students in the summer battles. A booklet published in their honour, in 1946, cites among others, "Deltreil, Jacques, aged 15, model pupil, grievously wounded by the Germans and atrociously killed by them on 26 June",[2] and "André Videau, taken with 6 comrades, tortured and murdered for not giving away the site of his F.T.P. camp."[3] The Sarlat college was a hotbed of illegal activity during 1944; the Principal's office was a centre for the *Armée Secrète*, and an asylum for Jewish refugees throughout the Occupation. After 6 June the College became a barracks, with a recruiting office for the F.F.I. set up in one of the classrooms. In two days, 800 volunteers were registered, ranging from seventeen-year-olds to veterans of 1914–18. La Boétie "changed from an educational

establishment to a nerve centre of insurrection". Labs and technical
workrooms became grenade factories and repair shops. The kitchens
were transformed into army canteens serving hundreds of meals in
the refectory and in the grounds. Classrooms were wardrobes for
supplying clothing and boots to the Maquis. The Germans got wind
of all this, and sent planes over Sarlat to spy on extra-mural activities. Three times a punitive expedition arrived in the town, searched
the College, breaking windows and doors, but finding nothing.
When they had gone, the "préfet of the Maquis", a former Inspector
of Education, visited the school, "wearing terrorist uniform", to
congratulate the staff on their good work. "On 18 July, an enemy
column returned, went straight to the College and proceeded to loot
and pillage. It was the last time. The Germans had to admit themselves helpless against the general insurrection, simultaneous with
the success of the Allied armies in Normandy."[3] After victory, the
square in front of the College was renamed "Place de la Libération".[4]

*   *   *

André Marty, a hero of the Resistance whom I met at Belvés,
Dordogne, made it very clear that the war did not end for him in
August 1944. He had been named Chef de Secteur in 1942, and had
worked indefatigably to build up groups of the Secret Army in
preparation for D-Day. By some miracle he escaped arrest (his house
was constantly watched and searched by the *Milice*) and was able
to celebrate the landings ceremonially in his little town; he noted in
his journal for 6 June: "*Débarquement*. Distribution of arms to the
A.S. Groups. Positions taken up on appointed posts. Proclamation
of the Fourth Republic. Bell Ringing. Resistance Town Council
elected." A later report describes his group's activities from then on:
"Belvés resistance. While the new civic authorities replace those
of Vichy in all the canton, the armed Resistance of Belvés becomes a
fighting unit, organised in sections and combat groups. It consists of
350 volunteers, chosen according to medical fitness and the arms
available. In spite of certain difficulties due to the terrible repressive
operations carried out by the enemy on 21–22 and 24 June in S.
Dordogne, it maintains its unity and its faith. But the Command is
now situated in the woods of Cartelade and keeps in contact with
Belvés by telephone. . . .
"On 16 July 1944 the Marsouin group is formed, incorporating
Senegalese soldiers, along with officers of the Colonial Army. Our
group are uniformed and supplied with arms and *prend grand*

allure" (look splendid). The group, incorporated in the mobile company, Driant, of 1,000 men, sets out on 22 August and travels all over the Garonne valley, "where the enthusiastic populace of towns and villages are greatly impressed by the behaviour and discipline of the Liberators. Contact made at Langon with the enemy who resists fiercely for two days. The company follows the retreating enemy to Bordeaux, where it drives the last German troops out of the town. They leave in haste and disorder towards the North West."[5]

The Marsouin group becomes *Bataillon* Marsouin, and, armed with artillery seized from the Germans, starts the siege of la Pointe de Grave, a coastal fort where some Wehrmacht men are dug in. They remain there for two and a half months; "despite bad weather, low temperature, poor equipment, with insufficient food, lacking shoes, warm clothing and blankets, in face of a strongly armed enemy the morale remains excellent. . . ." But on 8 December, "in view of the men's fatigue, the battalion is relieved and goes to Bordeaux. Regular army men are sent home, and volunteers are offered contracts of engagement in the regular army, if desired." The battalion was to be dissolved on 1 November by a military decision, but in view of the imperative need of forces to hold the position, it was not till 1 January 1945 that M. Marty could go home. Two hundred of the volunteers were incorporated in the Third Colonial Infantry regiment and sent to the Alsace front, where the battle against the Germans was still raging. "250 to 300 others, engaged for the Colonial Service, went to the Far East and fought in Indochina, returning after the defeat at Dien Bien Phu."[6]

This example of the aftermath of the Liberation is typical of what happened to a fair proportion of the F.F.I. De Gaulle had cleverly succeeded in disarming the "irregular" and most political partisans and in incorporating the less argumentative but patriotic F.F.I. volunteers into regular formations. This acted as a safety valve for the energy that might otherwise have gone into clearing out reactionaries (Vichyist or Gaullist) from posts of authority. There were clashes at that period, summary trials and executions by the partisans, efforts to put left-wing leaders into control, which the General could not countenance. In fact, the pre-Liberation executions of traitors, or suspected pro-Nazis, totalled 5,234; those carried out during Liberation, 3,114, and after later trials by authorised courts 1,325 executions—totalling 4,439 according to government figures: although a considerable number (and said by some historians to be an underestimate), it was a much less fearful vengeance than that wreaked on collaborators in Norway, Holland and Belgium.

To return to the question of the continuing war and of the army: In mid-September, 1944, for the first time in four years the question of political control came into the open. The Resistance movement was united in wanting to raise France's reputation by sharing in the final defeat of the Nazis and leaders from General Leclerc to Maurice Thorez (still in Moscow) called for continuation of the national struggle against the battered but not beaten Nazis; Germany was still fighting in Poland, Bulgaria, Greece, Hungary. France's first task, according to Thorez, was to help win the war, contributing her national army; her second, was to rebuild the economy, carry out the Resistance programme of reforms, abolish "Vichyism", and consolidate her alliance with the U.S.S.R. This was clearly what the French people wanted, as was shown by the rush of volunteers—maquisards whom de Gaulle had disarmed—totalling 500,000, in the late summer. The F.F.I. agreed to accept military authority, but refused to let themselves be completely dissolved, and after their repeated protests de Gaulle had to retract his order disbanding them. A volunteer force under Colonel Fabien, 2,500 strong, went to the Alsace front, but most of the F.F.I. were sent to camps in the Seine departments, in what Tillon saw as "an attempt from above to break the spirit of the Liberation, demoralising its youth and eliminating its leaders".[7] There was bitter discontent among thousands of would-be recruits who besieged the army offices during October, and were refused by the commanding generals, in spite of a degree of 25 September accepting volunteers for the front.

* * *

At the same time, the problems of the reconstruction of France had to be solved. The vast majority of people supported the C.N.R. programme which aimed at ensuring France's freedom and independence and guaranteeing democracy and civil rights. In outline, the Resistance programme, drawn up by the C.N.R. in March 1944, was as follows:

1. Unity after Liberation so as (a) to establish the Provisional Government of the Republic formed by de Gaulle to defend the political and economic independence of the nation, and to re-establish French power, grandeur and the universal mission of France; (b) to assure the punishment of traitors and black marketeers, confiscating their property and outlawing them from public life;

(*c*) to establish a progressive tax on war profits, and on all profits realised at the expense of the people and the nation during the occupation; (*d*) to ensure universal suffrage, freedom of the press, and equal rights of citizens.

2. Economic reforms to include the eviction of the great industrial and financial monopolies from the direction of the economy, and the rational organisation of the economy in the general interest. Social reforms included: the right to work and to leisure; readjustment of wages to give every worker security, and the chance of a decent life; guaranteed purchasing power; an independent trade union movement; a social security system; and reforms in the old age pension system, education, and the colonial administration; indemnification for war damages, and pensions for victims of fascist terror.

The manifesto ended: "Thus a new Republic will be founded, which will sweep away the reactionary regime of Vichy and return to our democratic and popular institutions the power which they lost through the corrupting and treasonable activity that preceded the surrender. . . ."[8]

Unfortunately, the unity which was a prerequisite to the carrying out of the programme was early threatened by de Gaulle's personal ambition, and by his determination to restore the pre-war French State with the support of the big bourgeoisie. "The General refused to proclaim the Republic, and as soon as things calmed down he adopted a contemptuous attitude towards the C.N.R.", says Tillon.

As de Gaulle himself writes, "To the C.N.R.'s unanimous complaints pressing me to reconsider the decision I had taken (on the dissolution of the militias) I could only answer by an absolute refusal."

When forming the National Assembly (single-handed!) the General wanted to make it as representative as possible: "Not that I gave such a body the capacity to act. I was well aware of the fact that Assemblies, despite their fine speeches, are ruled by the fear of action. Besides, I knew of the rivalries which already divided the men of the Resistance; therefore I had no expectation that the representatives would effectively support a resolved policy. But I did hope they would support a mystique of recovery which would inspire the French people. In any case, I thought it wise to offer a sop to their seething spirits."[9]

When a delegation went, representing the Resistance, to complain about the Assembly's limited role in Government, de Gaulle answered that "You are associated in the Government's actions by the questions you ask, the explanations you are given, and the opinions you express. . . . France is greater than the Resistance. It is in the name of France as a whole . . . that I am carrying out my mission. Until the future general elections, I am responsible for the nation's fate only to the nation."[10]

The Provisional Government was recognised on 9 September 1944 with the appearance of national unity; two very minor posts were all that were accorded to the Communists, although the P.C.F. had taken the lion's share of the struggle and in drawing up the programme of the C.N.R. which was used by de Gaulle as a screen for his own plans.[11] The General had made careful preparations, and the Communists and left-wing Resistants involved in the insurrection were far too busy fighting the Germans to occupy themselves with political manœuvring for future position. De Gaulle was thus able to seize the initiative, which until his arrival in Paris had seemed so clearly to be with the Resistance movement. He now presented himself as the only hope for stability and economic recovery in France.

Shrewd and far-seeing, he handled the situation very cleverly, and, as he no doubt thought, in the interests of France—but the France of his own class and beliefs. The long-term interests of the people were considered only in terms of essential reforms, avoiding drastic change, and ensuring law and order.

There is a revealing passage in the General's Memoirs, under the heading "Order": "Now the winds of change were sweeping over liberated France, but order had to be enforced or all would be lost." Then de Gaulle describes the suffering and lack of food: "1,200 calories a day was all the official rations allowed . . . there was no wool, no cotton, scarcely any leather . . . no heat in the cities . . . four million young men mobilised or prisoners, a quarter of the population displaced persons or refugees camping in the ruins or in shanties". His policy was to "revise social conditions so that work could begin again and subversion miscarry; to prepare for the moment when the people would have the power to speak, without allowing anything to breach my authority till then; to restore justice . . . repression taken out of partisan hands . . . to guide the country towards economic and financial equilibrium . . . avert excessive upheavals."[12]

"The mystique of Communism offered itself to the masses' enthusiasm and hopes", the General further writes. "Their aversion for the structure of the past was exacerbated by poverty, concentrated by the Resistance and exalted by the Liberation. Here then was an extraordinary opportunity for the 'Party' . . . the Communist Party had every chance of seizing control of the country, even if it could not do so by means of the Council of the Resistance, the committees or the militia"—unless de Gaulle "took the initiative, carried out a number of reforms . . . got support from the workers and ensured economic recovery on a new basis." This he set out to do.

Haunted by the spectre of workers' revolution, de Gaulle adopted a fair part of the workers' programme. Sources of energy were nationalised; coal, electricity, gas were put under government control; a petroleum bureau was created to regulate the fuel and oil industry; a social security programme was drawn up, largely inspired by the C.N.R. charter. De Gaulle writes that the Communists, who alleged that "the government was prevented from going any further by its reactionary connections", regarded his measures as inadequate but presented no real opposition. "I knew the Party aimed at seizing total power," says de Gaulle, "but its part in the Resistance, the influence it wielded over the workers, the desire of public opinion to see it return to the nation determined me to give the 'Party' its place in the tasks of recovery. Plunging, biting, rearing but strongly harnessed between the shafts . . . it was to help draw the heavy wagon. It was my job to hold the reins . . . I had the strength to do so because of the confidence of the French people."[13] In fact his strength was chiefly derived from the allied armies and from funds provided by Western monopoly capital.[14]

To make sure that Gaullism would be in control all over the country, the General made a tour of the "troubled" regions in November 1944, and his description gives a good idea of the conditions he saw and the measures he took to rectify things. In Lyons, where all but two bridges had been destroyed, where stations were out of commission and factories gutted, he found that "most of the inhabitants had no intention of overthrowing national life" and "given certain changes, spectacular but ill-defined . . . they hoped, instead, for order".[15] In Marseilles, "the atmosphere was ominous" —"German destruction, Allied bombing, the harbour demolished . . . the populace, fed at the cost of great effort and extremely badly, combating destitution at every turn". "The Communists . . . had established an anonymous dictatorship." Some F.F.I. units wanted to be sent into battle in Alsace, others, "subject to a secret allegiance", wanted to remain there. De Gaulle ordered the general on the spot "to give satisfaction to the former and to dissolve the latter" and "instructed the Minister of War to send a regiment from Algeria to Marseilles at once to facilitate matters". (De Gaulle's trump card of course was his control of the regular army and war machine: *"La raison du plus fort est toujours la meilleure."*)

Next, he went to Toulon where "nothing could surpass the scene of desolation of the arsenal, the Quai Cronstadt, the entirely demolished neighbouring districts and the hulls of ships scuttled in the roads", but where he was consoled by the sight of the Free French naval squadron, and the cheers of its crews. Arriving at Toulouse he found "a considerably disturbed city", where the leader of the Haute Garonne Maquis had assumed command, and leaders of the armed units had constituted something like a soviet, carrying out purges with their own men, while the *gendarmerie* and the *garde mobile* had been taken into detention. The General promptly "rescinded the order that kept the *gendarmerie* in barracks and restored these brave men to their normal duties". He appointed General Collet, from Morocco, to command the military sector, and had the First Army dispatch a good-sized unit to Tarbes and Perpignan to prevent the Spanish "division" of maquisards from returning to Spain. He reviewed the Toulouse patriotic militia, a mixed bunch of French partisans, Russians and Spaniards, and was wildly cheered. "I was not at all sure that this . . . would compensate for all we lacked in maintaining public order. At least I hoped that it would enable us to prevent either the dictatorship of the few or general anarchy." This certainly confirms his biographer's view that de Gaulle's provincial journeys were aimed at reducing to zero, if possible, the authorities which had arisen from the Resistance or from the Maquis.

In Bordeaux on 17 September, the atmosphere was strained. "Since the Germans, still entrenched nearby, had considerable stocks of material and since the F.F.I. were neither well organised nor armed, Bordeaux tempered its joy at being free with its fear of ceasing to be so. . . . Armed groups operated and refused to obey the official authorities." De Gaulle applied himself "as elsewhere, to reinforcing these authorities . . . to some leaders who appeared recalcitrant I offered the immediate choice of two alternatives, to submit to the orders of the Colonel in command of the sector, or to go to prison. All preferred the former." (*Force majeure* again!)

The Marsouin group was doubtless among the "several thousand poorly equipped but eager men" whom the General reviewed near Bordeaux, and described as "partisans, completely without heavy arms, artillery, armoured units or planes . . . banded together as they had been in the Maquis, infiltrated from the Gironde, Vienne, Dordogne departments". The "frequent confusion" in the area resulting from different factions claiming command was resolved by de Gaulle again putting one of his Colonels in control, over the heads of the local people.

Visiting Orléans, de Gaulle "with a shudder at the sight of the ruins, drove through the massacred city. . . . In contrast to the inhabitants of the Garonne, the people of the Loire seemed quite temperate." The maquisards "served as a guarantee of order".

In Nancy, just liberated by General Patton's troops, "law and order ran no risk of infringement . . . two thousand maquisards bore witness to this ravaged region's faith in France" as personified by de Gaulle, so he assures us.

At the beginning of November de Gaulle made a tour of the Alpine departments, "where life was beginning to resume its normal course despite great difficulties of provisioning, the problems of action by Alpine maquisards against the enemy, and incidents precipitated by clandestine fighters who wanted to mete out justice on their own". Ambérieu, Annecy, Albertville and Chambéry "overflowing with enthusiasm, gave me the measure of Savoyard loyalty". Grenoble's reception was "indescribable".[14]

All this led the General to conclude that "the nation saw that the confusion of the moment threatened it with anarchy and ultimate dictatorship unless I were there to serve as its focus and guide". "Today it pledged itself to de Gaulle to escape subversion," as it had yesterday, to drive out the invader. "By this token I considered myself reinvested by Liberated Frenchmen. . . . Hailed by the voice of the people, this was never contested. . . ." The administration, the magistracy and the educational authorities, the Council of State, the Audit Office, the Clergy all paid official respect. The former supporters of Vichy capitulated. Pétain, in Germany, kept silence, and those officials, diplomats, military men and journalists who had assiduously served him now lavished obeisances and justifications on the government. M. Albert Lebrun added the approval of the sad ghost of the Third Republic to the chorus.[15]

Backed by all this respectability, de Gaulle felt well able to deal with the Left and to push ahead with his limited programme, the object of which in the not-so-long run was the consolidation of France's bourgeois institutions, and—with a certain number of concessions to the working class—the restoration of capitalism.

NOTES

1. Michel, *Histoire de la Résistance* p. 117
2. R. Terreno, *Collégiens et Maquisards* (Sarlat, 1945) p. 16
3. ibid. p. 107
4. ibid. pp. 98–108
5. André Marty, *Report, Belvés*, August 1974
6. ibid.
7. Tillon, *Les F.T.P.* p. 341
8. Novick, *Resistance against Vichy*, pp. 199–200
9. De Gaulle, *Mémoirs: Salvation* pp. 93–95
10. ibid. p. 106
11. *PCF dans la Résistance* p. 333
12. De Gaulle, op. cit. pp. 15–20
13. ibid. pp. 100–101
14. Tillon, op. cit. p. 382, pp. 393–600
15. ibid. p. 27
16. De Gaulle, op. cit. p. 20

Chapter 21

CONCLUSION

L'aube est tissée de fils limpides
Les innocents ont reparu
Légers d'air pur blancs de colère
Forts de leur droit impérissable
Forts d'une terre sans défauts.

Paul Eluard, *Au Rendezvous allemand*

The dawn is woven with bright threads,
The innocents have reappeared,
Light with purity, white with anger,
With the strength of their undying justice,
The strength of a land that is purged.

Notwithstanding General de Gaulle's well-laid plans and the projection of his image as national saviour, on every possible occasion and by every available means of propaganda, which undoubtedly impressed a large section of French society, the Left and a great many Republicans were most unwilling to hand France over to him lock, stock and barrel. It was true that he held important cards in his hand—the deputing of local government to his men, and control of the Army, achieved by thoroughly undemocratic means. The disbanding of the F.F.I. was a heavy blow to the Resistance and meant that the people's army, which would have been a guarantee for the carrying out of the C.N.R. programme, was no longer available. Nevertheless, the Resistance movement, still largely intact in the autumn of 1944, answered the General in no uncertain voice, with a call for the carrying out of its programme and for unity in the building of a new, truly democratic France.

On the Left the first, most immediate task was seen as the winning of the anti-Hitler war. Maurice Thorez was tumultuously acclaimed on his return from Moscow in November (long delayed by the unwilling de Gaulle) when he called in the Vel d'Hiv, for union and action to defeat the Nazis still fighting the Russians and the Allies in Germany, and for a massive united effort towards national reconstruction. Seizure of power by the Left in France was not mooted; it was believed that Socialism could be won by a truly anti-fascist and

216

united front, led by the Communist Party; it was argued that the
Front Populaire situation with its innate weaknesses was not com-
parable to that of 1944; then, the Centre Parties and the Socialists
had acted as a brake on progress, and the P.C.F. had not been in the
government—from now on, there would be Communist ministers
and an immensely strengthened Party; the P.C.F. had now 500,000
members and a vast fund of popular credit, and it had won a quarter
of all votes cast in the 1944 autumn local elections on a programme
of far-reaching change. To implement this programme the P.C.F.
had the support of many powerful organisations: for instance, the
C.G.T., a formidable force for progress; the *Mouvement des
Intellectuels*, formed to unite Left-wing intellectuals, which grouped
100,000 writers, teachers and university people; the 4,000 agricultural workers' committees (C.G.A.), all former "resistants"
whose vice-chairman was the Communist deputy Waldeck-Rochet.

The majority of anti-fascists agreed with Thorez on the need to
build "a strong and democratic France" by parliamentary means,
accepting de Gaulle's leadership, and counting on the popular forces
to push through the Resistance programme. During the first post-
Liberation months, when the reconstituted Assembly was thick with
Resistance stalwarts, it seemed that really democratic changes might
be achieved through its laws and decrees. But the S.F.I.O. (Socialists)
and Radical groups soon reverted to their bourgeois attitudes
opposing serious economic and social change, and—as in the
Popular Front days—it became clear that they could not be counted
on to support the implementing of drastic reforms. Groupings arose
on the Right, the most important being the M.R.P., de Gaulle's
party, which included a number of ex-Pétainists and put forward a
frankly reactionary programme. Thorez warned that "we see
movements and groups proliferating. Delimitations and divisions
destroy hopes of unity, and prejudice our party's interests."[1] It was
disturbing to see the Roman Catholic Church enjoining the faithful
not to fall under Communist control, and urging Catholic workers
to join Christian trade unions outside the C.G.T.

Although Communists held office in the post-Liberation government (seven, indeed, after 1946), and the Resistance groups were
well represented in the Assembly, de Gaulle, as we have seen, was
determined not to allow them more than a consultative role. In his
plans to prevent a possible takeover by the P.C.F. (an idea which
obsessed him constantly if baselessly) or even by the C.N.R. after the
collapse of the Vichy regime, the General had pre-arranged (in

Algiers' decrees of 1 January, 21 April and 3 June 1944) a transfer of administrative power from Pétainists to Gaullists in every sphere; he had also made sure that his men controlled the Civil Service in Paris, so that Communist ministers met with sabotage *"tantot ouvert, tantot larvé, par les hommes de la bourgeoisie"* (sometimes open, sometimes veiled, by the representatives of the bourgeoisie). "Many Vichy relics survived, adversely affecting industrial and agricultural production. Parasitic services proliferated; the military apparatus was vastly and needlessly overgrown", François Billoux complained, struggling against red tape in the *bureau d'Economie nationale*.[2]

The Communist leaders and Resistance representatives fought hard to remedy these ills, but the fact was that, though they had joined the government, their position in it was not strong enough to push through the sweeping economic changes needed. It was certainly due to their pressure that important steps in social welfare, health and education were taken. They proposed re-organisation in industry, and helped achieve wide measures of nationalisation—Air France, Renault, the mines, gas, etc. But much remained on paper; in spite of vigorous protests by the P.C.F., vital areas which should have come under State control were left to private ownership—the great banks, heavy industry, chemicals and textiles among them.

The P.C.F. bitterly regretted that "the nationalisations were only partial and hardly touched the real power of the Trusts".[3] At the same time it recognised that "nationalisation is a socialist measure only when it is carried out by a Socialist State", and it had to be admitted that France, though purged of the Nazis and Vichy fascist regime, was still far from having achieved Socialism. It was a hard and unpalatable fact that in spite of high hopes the social revolution was not on the agenda. Owing to de Gaulle's strategic moves, and the tacit support of the Allies for French capitalism, a popular seizure of power was not envisaged. Even had it been, two million American and British troops were within call, and their attitude might only too well have resembled that of the men under Churchill's orders in Greece, where in December 1944 British tanks crushed the people's army and restored reaction.

Nor could help have been expected from Stalin who would not involve the Soviet Union in the Western sphere of influence (even Greece had had to be sacrificed to his agreement with Churchill).[4]

Many French patriots, especially in the towns and villages of central and southern France, who had been inspired by the faith and devotion of the Resistance, felt and still feel that their cause had been betrayed, as they resumed their shattered lives and the ideals of their struggle faded, leaving no tangible improvement in society. Whether their trust in future justice and hopes of a better life were pitched too high, whether things could have been different, are questions for another book. It can only be suggested here that if the masses of the French people had not been misled by the Gaullist legend, if the millions of prisoners and workers had been in France to press their claims instead of still rotting in Germany, if the F.F.I. had been able to keep their weapons and their insurrectionary formations, the will of the Resistance might have been imposed. But this was not to be. After August 1944, the bourgeoisie, frightened by the dramatic spectacle of the people in arms, closed their ranks, and willingly set to work under de Gaulle's leadership for the return of capitalism.

Once back in the saddle, the ruling class, while making a few concessions to the workers, concentrated on a policy of anti-sovietism, reformism and neo-imperialist expansion, in a programme where Communist and Resistance ideas had no place. The P.C.F. and left-wing representation in the Assembly declined, Communist ministers were excluded from office, and France returned to the rule of banks and industrialists. The structure of French economy though damaged was not basically affected by the war, and the superficial prosperity that marks much of the country today is based on the technological changes that monopoly capital has been able to carry out on the ruins of bombed towns and villages.

The Socialist State that Aragon, Lurçat, Eluard, and the majority of the French people hoped to see, is still far away, and, as yet, few of the ideas of the Resistance have been put into practice.

But to suggest that the Resistance with all its glory, sacrifice and struggle had merely ended in a restoration of the old regime and without positive gains would be misleading and negative. In fighting and defeating the Nazi invader, and exposing and vanquishing Vichy obscurantism, the French people gained a quite new national consciousness, an unforgettable knowledge of their own strength when united and determined. The working people and their allies have realised that they need only apply the principles of the wartime Resistance to create a new France. The lessons learned during those terrible years of united anti-fascist struggle were much too impressive not to have sunk into the nation's consciousness and to serve infallibly when the future brings opportunity.

A group of patriots, in a book of war-time recollections, *Maquis de Corrèze*, wrote on the thirtieth anniversary of Liberation: "The aspiration of the people in the Resistance to democratic power was embodied in the C.N.R. programme, which we wanted carried out immediately after Liberation. We, the survivors, will never abandon this hope, the hope of our martyrs. They fell in battle, on the snow-covered plateaux, in the gorges, in the forests, on the roads, in the torturers' gaols, in the city streets, or on the moors north of Egletons in the red glow of the flowering heather. All, French and foreigners alike, fought and died for the power of the People, which they saw embodied in the fraternal army of the F.T.P. . . . This was the ideal of believers and non-believers alike, of those who died and of those who survived. It is deeply rooted in our hearts and in the conscious-ness of our people, in spite of all and because of all that has happened. With our children and our children's children, we shall make it come true."[5]

NOTES

1. Le P.C.F. *dans la Résistance*, pp. 335–336
2. F. Billoux, *Quand nous étions Ministres* (Paris, 1972) p. 69
3. E. Fajon, *Cahiers du Communisme*, February 1945, quoted in J. Ellenstein, *De la Guerre à la Libération* p. 106
4. Churchill, *Second World War*, Vol. VI p. 198
5. *Maquis de Corrèze* (Paris, 1970) p. 619

ABBREVIATIONS

A.S.	Armée Secrète
B.C.R.A.	Bureau Central de Renseignements et d'Action
C.F.L.N.	Comité Français de Libération Nationale
C.F.T.C.	Confédération Française de Travailleurs Chrétiens
C.G.T.	Confédération Générale du Travail
C.G.T.U.	Confédération Générale du Travail Unifiée
C.N.R.	Conseil National de la Résistance
C.O.M.A.C.	Comité d'Action
D.M.R.	Délégué Militaire Régional
F.F.I.	Forces Françaises de l'Intérieur
F.F.L.	Forces Françaises Libres
F.N.	Front National
F.T.P.	Franctireurs et Partisans
Gestapo	Geheime Staatspolizei
G.P.R.F.	Gouvernément Provisoire de la République
L.V.F.	Légion de Volontaires Français (contre le Bolchévisme)
M.U.R.	Mouvements Unifiés de la Résistance
O.C.M.	Organisation Civile et Militaire
O.S.	Organisation Spéciale (P.C.F.)
P.C.F.	Parti Communiste Français
P.T.T.	Postes, Télégraphes, Téléphones
S.H.A.E.F.	Supreme Headquarters Allied Expeditionary Force
S.N.C.F.	Société Nationale des Chemins-de-Fer Français
S.O.E.	Special Operations Executive
S.S.	Schutzstaffel
S.T.O.	Service du Travail Obligatoire
Z.N.O.	Zone Non-Occupée
Z.O.	Zone Occupée

CALENDAR OF EVENTS
1933–1945

Published in Ivry Memorial Volume, 1970

1933

30 January	Hitler appointed Reichs Chancellor by Hindenburg.
31 January	Daladier forms ministry.
1 February	Hitler dissolves Reichstag. German C.P. calls for general strike.
27 February	Nazis burn Reichstag and start repression against communists and democrats.
5 March	Communist International appeals for struggle against fascism. P.C.F. (Communist Party of France) calls for united front.
9 March	Dimitrov accused of burning Reichstag.
9 April	60,000 workers demonstrate against fascism at Bagnolet.
7 June	4-power pact giving free hand to fascist powers.
20 August	Formation of world movement against war and fascism.
21 September	Opening of Dimitrov trial.
23 December	Dimitrov acquitted.

1934

6 February	Fascist leagues riot in Place de la Concorde against Daladier government, which resigns.
9 February	Demonstration by 50,000 workers all over E. Paris. Many arrests. Formation of Doumergue government, to appease fascists.
12 February	General strike of 150,000 workers.
17 February	200,000 attend funeral of victims of 9 February.
19 February	General strike in Spain, in sympathy with French.
5 March	Formation of *Comité de vigilance des intellectuels* led by Rivet, Langevin and Emile Alain.
20 May	30,000 Parisians demonstrate for liberation of Ernst Thaelmann.
23 June	National conference of P.C.F. at Ivry for unity of action.
27 July	United front pact signed between P.C.F. and Socialists.

18 September	U.S.S.R. joins League of Nations.
8 October	Thorez calls for a Popular Front.
8 November	Flandin forms government.

1935

7 January	Laval and Mussolini sign agreement at Rome.
6 February	Fascist leagues organise commemoration service at Notre-Dame.
10 February	100,000 at demonstration in memory of 9 February 1934.
2 May	Franco-Soviet pact signed.
19 May	200,000 at Commune memorial meeting at Père Lachaise.
6 June	Ministry of National Union, led by Laval.
29 June	First great meeting of Front Populaire, Mutualité.
14 July	500,000 at F.P. demonstration.
28 August	P.C.F. calls for common action against fascism.
3 October	Mussolini attacks Ethiopia.
5 October & 27 October	P.C.F. approaches Socialist and Radical Parties to form Popular Front. Radical Congress agrees.
6 December	French Parliament votes to dissolve fascist leagues.

1936

7 March	Remilitarisation of the Rhineland.
28 April	F.P. victory at elections.
1 May	Mass demonstrations all over France.
11 May	Factories occupied. Strikes continue through May and June.
4 June	F.P. government formed under Léon Blum.
7 June	*Accords Matignon:* Freedom of T.U.s respected. Increase in wages and salaries.
11 June	Collective agreements, paid holidays and 40-hour-week voted by Chambre in majority vote.
18 June	Dissolution of fascist leagues, Croix de Feu, Jeunesses patriotiques, Solidarité Française, etc.
14 July	A million demonstrators at Bastille.
18 July	Franco starts war on Spanish republic.
20 July	Madrid asks F.P. government for help. Blum decides on non-intervention.
8 August	French Government refuses war material to Spain.
9 August	Pro-Spanish demonstrations all over Paris—40,000 at St Cloud.
29 September	Devaluation of franc.

November	International Brigade leaves for Spain.
25 November	Germany and Japan sign anti-communist pact.
December	Blum puts brakes on talks with U.S.S.R. about anti-fascist alliance against Germany.

1937

13 February	Blum announces "pause". Suspends economic and social measures at demand of employers.
21 June	Blum resigns. Succeeded by Chautemps, supported by Socialist Party.
30 June	New devaluation of franc.
6 November	Italy joins Anti-Comintern pact.
25 December	11th congress of P.C.F. reaffirms F.P. programme.

1938

14 January	Chautemps resigns, after anti-P.C.F. moves.
18 January	Chautemps returns, without Socialist support.
12 March	German troops enter Austria (*Anschluss*).
13 March	Blum's second government. Daladier succeeds him on 10 April.
29 September	Munich agreement, abandoning Czechs.
5 October	73 P.C.F. deputies vote against Munich.
14 November	Daladier government *décrets-lois* abolishing many F.P. decrees and 40-hour-week.
30 November	Twenty-four-hour general strike. Police repression.
December	Franco-German pact signed by Bonnet/Ribbentrop.

1939

| 6 September | Hitler attacks Poland. War declared. Repression of Left. |
| 30 November | U.S.S.R.–Finnish war. |

1940

20 January	Communist Deputies deprived of rights by law.
20 March	Trial of 44 P.C.F. Deputies.
	End of war in Finland.
20 March	Daladier resigns; replaced by Reynaud government.
10 April	Law published announcing death penalties for Communists.
10 May	German invasion of Belgium.
	Advance into France.
28 May– 3 June	Dunkirk. Six million civilian refugees. Small groups resisting.
6 June	P.C.F. appeals through G. Politzer to Government for organisation of defence of Paris.

10 June	Italy declares war on France.
14 June	German army enters Paris.
16 June	Reynaud resigns, partisans of capitulation take over.
18 June	De Gaulle's appeal from London.
19–21 June	Soldiers carry on in places—Saumur, Loire, etc.
22 June	Armistice signed at Rethondes.
2 July	Pétain sets up Vichy government.
July	Nine underground organisations printing and distributing tracts destroyed, ninety militants arrested.
10 July	Thorez and Duclos appeal for resistance.
	Agreements between Vichy and Germans: internment of dissidents, oppressive measures.
1 August	*La Vie Ouvrière* starts campaign setting up *Comités populaires* in factories.
9 August	German and French industrialists agree (Kuhlmann, I.G. Farben, Renault, Schneider) on production for Germany.
14 August	Royan town is fined 3 million fr. after death of a German sailor.
	Thorez' *Appel* circulates in both zones. Ten issues of *Humanité* monthly, 140,000 copies. Jeunesse publishes *L'Avant-garde*.
	During summer Jean Baillet, secretary of Com. Fed. of W. Paris, delegated to carry directives in several departments, such as l'Aube, organising collection of arms abandoned during débâcle.—Action groups in North carry out sabotage, cutting cables, burning vehicles.
16 August	General Delestraint's *Appel*. *Vie Ouvrière* appears.
	Big capitalists form economic councils.
10 September	German notice forbidding "damage to means of communication" on pain of death.
	600,000 unemployed in Paris region. Bread 350 gr. daily and meat rationed (350 gr. weekly).
September–October	*Les Bataillons de la Jeunesse*, and O.S. formed by P.C.F. Campaign against French culture launched by Vichy. Anti-Jewish law passed. *L'Œuvre* announces (18 October) legal inquiries into many militants distributing underground press.
	Paris police announce 871 arrests and thirty-five

	printing presses closed since July.
9 November	Demonstration by students "Libérez Langevin", at Sorbonne.
11 November	Demonstration by students in Champs Elysées.
December	Poster up in Paris announcing execution of Jacques Bonsergent.

1941

14 May	First mass arrest of Jews, in Paris.
15 May	P.C.F. calls for Front of national unity.
26 May	Miners' strike, organised by P.C.F., in Northern France (100,000 on strike, 472,000 working days lost plus 500,000 tons of coal) lasting till 9 June when demands met.
2 June	Vichy announces new law on Jews.
21 June	Hitler attacks U.S.S.R.
29 June	Three lawyers arrested in Paris.
7 July	Vichy approves creation of *Légion de Volontaires Française contre le Bolchévisme*.
21 July	Seventy-two arrests in l'Aube.
23 July	Twenty-seven shot at Beauvais.
14 August	Pétain's special tribunals set up. Atlantic Charter signed.
23 August	Colonel Fabien shoots a German officer. Reprisals. Shooting of hostages announced.
September	"France d'Abord" F.T.P. paper appears. Beginning of siege of Leningrad.
16 September	Keitel announces 100–500 Communists to be shot for every German killed.
19 September	*Vie Ouvrière* calls for sabotage in factories producing tanks, etc., for Russian front.
22 September	Gabriel Péri sentenced to hard labour for life.
23 September	De Gaulle forms Free French Committee in London. Executions of Voog, Adolphe Guyot and Jean Catelas.
26 September	Soviet Government recognises de Gaulle's Committee.
9 October	Dietrich declares that Russia no longer counts as military factor.
20–22 October	Patriots kill German officers at Nantes and Bordeaux.
22 October	Twenty-seven shot at Chateaubriant. Twenty-one at

	Nantes, fifty at Bordeaux. Pétain on radio: "We have laid down our arms, we have no right to take them up to stab the Germans in the back."
23 October	Five-minute strike all over France in honour of martyrs.
25 November	Anti-Comintern Pact renewed.
26 November	Great Britain recognises de Gaulle as Free French Government.
27 November	Million-franc fine for strike, imposed on Paris.
5–7 December	Soviet offensive. Germans retreat to 200 km. from Moscow. More German officers killed in Paris followed by reprisals, and 1,615 arrests.
8 December	Japan attacks Pearl Harbour, landings in Siam and Borneo.
14 December	Deportation of Jews. 100 hostages executed in Paris.
15 December	Péri executed at Mont Valérien, Lucien Sampaix at Caen.

1942

January	12 days' strike by miners of Montceau-les-Mines, 100,000 tons lost. German submarine offensive.
6 February	Hunger riots at Sête.
13 February	Twenty executed at Tours, thirty-two in Paris, forty-five in other parts.
25 February	German 16th Army encircled at Staraia-Roussa.
28 February	U.S.A. recognises de Gaulle's National Committee.
3 March	R.A.F. bombardment of Renault at Billancourt.
7 March	Execution of Pierre Semard, General Secretary of Railwaymen.
10 March	Twenty hostages executed in Paris.
27 March	First big convoy of Jews deported to camps.
27–28 March	British bomb St Nazaire, putting submarines out of action. Sauckel appointed commissar of labour in Z.O.
14 April	Thirty-five executed in Pas-de-Calais. Suspension of Riom trial (opened on 19 February).
19 April	Thirty executed at Rouen.
20 April	Laval (head of Vichy government, 18 April, with Darlan as C. in C. of armed forces). "I wish for a German victory" speech. Doriot attacked at Rennes. Fifteen hostages shot in Paris; curfew, 11 p.m.
1 May	Allied bombings of Germany. Many demonstrations in France, protected by F.T.P.

5 May	Heydrich (*S.S. chief*) arrives in Paris, Oberg S.S. appointed head of police there. Darquier de Pellepoix named Commissar-General of Jewish questions.
6 May	Forty executed at Lyons.
10 May	Churchill asserts bombings are equivalent to Second Front.
12 May	Twenty executed at Rouen. Russian offensive, Kharkhov.
16 May	Seventy-one F.T.P. arrested in Paris.
19 and 23 May	Five shot in Paris, eleven at Clairvaux.
27 May	Heydrich killed at Prague (Lidice reprisal, 10 June). Rommel offensive in Libya, Koenig at Bir-Hakeim.
28 May	Waggons of wheat emptied by crowd at Onnaing.
29 May	German decree on wearing of Yellow Star by Jews.
30 May	Felix Cadras, J. Decour, G. Politzer, J. Solomon executed.
31 May	Leaflets distributed in Paris. Housewives raid shops.
1 June	Escape of nineteen Communists from Compiègne camp. Eichmann proclaims Hitler's "final solution" for all Europe.
22 June	Laval announces the "relève".
27 June	Churchill and Roosevelt say no Second Front yet. Five sentenced to death after "rue de Seine affair".
3 July	Patriots set fire to Bonneuil works.
13 July	De Gaulle's Committee becomes *France Combattante*. Demonstrations at Lyons, Toulouse, Marseilles.
15 July	Five executions at Lille.
16 July	22,000 arrests of Jews in Paris area, later deported from Vel d'Hiv to Auschwitz.
20 July	Fifteen sentenced to death at Nancy.
29 July	First bombing by U.S.A.F. of Germany.
1942	
	Agreement signed "harmonising" French and German police. "Brigades Spéciales" work with Gestapo in hunting down Communists.
30 July	Demonstration in Gare d'Orléans against departure of 200 deportees.

1 August	200 hostages short in France. Under *Nacht und Nebel* decree 104 patriots sent to unknown destination in Germany.
8 August	Laval promises Germany 350,000 French workers. Mussolini claims Corsica and Tunisia.
11 August	Execution of ninety-three "terrorists", all from Ivry.
15 August	German officers attacked in Paris boulevards, Clamart, Ivry and Chelles.
20 August	Germans attack Stalingrad, after reaching Volga.
21–27 August	Russian bombings of Poland and E. Prussia.
28 August	Russian offensive at Leningrad.
31 August	Rommel offensive halted at El-Alamein.
1 September	French bishops protest at persecution of Jews.
4 September	Law of S.T.O. for all French. Battle of Stalingrad begins.
19 September	116 executions in Paris.
20 September	Demonstration (called by P.C.F.) in Paris for 150th anniversary of Valmy. Sanctions following attacks by patriots on Rex Cinema and Metro Marbeuf. Cinemas, sports events, etc., banned. Curfew 3 p.m.
25 September	C. Lebarge, leader of F.T.P. of Calais, executed.
30 September	Death sentence on 21 F.T.P. by German military tribunal.
5 October	Execution at Issy of Pierre Rébière, member of E.C. of P.C.F.
17 October	Shootings at Lyons, Marseilles, etc., after demonstrations against deportations to Germany.
30 October	Rail strikes in Savoy.
1 November	German-Italian front broken at El-Alamein.
8 November	Allied landings in N. Africa. Pétain orders resistance.
11 November	Germans occupy southern Zone (Z.S.) of France.
12 November	Egypt entirely liberated. British cross Libyan border.
19–23 November	Soviet counter-offensive at Stalingrad. Von Paulus encircled.
27 November	German occupation of Toulon, scuttling of Fleet.
24 December	Twenty-four executions at Rennes. Giraud in power in N. Africa after assassination of Darlan.

25 December	Von Manstein's counterattack broken at Stalingrad.
31 December	F.T.P. communiqué announces nearly 300 operations against railways, and 750 officers and other members of German army killed, 1,780 wounded, 42 barges of material sunk.

1943

January	Final offensive of Red Army at Stalingrad.
11 January	Fernand Grenier arrives in London to represent P.C.F.
24 January	Danièlle Casanova and M. C. Vaillant-Couturier leave fort of Romainville for Auschwitz in first convoy of women.
28 January	Hitler mobilises all men from 15 to 65, women of 14 to 45.
29 January	F.T.P. announce derailing at Chagny, a train full of German soldiers for the E. Front—250 killed, many wounded.
2 February	Final victory at Stalingrad.
5 February	P.C.F. deputies in Algiers prison set free; issue *Appel*, "S'unir, s'armer, se battre".
25 February	Hitler's speech: "Germany will mobilise and use the forces of other nations".
11 March	In Paris, patriots attack Wehrmacht at Boulevard Souchet and Odéon.
10 April	F.T.P. reports 1,500 actions against the enemy, between 1 January and 31 March. 158 derailings; 180 locomotives and 1,200 waggons with material, or troops, destroyed; sabotage of 110 locos, 3 bridges, 14 barges, 8 locks; 800 Wehrmacht killed or wounded.
11 April	Laval and Sauckel transform P.O.W.s into "free workers". Since January 1943 Laval mobilised seven classes, deported 250,000 workers, turned 250,000 prisoners into factory workers (so-called "free").
2 May	Georges Wodli hung, in Struthof camp.
10 May	Danièlle Casanova dies at Auschwitz.
12 May	German-Italian resistance ends in Tunis.
15 May	Conseil National de la Resistance formed in France (C.N.R.).
3 June	Comité Française de Libération Nationale (C.F.L.N.)

4 June	formed in Algiers. Churchill meets leaders (de Gaulle and Giraud).
6 June	Beheading by Gestapo of Bertie Albrecht.
21 June	Jean Moulin (chairman of C.N.R.) arrested.
5–19 July	German offensive Bielgorod, Kursk-Orel. "Normandie" squadron active in battle.
10 July	Landings in Sicily. Attacks by F.T.P. on Germans in Paris.
25 July	Mussolini resigns and is arrested. Badoglio cabinet.
31 July	C.F.L.N. reorganised: De Gaulle President, Giraud C. in C.
August	German Eastern Front broken.
23 August	Red Army takes Kharkhov.
26 August	U.S.S.R. recognises C.F.L.N.
3 September	Allied landings in Sicily.
8 September	Italy capitulates. Allied landings at Salerno.
13–17 Sept.	Arrival in Corsica of French troops to join partisans, under Giraud.
20 September	Zone interdite on Mediterranean coast.
29 September	Ritter, Sauckel's representative in France, killed by F.T.P.
30 September	Occupation costs for France: 321 milliard francs.
3 October	Liberation of Corsica.
8 October	Seventeen patriots executed at Orléans.
10 October	Caucasus liberated.
13 October	Italy declares war on Germany.
16 October	Miners strike (30,000) in Nord and Pas-de-Calais.
24 October	Four young F.T.P. assassinated at Grenoble.
9 November	Giraud retires, de Gaulle head of C.F.N.L. at Algiers.
25 November	Arrests and deportation of staff and students of Strasbourg university, Clermont-Ferrand.
28 November	Teheran meeting (Churchill, Roosevelt, Stalin).
5 December	50 arrests, 50 deportations, curfew at 3 p.m., at Grenoble, following attack on German H.Q. (10 killed, 50 wounded).
20 December	Arrests and curfew at Annecy, German officer killed by patriots. Occupation costs now 350 milliards.
24 December	General Eisenhower named commander of Allied Forces for landings in Normandy (Overlord).

1944

20 January	Promulgation of law on courts martial against "terrorist" activities.
26 January	400 students demonstrate in Sorbonne Chemistry Theatre.
1 February	Repressive operations begun by Vichy police against the Maquis of Haute Savoie.
18 February	Twenty-three F.T.P. sentenced to death in Paris (and shot on 21st).
23 February	Chemistry students demonstrate in Marseilles.
2 March	Seventeen executions of "réfractaires" at Nîmes.
15 March	Announcement of C.N.R. programme.
20 March	Pucheu (Pétain's minister) shot in Algiers. Consultative Assembly votes for plan for France after Liberation.
22 March	Death of Pierre Brossolette, escaping from Gestapo.
25 March	460 patriots on plateau of Glières attacked by 20,000 Germans and Milice.
26 March	Severe repression in Dordogne by German troops.
30 March	Cost of occupation, now 381 milliard francs.
1 April	At Ascq, near Lille, eighty-six inhabitants massacred by S.S. after German military train derailed.
3–14 April	Grenier and Billoux enter C.F.L.N. as ministers. Giraud pushed out by de Gaulle.
11–15 April	Odessa re-taken by Red Army; Jukov enters Galicia.
9 May	Red Army liberates Sebastopol.
1 June	Bombings of bridges and fortifications by R.A.F. and U.S.A.F.
3 June	C.F.L.N. at Algiers becomes Provisional Government of French Republic (G.P.R.F.).
4 June	Rome taken by Allies, including French forces.
5 June	Churchill-Eisenhower conference on administering liberated territories.
6 June	Allied landings in Normandy. Activity of F.F.I., specially on railways used by enemy. F.F.I. frees many departments. Normandy towns bombed by U.S.A.F.
8 June	Germans recapture Tulle freed by F.F.I. Ninety-nine hostages hanged in streets. Bayeux, first town to be freed.

10 June	Massacre of 700 (250 children) at Oradour-sur-Glane, by 3rd company of 2nd regiment of S.S. division *Das Reich*.
12 June	Telecommunications suspended in northern zone.
13 June	Germans continue offensive against Vercors. Maquis waits in vain for arms from Algiers. De Gaulle refuses to send planes asked for by Grenier.
15–30 June	Growing battle of F.F.I. against Germans, liberation of much of country, particularly Brittany where resistants help progress of Allies. Increased repression by Germans and Milice in "punitive columns".
20 June	Suspension of telecommunications in Z.S.
25 June	General Koenig named C. in C. of F.F.I.
27 June	Siege of Cherbourg, where Germans installed.
July	Massive exterminations in German concentration camps. Occupation costs now 409 milliard francs.
14 July	Great demonstrations all over France. 45,000 in Paris, thousands more in suburbs. Work stopped in factories.
27 July	Execution of five hostages in Lyons, bodies shown in street.
6–10 August	Liberation of St Brieuc, Quimper, etc., by F.F.I. Allied tanks arrive at Mans. Rail strike, signal for final battle.
11 August	F.F.I. free Aurillac, Nantes, Angers.
15 August	Allied landing in Provence, with De Lattre de Tassigny.
16 August	Thirty-four partisans executed in Bois de Boulogne, Paris.
19 August	Beginning of insurrection in Paris and Marseilles. F.F.I. occupy Préfecture and Hôtel de Ville. F.F.I. free Perpignan, Agen, Castres, Foix, Le Puy.
19 August to 12 September	Retreat of German troops from South-west and centre. 18,000 prisoners at Tours; 20,000 at Issoudun; 20,000 Autun.
20 August	Allies cross Seine at Mantes. Liberation of Montauban, Toulouse, Saint-Girons, Vichy. Massacre of 100 at St Genis-Laval near Lyons.
21 August	*L'Humanité* publishes first legal number since 1939. Bordeaux, Gap, Limoges freed. Massacre of 126 at Maille (Indre et Loire) by S.S.

22 August	Vain attempt on Préfecture and Hôtel de Ville, Paris, by German tanks. Fighting around Pantheon, Boulevard Saint-Germain, Tuileries, Batignolles. Communiqué announces fourteen departments freed by F.F.I.
23 August	Street fighting intensified in Paris. Allies arrive in Marseilles.
24 August	F.F.I. in Nîmes and Villeurbanne. Leclerc division enters Paris 9.30 p.m.
25 August	Last battles in Paris, and surrender of Germans by Von Choltitz (Gare Montparnasse) to Rol Tanguy and Leclerc.
26 August	Germans bomb Paris. Many killed.
27 August	F.F.I. take Clermont-Ferrand. Germans surrender at Toulon.
28 August	F.F.I. take Soissons before Americans arrive. Germans surrender at Marseilles. De Gaulle who wanted to dissolve the F.F.I., has to change his mind after massive protests of Resistance movement.
1 September	Red Army enters Bucharest.
3 September	Many militants leave for front, led by Colonel Fabien.
5 September	Germans evacuate Greece and Aegean islands.
6 September	Fighting in Doubs. Red Army enters Bulgaria.
7 September	Liberation of Poitiers. Goebbels demands intensification of war effort. Red Army on Danube, Rumanian border.
8 September	German troops in south-west and central France retreat along Loire trying to rejoin Wehrmacht in Lorraine.
9 September	Patton's thrust between Metz and Thionville.
13 September	Allied troops enter Germany, towards Trêves.
14 September	U.S. army enters Germany. Leclerc and De Lattre meet at Chantillon-sur-Seine.
17 September	Red Army at Sofia (Bulgaria).
23 September	Publication of F.F.I. statute in *Journal Officiel*.
26–27 September	French Ministers' Council publishes decisions on industry, nationalisation, purge of collaborators.
13 October	Athens freed by Greek patriots.
16 October	Liberation of Belgrade; 4 November, Budapest.
23 October	Provisional Government recognised by Allies.

28 October	Dissolution of armed movements outside police and army in France.
8 December	Creation of Comp. Républicaine de Securité (C.R.S.).
13 and 23rd December	Nationalisation of mines in North and Pas-de-Calais and of Renault factories.
10 December	Signing of Franco-Soviet Pact of alliance and mutual assistance.
30 December	Deaths of Colonel Fabien, Commandant Dax, and Captain Lebon on Rhine front.

SELECT BIBLIOGRAPHY

On the Resistance (local and specialised)

Bellanger, R. *Dordogne en armes*, Périgueux 1946

Bonte, F. *Le Chemin de l'Honneur*. Editions Sociales, Paris, 1970

Chapsal, J., *La Vie politique en France*, Paris

Delanoue, P., *Les Enseignants*, E. S., Paris, 1973

Ellenstein, J., *De la Guerre à la Libération*, Paris, 1970

Gosset, A., *Caen pendant la Bataille*, Caen, 1946

Grenier, Fernand, *C'était ainsi*, E.S., Paris, 1970

—, *Ceux de Chateaubriand*, E.S., Paris, 1942

Guéguen-Dreyfus, G., *Résistance Indre et Vallée du Cher*, E. S., Paris, 1972

Ivry, fidèle à la Classe ouvrière, Ivry, 1970

Maquis de Corrèze, E.S., Paris, 1971

Massiet, R. (Dufresne), *La Préparation de l'Insurrection et la Bataille de Paris*, Paris, 1945

Moine, André, *Déportation et Résistance, Afrique du nord*, E. S., Paris, 1969

Moulin, Laure, *Jean Moulin*, Paris, 1969

Ouzoulias, A., *Les Bataillons de la Jeunesse*, E.S., Paris, 1969

P.C.F. *Le Parti Communiste Français dans la Résistance*, E.S., Paris, 1967

Oradour-sur-Glane, Vision d'épouvante, Limoges, 1970

Pestourié, Roger, *La Résistance c'était cela aussi*, E.S., Paris, 1969

Terreno, R., *Collégiens et Maquisards*. Sarlat, 1946

Tillon, Charles, *Les F.T.P.*, Paris, 1962, Juilliard

Tollet, Andre, *La Classe ouvière dans la Résistance*, E. S., Paris, 1969

Willard, Germaine, *De Munich à Vichy*, E.S., Paris, 1969

Memoirs, Biography, History

Aron, Robert, *De Gaulle before Paris*, trans. London, 1962

Baudouin, Paul, *Neuf mois au gouvernement*, Paris, 1948

Bidault, Georges, *Resistance*, trans. London, 1967

Bloch, Marc, *Strange Defeat*, trans. London, 1949

Bourdet, Claude, *L'aventure incertaine*, Paris, 1975

Bradley, Omar, *A Soldier's Story*, New York, 1951

Churchill, Winston, *The Second World War* (5 vols.), Reprint Society, London, 1954

Collins, L., *Is Paris burning?* Penguin, 1966

D'Astier, E., *Seven Times Seven Days*, trans. London, 19

Esquier, G., *8 Novembre 1942*, Paris, 1946

Foot, M. R. D., *S.O.E. in France*, London, 1966

Gallo, Max, *Spain under Franco*, trans. London, 1973

Gaulle, Charles de, *Memoirs* (3 vols.), trans. London, 1955

Hawes, S. and White, R. ed. *Resistance in Europe*, London, 1975

Malraux, André, *Anti-mémoires*, Paris, 1970

Maurois, André, *Call No Man Happy*, trans. London, 1944

Michel, Henri, *Histoire de la Résistance*, Paris 1952

—, *Vichy Année 40*, Paris, 1966

—, *The Shadow War*, trans. London, 1970

Novick, Peter, *The Resistance against Vichy*, London, 1968

Paxton, Robert, *Vichy France*, London, 1970

Pelling, Henry, *Britain and the Second World War*, London, 1970

Pritt, D. N., *The Fall of the French Republic*, London, 1941

Reynaud, Paul, *La France a sauvé l'Europe*, Paris, 1947

Sérigny, A. de, *L'Enigme d'Alger*, Paris, 1947

Simone, André, *J'accuse*, London, 1942

Stewart, Frida, *Dawn Escape*, London, 1943

Teissier Ducros, Janet, *Divided Loyalties*, London, 1966

Tournoux, J. R., *Pétain and de Gaulle*, trans. London, 1966

Warner, G., *Pierre Laval*, London, 1972

Werth, Alexander, *The Destiny of France*, London, 1938

—, *The Last Days of Paris*, London, 1940

Weygand, General, *Memoirs*, Paris, 1955

Willard, Germaine, *De la Guerre à la Libération*, Paris, 1971

Zilliacus, K., *Why we are losing the Peace*, London, 1939

Books by or about British (S.O.E.) and French (B.C.R.A.) Agents

Benouville, G. de, *Le Sacrifice du Matin*, Paris, 1947

Braddon, Russell, *Nancy Wake*, London, 1956

Buckmaster, M., *They Fought Alone*, London, 1958

Cookridge, E. H., *They came from the Sky*, London, 1965

Fourcade, Madeleine, *Noah's Ark*, trans. London, 1973

Millar, G., *Maquis*, London, 1945

—, *Horned Pigeon*, 1946

Moulin, Laure, *Jean Moulin*, Paris, 1969

Rémy, *Une Affaire de Trahison*, Paris, 1947
Sherwood, R. E. The White House Papers of Harry Hopkins (U.S.A. 1949)
Sweet-Escott, Bickham, *Baker Street Irregular* (1965)
Weil-Curiel, *Eclipse en France*, Paris, 1946
Xavier, *Memoirs of an Agent*, London, 1970

Poetry and Literature in the Resistance

Aragon, Louis, *Les Yeux d'Elsa*, 1943
—, *Le Crêve cœur*, Paris, 1944
—, *La Diane française*, 1945
—, *Le Musée Grévin*, 1946
—, *Matisse, a novel*, trans. London, 1973
—, *Servitude et Grandeur des Français*, 1946
De Beauvoir, Simone, *La Force de l'Age*, Paris, 1960
Eluard, Paul, *Poèsie*, Paris, 1945
—, *Au Rendezvous allemand*, 1945
Lurçat, Jean, *La Tapisserie française*, Paris, 1950
Mauriac, François, *Le Cahier noir*, Paris, 1945
Parrot, Louis, *L'Intelligence en guerre*, Paris, 1947
Penrose, Roland, *In the Service of the People*, London, 1945
Sartre, Jean Paul, *The Age of Reason*, Penguin, 1961
Vailland, Roger, *Drôle de Jeu*, Paris, 1948
Vercors, *Le Silence de la Mer*, London, 1943

Periodicals and unpublished material include:

La Lettre de la France Libre, 1942–44
Documents, France Libre service 1943–44
Illegal Press, particularly *l'Humanité, Combat, Libération, Vie Ouvrière, France nouvelle*
Bulletin du Musée de l'Homme
Police Report, Paris, 1938–39. *Maquis report*, Belvés, 1944

INDEX

Abetz, Otto, 28, 39, 193, 195
Aboulker, José, 103, 105
Action Française, 11, 12, 28
Albrecht, Berthy, 179
Alibert, Raphaël, 82
Anjot, Captain, 153
Aragon, Louis, 52, 116, 143–6, 148, 219
Aron, Raymond, 17
Aron, Robert, 172–3
Astier de la Vigerie, Emmanuel, 138
Atholl, Duchess of, 27
Aubrac, Raymond, 169

Babeuf, 37
Barbusse, Henri, 14, 39
Barre, General, 105
Baudouin, Paul, 22, 43, 49, 54
B.C.R.A., 76, 117, 128, 151, 157, 165, 169–72, 181
Beauvoir, Simone de, 52, 72, 164
Béraud, Henri, 146
Bergery, Gaston, 29
Bidault, Georges, 46, 55, 75, 98, 119–21, 141, 196
Billoux, François, 37, 156, 218
Blanqui, Auguste, 36
Bloch, Marc, 46–8
Blocq-Masquart, Maxime, 121
Blum, Léon, 15, 21, 22, 24–5, 57, 82, 124
Bonnard, Abel, 143
Bonnet, Georges, 26, 28, 37, 40, 44, 82
Bonsergent, Jacques, 71–2
Bonte, Florimond, 38, 125
Bost, Pierre, 148
Bouffet, Préfet, 189
Bourdet, Claude, 98
Bradley, General Omar N., 187, 198
Brault, Michel, 138
Brécard, General, 194

Brinon, Fernand de, 28
Bourgoin, Captain, 170–1
Brossolette, Pierre, 98, 179
Brunschvicg, Professor Léon and Mme, 17
Buettner, Elizabeth (Mme Des Marres), 28

Campinchi, César, 49, 54
Camus, Albert, 146, 148
Caraman-Chimay, Prince Jean de, 15
Casanova, Danielle, 109
Cassou, Jean, 88, 147
Catroux, General Georges, 108
Caziot, Pierre, 84
Céline, Louis-Ferdinand, 29, 146
C.F.L.N. (French National Liberation Committee), 126–9, 173
C.G.T., 11, 13, 15, 16, 26, 84, 132, 141–2, 185, 188, 217
C.G.T.U., 13
Chaban-Delmas, Jacques, 195–7
Chamberlain, Neville, 24–5, 28–9, 39, 41
Chamson, André, 21, 23
Chaudier, Pasteur, 160
Chautemps, Camille, 23–5, 54
Chevigné, Colonel Pierre de, 172
Citroën, 132
Clark, General Mark, 103–4
Clemenceau, Georges, 43, 70
C.N.R. (Conseil national de la Résistance) 117–22, 132, 151, 166, 195–7, 201, 209, 210–12, 216–17, 220
Combat, 98, 117–18, 141, 147, 176, 179, 198
Communist Party of France (P.C.F.), 11, 14, 15, 36, 55–6, 60, 62, 66–7, 71, 109, 111–12, 127, 140, 151, 173, 176, 179, 197, 212, 217–19

239

Coston (*La libre Parole*), 29
Cot, Pierre, 22, 76
Courbet, Gustave, 36
Croix de Feu, 11, 12, 28

Daladier, Edouard, 12, 14, 22, 24–9, 33, 35–7, 39, 42, 54, 57, 82
Dalloz, Pierre, 153–4
Danton, 37
Darlan, Admiral François, 49, 54, 57, 86, 103–7, 124
Darnand, Joseph, 82, 115, 135, 169, 178–9, 184, 197
Darquier, de Pellepoix, Louis, 28, 29, 82
Déat, Marcel, 29, 53, 86
Decour, Jacques, 146
Delanoue, Paul, 142
Delestraint, General, 151, 153
Deloncle, Eugène, 23
Doriot, Jacques, 11, 12, 96
Dormoy, Marx, 23
Doumergue, Gaston, 13
Drossier, Marcel, 65
Duclos, Jacques, 38, 63, 198
Duclos, Jean, 38
Dufresne, Commandant (Raymond Massiet), 189, 194, 200–1
Dufy, Raoul, 145
Duhamel, Georges, 146, 148, 161

Earnest, General, 168
Eden, Anthony, 107, 124
Eisenhower, General Ike, 103–4, 107, 126–7, 163, 165, 171, 198–9
Eluard, Paul, 143–8, 180, 219
Eon, Colonel, 168, 171

Fabien, Colonel, 200, 209
Farges, Yves, 153
Fiocca, Mrs (Nancy Wake), 88
Flandin, Paul-Etienne, 25, 44
Frachon, Benoit, 13, 198
Franco, General Francisco, 20, 23–5, 43

Franctireurs-Partisans (F.T.P.), 55, 66, 113, 118, 129, 151–2, 156–7, 165, 167–9, 171–3, 178–9, 181, 186–90, 197, 204, 220
French National Liberation Committee (C.F.L.N.), 126–7, 173
Friedmann, Professor Georges, 89

Gallacher, William, 25
Gallois-Cocteau, Captain, 198
Gamelin, General Maurice-Gustave, 16, 22, 24, 42–3
Gaulle, General Charles de, 49, 54–5, 62, 66–7, 70, 75–6, 79, 82, 85, 87–8, 90–5, 101, 106–9, 111–12, 117–22, 124–8, 150–1, 155–7, 163, 166, 169–71, 182, 187, 193, 199, 200–2, 209–19
Gestapo, 135, 184
Gide, André, 14, 85–6, 130
Giraud, General Henri, 104, 106–8, 125–6, 128
Giraudoux, Jean, 143
Gitton, Marcel, 86
Goebbels, Dr Josef, 39
Goethe, 146
Gort, Lord, 42
Gouvernement Provisoire de la République Française (G.P.R.F.), 195, 209, 211
Grenier, Fernand, 71, 111–12, 129, 155–6
Grinbaum, Jacques, 64
Guéhenno, Jean, 83, 146
Guitry, Sacha, 75

Hazard, Paul, 146
Henriot, Philippe, 82, 169
Herriot, Edouard, 36–7, 57, 193
Heslop, R. H., *see* Xavier
Heydrich (S.S. Gauleiter), fn. 30, 99
Hitler, Adolf, 11, 14, 18, 20, 24, 26, 28, 32, 35, 50, 74, 95, 104–6, 192
Hoare, Sir Samuel, 14, 24

Humanité, l', 29, 32, 36, 43, 64, 79, 140, 198
Huntziger, General, 56

International Brigades, 21, 24–5, 31

Jaujard, Jacques, 143
Joliot-Curie, Frédéric, 69, 198
Jouhaux, Léon, 13
Juin, General Alphonse, 103, 105, 125

Keitel, General Wilhelm, 5, 56, 78
Koenig, General Pierre, 154, 157, 166–7, 170, 183, 196
Koestler, Arthur, 27
Krupp, 131

Labarthe, André, 93
Laborde, Admiral, 106
Lacour Gayet, Jacques, 126
Langevin, Professor Paul, 14, 69
Laval, Pierre, 14, 24–5, 29, 44, 54, 57, 82, 86, 96, 104–5, 113–15, 135, 193
Lebrun, Albert, 12, 214
Leclerc, General Philippe, 198–201, 209
Leopold, King of Belgium, 44
Leroy-Ladurie, Jacques, 84
Le Troquer, André, 195
Lettres françaises, Les, 145–8, 161
Lévy, Louis, 93
Libération, 98, 141, 147, 176
Lifar, Serge, 75
Lurçat, Jean, 143–5, 219

Macmillan, Harold, 126
Malraux, André, 14, 21
Mandel, Georges, 49, 54, 82
Marion, Paul, 82
Marquet, Adrien, 29
Marres, Count Jaunez des (*see also* Buettner), 28
Martin Dugard, Roger, 85
Massiet, Raymond, *see* Dufresne

Masuy, Henry, 134–5
Matisse, Henri, 143–4
Mauriac, François, 145–6, 148
Maurois, André, 33
Maurras, Charles, 11, 146
Mendès-France, Pierre, 90, 128
Michels, Henri, 71
Moine, André, 32, 103, 123
Montgomery, General Sir Bernard, 125, 164
Morandat, Yvon, 98
Morel, Captain, 153
Morlaix, Captain (airforce), 155
Morgan, Claude, 146
Moulin, Jean, 22, 97, 117–20
Murphy, Robert D., 103
Murville, Jacques Couve de, 126, 128
Musée de l'Homme, 59–60, 97
Muselier, Admiral, 93
Mussolini, Benito, 14, 18, 20, 50, 105, 127

Noguès, General Charles, 102, 105
Nordling, Raoul, 193–5, 199
Nordling, Rolf, 199

O.S. (Organisation spéciale), 66, 71, 176

Palewski, Gaston, 90
Parodi, Alexandre, 195, 199
Parrot, Louis, 143
Passy, Colonel (Wavrin), 90, 151, 154, 157
Patton, General George S., 198, 201
Paulus, General von, 99
Paxton, Dr Robert, 67, 71, 81
Pellepoix, *see* Darquier
Péri, Gabriel, 38, 148
Pétain, Marshal Philippe, 22, 33, 43, 46, 49, 50, 54, 56–7, 66–7, 70, 80–8, 104, 106, 124, 142, 169, 172, 176, 193, 214
Peugeot, 137
Peyrouton, Marcel, 123, 125
Philip, André, 90, 128

Picasso, Pablo, 23, 143–5
Pleven, René, 90
Popular Front (Front populaire), 15, 17, 20, 23, 25, 34, 217
Poincaré, Georges, 14
Politzer, Professor Georges, 45, 69
Portes, Mme de, 39, 44
Pucheu, Pierre, 82, 86, 129, 135

Radical Party, 14, 37, 217
Rée, Harry, 137
Reibel, Senator, 43, 50
Rémy (Roulier), 133, 156
Renault, 33–4, 63, 132
Reynaud, Paul, 16, 35, 39, 42–6, 49, 52, 54, 57, 82
Ribbentrop, Joachim von, 26
Richet, Professor, 130
Rivet, Paul, 14
Roch, Pierre, 65
Rochet, Waldeck, 112, 217
Rocque, Colonel de la, 11, 12, 17, 81
Rol-Tanguy, Colonel Henri, 169, 196, 198–9, 200
Rolland, Romain, 14
Rommel, General Erwin, 125
Roosevelt, Franklin D., 104, 107–8, 126
Roussy, Recteur, 68–9, 71
Roustouil, Bishop, 160

Sadon, Professor, 131
Saint-Phalle, Alexandre de, 199
Saint-Saëns, Marc, 145
Saliège, Cardinal, 87
Sarraut, Maurice, 14, 36
Sartre, Jean-Paul, 21, 47, 143, 146, 148
Sauckel (Labour chief), 95–6, 113–15, 131
Schneider-Creuzot, 63
Schumann, Maurice, 90
Schuman, Robert, 16
Séghers, Pierre, 148
Semard, Pierre, 96
Sérigny, Alain de, 103

S.F.I.O. (Socialist Party), 217
S.O.E. (Secret Operations Executive), 117, 128, 133, 137, 165, 176
Solomon, Professor Jacques, 69
Soustelle, Jacques, 112, 151, 154–5
Speidel, General Hans, 85
Sperrle, Marshal Hugo, 191
Stalin, Marshal Joseph, 218
Stavisky, Pierre, 12
Streicher, Julius, 28
Stulpnagel, General Karl-Heinrich von, 188

Taittinger, Pierre, 11, 193–5
Thaelmann, Ernst, 13
Thomas, Edith, 148
Thorez, Maurice, 16, 38, 59, 62, 63, 209, 216–17
Tillon, Charles, 55, 151, 171, 209
Tillion, Mme Germaine, 59, 60
Tollet, André, 186
Triolet, Elsa, 148
T.U.C., 13

Vaillant-Couturier, Marie-Claude, 109
Valéry, Paul, 146, 148
Valléry-Radot, Pasteur, 198
Valrimont, Captain (COMAC), 200
Vercors (Jean Bruller), 145
Vie Ouvrière, La, 63, 141, 182
Vildrac, Charles, 148

Wahl, Professor Jean, 17
Wendel, M. de, 34, 63
Weygand, General Maxime, 43–4, 49, 50, 54, 102
Willard, Maître Marcel, 37

Xavier (R. H. Heslop), 117–18, 137

Ybarnégaray, Jean, 43, 50, 82
Yeo-Thomas, F. F. E., 130, 137–9, 150, 179

Zilliacus, Konni, 24